D1289633

NATIONAL UNIVERSITY PUBLICATIONS
KENNIKAT PRESS CORP.
90 SOUTH BAYLES AVENUE
PORT WASHINGTON, N. Y. 11050 · (516) 883-0570

Book No. 9197

We take pleasure in sending you this review copy of

WALTER WHITE AND THE HARLEM RENAISSANCE

By Edward E. Waldron

DATE OF PUBLICATION   October 27, 1978

PRICE $12.50

Direct quotation in reviews is limited to 500 words unless special permission is given.

Please send us two copies of your review

WALTER WHITE AND THE HARLEM RENAISSANCE

Kennikat Press
National University Publications
Literary Criticism Series

General Editor
John E. Becker
Fairleigh Dickinson University

WALTER WHITE *and the*
HARLEM RENAISSANCE

EDWARD E. WALDRON

National University Publications
KENNIKAT PRESS // 1978
Port Washington, N. Y. // London

The author and publisher acknowledge, with gratitude, the kind permissions of various individuals and institutions for the use of certain materials: *CLA Journal* and the College Language Association; Mrs. Countee (Ida M.) Cullen; estate of Claude McKay; estate of Sinclair Lewis; Random House Inc. and Alfred A. Knopf, Inc.; Doubleday Communications Corporation; Mrs. Thomas S. Stribling; Mercantile-Safe Deposit and Trust Company, Trustee under the Will of Henry L. Mencken; and National Association for the Advancement of Colored People.

Manufactured in the United States of America

Published by
Kennikat Press Corp.
Port Washington, N.Y./London

Library of Congress Cataloging in Publication Data

Waldron, Edward E
    Walter White and the Harlem Renaissance.

    (Literary criticism series) (National university publications)
      Bibliography: p.
      Includes index.
      1. White, Walter Francis, 1893–1955. 2. Novelists, American–20th Century–Biography. I. Title. II. Title: Harlem Renaissance.
PS3545.H6165Z95   913'.5'2[B]   77-6241
ISBN 0-8046-9197-5

To Jo
A person in her own right

CONTENTS

ACKNOWLEDGMENTS

As always there are many people to thank for helping in various stages of this book's production. First of all, I would like to acknowledge the National Endowment for the Humanities, whose Fellowship in Afro-American Studies in 1970–71 enabled me to begin the research which eventually led to this publication. I would also like to express my gratitude to an impeccable scholar and a wonderful gentleman, Professor Arthur P. Davis, with whom I studied at Howard University under that fellowship. It was Professor Davis who first told me of the NAACP letters and suggested that I might want to work with them for a seminar project. I shall always remember fondly the time I spent under Professor Davis's guidance.

Special gratitude for his untiring efforts on my behalf must be shown to Mr. Charles Cooney, formerly of the Manuscript Division of the Library of Congress. Professor Richard B. Erno of Arizona State University gave constant guidance and encouragement as work on the book progressed.

Finally, I would like to thank my family for their patience and their help. My son, Chris, is too young to know how much time my working on this book took from him, but my wife, Jo, to whom this book is dedicated, knows full well. Her demanding reading of the drafts and her typing of most of them were tremendously helpful, and her understanding and encouragement were invaluable.

E. E. W.

PREFACE

When I first started researching the material for this book, I knew nothing about Walter White. I might have known, vaguely, that he had been connected with the National Association for the Advancement of Colored People, but not much more. After reading hundreds of his letters, his biography, and other related material, however, I feel that I have known Walter White forever. His personality comes through his writing so predictably that it is impossible not to feel that way. This was brought home to me quite unexpectedly a few days ago as I was reading Thomas Cripps's study of the Negro in the early days of American film, *Slow Fade to Black* (Oxford University Press, 1977). As I read what Cripps had to say about White and his reaction to such matters as the screening of *The Birth of a Nation* and Hollywood's use and abuse of black actors and themes, I found myself thinking, "Yes, that's Walter White, all right." The occasions might have changed from the ones with which I worked, but the man was the same: feisty, yet always aware of what would best serve his cause—and the cause of the NAACP.

There are many fascinating aspects to the life of this multifacted man. His friendships with men like Sinclair Lewis and H. L. Mencken, his work as an "undercover" investigator of lynchings for the NAACP, his sometimes behind-the-scenes maneuvering with publishers and editors on behalf of a young Countee Cullen or a Claude McKay combine to form the portrait of a man who loved the active life he led and who constantly basked in the glow of being a "race leader." There were those who, like W. E. B. Du Bois, did not particularly like White and distrusted his motives on occasion, especially later in his long career, but there were as many—if not more—who thought of Walter White as *being* the NAACP and as an ever visible figure to whom they might turn for help in one form or another.

To date, most of what has been written concerning the Harlem Renaissance has neglected Walter White almost entirely, and most of what has been written about White has focused on his later years of leadership in the NAACP and his work with presidents and other national figures. This study is an attempt to put Walter White's contributions to the Harlem Renaissance in perspective. The biographical first chapter presents a brief introduction to the man, while the second chapter presents a brief introduction to the times; neither is meant to be exhaustive, but both are necessary to present the heart of the study, the chapters on White's novels and the final chapter, which examines his role in aiding other Black artists in reaching the American marketplace.

It is hoped that the reader will leave this book with a clearer understanding of Walter White's rightful place in one of the most important decades in Black American literary history. Until now, that place has not been recognized.

WALTER WHITE AND THE HARLEM RENAISSANCE

ABOUT THE AUTHOR

Edward E. Waldron (Ph.D., Arizona State University) has taught at all three state universities in Arizona, and at Howard University. His articles have been published in the CLA *Journal,* the Arizona English *Bulletin, Negro American Literature Forum,* and *Phylon.* In 1970 he received an NEH Fellowship in Afro-American Studies. Currently he is an assistant professor of English at Yankton College in Yankton, South Dakota.

1

THE MAN CALLED WHITE

To many people Walter White and the National Association for the Advancement of Colored People were synonymous. For over three decades White enjoyed positions of power and leadership in the NAACP, and from 1931 until his death on March 21, 1955, he served as its executive secretary. Indeed, he participated in all phases of the Association's activities, from his earliest investigations into southern lynchings to his fights in Congress for legislation to end that most horrendous of America's institutions of justice. He was an advisor to presidents, yet he was always willing to lend his services to someone looking for a job or for a place to publish a book. While there were those within the Association and without who thought White was too egocentric, his writing and his correspondence show that whatever his inclination toward vanity and showmanship, Walter White was a warm, likable man who seemed to enjoy being in a position to help people almost as much as he enjoyed the formal position itself.

Walter Francis White was born on July 1, 1893, in Atlanta, Georgia, the son of George and Madeline White. Both of White's parents were light-skinned, and White himself was blond and blue-eyed, which often confused white folks who found themselves addressing a "Negro" who was fairer than they. As a matter of fact, through some marvel of computation, the Harvard anthropologist Earnest Hooton arrived at the conclusion that White was 63/64 white, enough to make him "legally white" in most states; this idea was evidently so fascinating to people that it was inevitably noted in White's obituaries.[1] In his autobiography *A Man Called White* (1948) White cites several instances in which he was attacked or almost attacked by blacks who, finding him walking in their part of town and not recognizing him, thought him just another white man looking for trouble. His fair complexion, in addition to his Anglo facial characteristics, served White in good stead, however, during his investigation of lynchings.

From what little he tells us in his autobiography, White's early years in Atlanta must have been relatively pleasant, although his parents were not wealthy and there were moments of anxiety and fear. His father, George White, worked for the post office as a mail collector, one of the best jobs available to a black man in the turn-of-the-century South. In 1906, when Walter was thirteen, a terrible riot broke out in Atlanta, the result of a number of events: the late summer's heat; a bitterly contested gubernatorial campaign; an inflammatory series of headline stories about brutal attacks by black men on white women, designed mainly to spur sales of the newly established *Atlanta News;* and a dramatization of Thomas Dixon's *The Clansman.* It was during that riot, when his home was almost attacked by a torchbearing mob out to get the "nigger mail carrier" who lived in a house that was "too nice for a nigger," that, White said, he learned who he was:[2]

In the flickering light the mob swayed, paused, and began to flow toward us. In that instant there opened up within me a great awareness; I knew then who I was. I was a Negro, a human being with an invisible pigmentation which marked me a person to be hunted, hanged, abused, discriminated against, kept in poverty and ignorance, in order that those whose skin was white would have readily at hand a proof patent and inclusive, accessible to the moron and the idiot as well as to the wise man and the genius. No matter how low a white man fell, he could always hold fast to the smug conviction that he was superior to two-thirds of the world's population, for those two-thirds were not white.

In the moments when the mob began to close upon the lawn of the Whites' house, he felt his alliance with the nonwhite people of the world tighten and solidify; and when the mob was turned back by gunfire from friends who had barricaded themselves in a nearby house, White said, "I was gripped by the knowledge of my identity, and in the depths of my soul I was vaguely aware that I was glad of it. . . . I was glad I was not one of those who hated; I was glad I was not one of those made sick and murderous by pride." In this particular experience in White's early life, we can see the foundation of his later dedication to the fight to gain for black Americans all the rights of American citizenship.

White's family life was very stable. His father was a religious man who conducted Bible reading sessions in the parlor every Sunday morning, and his mother was a meticulous woman who evidently demanded that her children exhibit similar attitudes toward their home and persons. There was a closeness in the White family, a closeness made particularly apparent

in the later correspondence between Walter and his brother George. Altogether there were seven children: five girls and two boys. Interestingly, the
White home was situated almost exactly on the border between the black
community and the white, thus paralleling the family's own racial makeup.
In fact, it was the neatness of the White home that elicited envy from some
of their white neighbors and laid the groundwork for the assault during
the 1906 riot.

Although White's father was unable to complete his own college career
because his mother and father both died when he was a freshman, he encouraged his children to pursue their education, as did Mrs. White, a former
teacher. Long before he enrolled at Atlanta University, however, Walter
White had grown familiar with the classics from the family's meager stock
of books and from books borrowed from the church library. By the time
he was twelve or thirteen, White had read Shakespeare, Dickens, Thackeray,
Trollope, and some of the other Harvard Classics. Like many other young
black students in Atlanta, White did his secondary school work at Atlanta
University starting in 1908; because the schools opened to black children were
so inferior, a student hoping to attend an institution of higher learning did his
secondary work at that institution before entering the college program.
This was true all over the South; the black colleges instituted secondary
school programs for just that reason.

White did not discuss his work at Atlanta University, other than to say
he received his B.A. there in 1916. He must have been a fairly good student
and a popular one, for he was elected president of the class of 1916. Several
of the biographical sketches of White in the NAACP files, composed for
one reason or another, indicate that he also did graduate work "in economics
and sociology in the College of the City of New York" after he moved
to New York to work for the NAACP.[3] During his senior year at Atlanta,
in addition to "playing not too good football, . . . being a member of the
university debating team," and serving as class president, White prepared
for the Standard Life Insurance Company "simple mathematical tables
dealing with net and deferred premiums and . . . actuarial tables which
required simply care and the following of formulae."[4] Because of this
work, and his work the previous summer as a salesman in parts of rural
Georgia, White was offered a clerical position in the Standard Life Insurance Company when he was graduated from Atlanta University. His experiences with this company probably explain his meticulous concern
with money matters in later life and also supplied him with material for his
first novel, *The Fire in the Flint* (1924), the setting for which, as he often
stated in his correspondence, grew out out of his summer experiences selling life insurance in rural Georgia.

The chain of events which eventually led to White's decision to go to

New York to work for the NAACP began with a local problem. The Atlanta school board had decided to cut back even further the small budget allotted its black schools. In 1914 the board had abolished the eighth grade in those schools, to free more money for white schools; in 1916 it was threatening to cut off the seventh grade in black schools. An indignant group of men from Atlanta's black community, including Walter White, decided to petition the fledgling NAACP for help, and White was elected to write the letter. Their plan, however, was disclosed to the school board, and it was only through their own informers that they learned of the board's plans to move up a scheduled meeting to rush through the proposal. After a series of meetings with the citizens' group, the school board decided to keep the black schools' seventh grade and to obtain additional money for the white schools by floating a bond issue, the revenues from which would go only to the white schools. It was to fight this issue that the Atlanta branch of the NAACP was formed, the members electing Walter White secretary. In an effort to promote support for their cause, the local branch invited James Weldon Johnson of the national office to speak. At the mass meeting held for Johnson, White was pushed into an impromptu speech about the NAACP, a presentation which, he said, was "an impassioned . . . rabble-rousing speech," that concluded with Patrick Henry's "Give me liberty or give me death."[5] Apparently on the strength of this speech and private conversations between the two men, Johnson returned to New York and recommended that the board of directors of the NAACP hire White as an assistant secretary in the national office.

The decision to leave Atlanta was not an easy one for White. The job in New York paid only $1,200 a year, less than he was making at the life insurance company, and the Association was still rather shaky. In 1917 its membership was less than nine thousand, and there were only two full-time officials in the national office, Roy Nash as secretary, and Johnson as field secretary. One of White's former professors at Atlanta University, Edgar Webster, later recalled cautioning White against the move; he had told White that "the only independent man is the business man."[6] But two other important figures in White's life advised him to go. His father thought he could do much good in such a position and, therefore, would serve as God's tool. Dr. Louis Wright, the man who quite possibly was White's model for Kenneth Harper in *The Fire in the Flint* and who was a lifelong friend, was more blunt in his advice:[7]

You'd be a damn fool to stay here in Atlanta. Go to New York by all means. Life will mean much, much more to you when you are fighting for a cause than it possibly can if you stay here just to make money. You'll stagnate and eventually die mentally.

Taking the advice of the two men he most admired, White made the move and reported to work in New York on January 31, 1918.

According to White, it was quite by accident that he fell into one of his most important and dangerous activities in the NAACP, investigating lynchings. When James McIlherron, a black sharecropper in Estill Springs, Tennessee, was burned to death by a lynch mob after he had defended himself from a beating by his employer, White asked Johnson's permission to go to Tennessee and investigate first-hand what had happened. Posing as a white man interested in buying some cotton land nearby, White insinuated himself into the local gossip circle at the country store and, by feigning indifference, goaded the locals into telling all. Returning to New York, he published the facts he had uncovered about the lynching and began a phase of work within the Association which, he noted, "neither it nor I had contemplated when I was employed."[8]

While engaged in one of his investigations, White himself was almost lynched. During the summer of 1919 a group of black sharecroppers had formed the Progressive Farmers and Household Union of America in Phillips County, Arkansas, in order to pool their resources and free themselves from the slavelike conditions imposed by sharecropping. In the middle of a meeting the sharecroppers were attacked by a group of white men who later accused the sharecroppers of organizing to kill whites in the county. Although the total number of blacks killed during the senseless slaughter was never officially fixed, White estimated it at over two hundred men and women. It was while he was in Arkansas trying to uncover evidence to use in the defense of seventy-nine black men who had been accused of "murder, insurrection, and a variety of other 'crimes,' " that White was almost caught. On October 13, 1919, he wrote James Weldon Johnson from the Hotel Marion in Little Rock:[9]

I have just been informed that if I go to Helena [the county seat where the men were being held] tomorrow, I may meet with foul play. I leave here at seven tomorrow morning for Helena. If you haven't received a telegram from me by Thursday night, it might be well for you to start a discreet inquiry. . . . As for myself, I don't believe there is going to be any trouble and I think I can get away with it.

What White was "getting away with" was posing as a white reporter for the *Chicago Daily News,* a cover he used often in his investigations. (One of his fake business cards is attached to this letter to Johnson in the files.) White also told Johnson some of what he had already uncovered about the case:

My work so far has already revealed a system of economic exploitation that is fearful. The whites themselves haven't the slightest notion that a massacre was thought of and some of them admit that stories that have been sent out were sent solely to hide the system behind such a fog. Hill, the 26 year old Negro accused of being the ring leader is an ignorant, illiterate country farmhand without sense enough to "get in out of a shower of rain." To think that he built up an organization to massacre whites is so absurd that it is almost laughable, if it were not so serious. They are planning to railroad innocent Negroes to death and they'll do it. If ever a Congressional investigation were needed on anything, it's needed here and *we have got to get it through*. The report on this will be mighty good material. I am getting actual cases—no theories.

In closing the letter, White said that it was being sent by registered mail and that Johnson should note whether the seals were tampered with because "they are watching rather closely every stranger."

Whether this letter was tampered with or not, somehow the white folks in Helena discovered who White was. In *A Man Called White* he tells of his narrow escape. A black stranger intercepted White, who was on his way to the county jail house to meet with the prisoners, and warned him that the white folks were talking about him and were out to get him. Not hesitating, White dashed for the train depot and arrived just in time to catch one of the two daily trains out of Helena. Relieved, he explained to the conductor that he had not had time to purchase a ticket, as he had just been notified of an important business meeting in Memphis:[10]

"But you're leaving, mister, just when the fun is going to start," he told me. In answer to my question as to the nature of the "fun," he replied, "There's a damned yellow nigger down here passing for white and the boys are going to get him."

"What'll they do with him?" I asked.

Shifting his cud of tobacco, he shook his head grimly and assured me, "When they get through with him he won't pass for white no more!"

Although White encountered many moments of anguish and discomfort during his years as a public figure in the NAACP, none was more terrifyingly close to being final than this.

In addition to his work investigating lynchings, White also was involved in many of the important court cases fought by the NAACP. One of the most crucial of these involved the family of Dr. Osian Sweet, a black physician in Detroit. On September 8, 1925, the Sweets moved into an all-white neighborhood, and that night a mob of angry whites gathered outside their home, tossing stones and shouting threats. Sweet called the police for protection, but no policemen came. The next night the mob was larger and more hostile. This time bullets crashed into the house instead of rocks. Only after the gunfire was returned from within the house, however, did the police go into action—arresting the occupants of the house. At the request of the defendants and the Detroit branch of the NAACP, the national office was brought in to help. The importance of the Sweet case is underscored by White in his autobiography:[11]

If the Sweets were not given adequate legal defense, if the ancient Anglo-Saxon principle that "a man's home is his castle" were not made applicable to Negroes as well as to others, we knew that other and even more determined attacks would be made upon the houses of Negroes throughout the country. We were equally convinced that legal affirmation that a Negro had the right to defend his home against mob assault would serve to deter any other mobs in Detroit and elsewhere.

At a time when a large mass of the black population was still migrating to the urban North, such a problem was indeed acute. Many more black families would be the first to integrate all-white neighborhoods, and the wrong decision in the Sweet case could, in effect, declare an open season on those families.

The Association persuaded Clarence Darrow to take the case and direct the defense of the Sweet family, but only after Darrow was assured by White that the defendants had fired in self-defense. As he told White, "If they had not had the courage to shoot back in defense of their own lives, I wouldn't think they were worth defending."[12] The first trial, which ended in a mistrial after the jury could not decide on a verdict, cost the Association almost $22,000. The second trial, in which the defendants were tried separately, ended with a "not guilty" verdict in the case of Henry Sweet, a college student. Since the prosecution's case against him was the strongest, the state dropped the charges against the others. Apparently White was at least partially satisfied that the Sweet case had done some good. In a memo dated September 13, 1926, and headed, simply, "Memorandum on Sweet Case," White presented his findings:[13]

The Assistant Secretary [White] found that there had been a very great change in public sentiment since the acquittal of Henry Sweet. There is, of course, still opposition on the part of a certain class of white people but, apparently, the majority of people have realized the justness of the Sweet Case. There have been no further attacks upon the homes of colored people and race relations apparently are in a better condition than they have been within the last ten years in Detroit.

The toll inflicted on the Sweet family as a result of their confinement during the trial was heavy. Mrs. Sweet and Henry, a brother-in-law, both died of tuberculosis, a disease directly linked to heavy colds they had contracted during their stay in jail. Although White never explicitly mentioned any

conscious association on his part between the Sweet family's experience
and the experience of the White family in Atlanta in 1906, subconsciously,
at least, the Sweet verdict must have satisfied some deeper sense of justice
within White; he certainly expended a tremendous amount of energy in
pursuing a just decision for Dr. Sweet and his family.

For all its gravity, the Sweet trial had other moments of importance
for White. During the course of the trials he became friends with a number
of men involved in the case, including Judge Frank Murphy, later to become
a Supreme Court justice, and Robert Toms, the prosecutor. One of the
amusing anecdotes in White's autobiography centers around the initial con-
frontation between White, Arthur Spingarn, Charles Studin, and James
Weldon Johnson of the NAACP, and the legendary Clarence Darrow:[14]

Arthur Spingarn told the tragic story [i.e., about the Sweet case]. Mr.
Darrow listened with deep sympathy and when Arthur had finished, he
said softly, "I understand. I know the suffering your people have endured."
Arthur's naturally dark skin had been deeply tanned during his service
in the Army and week ends at his country place in Dutchess County. He
informed Mr. Darrow, somewhat to the latter's embarrassment, that although he was deeply concerned with the Negro question, he himself was
not a Negro. Mr. Darrow turned to Charlie Studin, also swarthy-skinned,
and said, "Then you understand." Charles laughed and told him that he
also was white.
In desperation Mr. Darrow turned to me. "Well, with your blue eyes
and blond hair I could never make the mistake of thinking you colored."
I smiled and told him I *was* colored.

Shortly after that meeting Darrow decided to take the Sweet case.

From his earliest days in the Association, White maintained a fairly
rigorous speaking schedule, part of the routine of an NAACP official. In
1918, his first year in the national office, he traveled over 12,500 miles,
and in 1919 he traveled 26,000 miles and made eighty-six speeches. This
was in addition to his work in the late summer of 1919 investigating the
massacre in Arkansas. In later years the schedule grew more hectic as the
Association—and White—grew in importance. For a twelve-day period in
February, 1927, for example, he made seventeen speeches and had several
conferences in the course of a tour that went from Buffalo to Akron and
Indianapolis, then back to New York City.[15] His audiences were varied.
Included in the groups before which White spoke were college students
from Butler University and the P. T. A. of Public School 23 of Indianapolis,
as well as the local branches of the NAACP in the various cities. He spoke
at meetings of five hundred and more, and he met with small groups of
people for more informal chats. His personal charm and wit made him
popular wherever he spoke, whether at a society ladies' luncheon or at a

meeting of professional men from whom he hoped to glean money for
the Association.

The mid-twenties were very busy years for White. In 1922 he married
Leah Gladys Powell, a member of the NAACP staff. Then in 1924, after
an initial rejection by Doran, his first novel, *The Fire in the Flint* (discussed
in chapter 3), was published by Alfred A. Knopf. While the novel was no
literary masterpiece, it did receive much critical attention and was hailed
at the time as an innovative novel on the "race question." Two years later
he published his second and last novel, *Flight* (discussed in chapter 4),
again with Knopf. Although this book did not sell as well as his first effort,
perhaps because it was less inflammatory in theme, many critics thought
it better written than *Fire*. White was also busy during these years writing
articles for such magazines as the *American Mercury* and the *Century,*
as well as numerous book reviews and articles for newspapers. In 1926
he began his column for the *Pittsburgh Courier,* one of the most influential
black newspapers in the country.

Also in 1926 White was awarded a Guggenheim Fellowship, ostensibly to
write a three-generation novel of Negro life, a project which he never completed. Included among those asked to write letters of recommendation
for White to the Guggenheim Foundation were Carl Van Vechten, Carl
Van Doren, H. L. Mencken, J. E. Spingarn, and Sinclair Lewis, all of whom
were personal friends. (White had met Lewis through J. E. Spingarn when
White was revising *The Fire in the Flint.*) In his letter to the Guggenheim
Foundation, Lewis stated: [16]

It seems to me that Walter F. White is ideally the type of person, and that
his work is ideally the kind of work, which the Guggenheim Foundation
desires to assist. In recommending him I am not doing so merely as a personal friend, though I am very glad and proud to have him as a friend.
Before I had ever met him or learned anything whatsoever about him personally, I had read his "Fire in the Flint" and found that although there
was too much propaganda in it, there was also an authentic and important
literary quality, a fidelity to life combined with a sense of beauty, which
I was very glad to praise publicly.

After stressing that he felt White was "rapidly freeing himself from the bond
of mere propaganda" and noting that White would do even better work
"in the security and tranquility of a country like France," Lewis added
this observation about White's style:

He has the integrity combined with beauty of which I spoke: he has a sense
of drama; he is not afflicted by the triviality which makes so many of our
clever young writers insignificant, but rather a feeling of dignity and importance in his work; he has sharp observation and an admirable sense of words.

Praising White's decision not to pass but to "remain with and work for the negroes," Lewis closed by saying, "As I think over this account it strikes me that it may seem so laudatory as to cause it to be questioned but I quite sincerely mean every word of it." A few days later White wrote to Lewis:[17]

Good Lord, man, I ought to charge you for a new hat! After reading your report to the Guggenheim Foundation, I don't know how I shall ever be able to notice ordinary mortals again. Honesty compels me to say that you were too laudatory but the same affliction causes me to say that I am damned glad you were and I shall ever be grateful to you whether I get the fellowship or not.

White received the Fellowship and he, Gladys, and their two children sailed for France in July, 1927.

While in Europe, White did begin work on a major project—his study of lynching in the United States, *Rope and Faggot: The Biography of Judge Lynch,* which was published by Knopf in 1929. While the book was received with mixed critical reaction, mainly centering on the success—or failure—of the "scientific detachment" White had tried to maintain within his study, *Rope and Faggot* was an important work; in writing it, he relied heavily on his own experiences in investigating lynchings as well as upon documented evidence of a more objective nature. In nominating White for a Harmon Award in Literature for 1929, James Weldon Johnson said:[18]

His last book, "Rope and Faggot," is, up to this time, the most complete and authoritative treatise on lynching. He discusses the subject from historical, economic, psychological, sex, religious, and political viewpoints, and with regard to the various theories of race superiority and inferiority.

Mr. White's book on lynching supersedes all other publications on this topic and makes it unnecessary for any other book on the subject to be written for many years to come. I believe that upon this piece of work alone, embracing as it does literary merit and civic value, he is entitled to serious consideration of the Committee for the first award in Literature.

There was no first award given by the Harmon Foundation in 1929 because, as Lewis Mumford put it, none of the work was "sufficiently distinguished, as literature, to be put in the same category as, say, Mr. James Weldon Johnson's; . . . it would be fairer to those who have reached a high standard before to give a second prize rather than a first one this year. . . ." The choice for the second (bronze) prize was Walter White, who was the only person under consideration to receive two votes for first prize, from Dorothy Scarborough and John Farrar. White queried both George Haynes and J. E. Spingarn, one of the judges, about the decision, and Spingarn advised him "not to give another thought to the matter," for his own sake and "the dignity of letters." Spingarn added:

Prizes are of such slight importance except for the sake of advertisement and encouragement that the less said or thought about them the better. . . . It is best of all not to seek prizes at all, and second best, not to worry about the kind of prize one seeks and fails to get.

White had also been nominated for an award in race relations that year, but he was not in the final list of candidates considered, perhaps for reasons expressed by W. C. Jackson, Chairman of the North Carolina Commission on Inter-Racial Cooperation:[19]

. . . I think that [Mr. White's] name should go before the judges in the Literature Award rather than that of Race Relations. As able and effective as Mr. White has been, and as highly as I regard him and his abilities, I feel that the award in Race Relations is not to be given upon the character of the work that he has done up to the present time. To illustrate in part what I mean, I may say that, whether rightly or wrongly, Mr. White has probably increased race antagonism in the South rather than diminished it. This may or may not be a good thing. The only point I am making is that, in my opinion, it is a part of the reason why the award should not go to him in promoting race relations.

White would have argued that his greatest strength was exactly what Jackson asserted should prevent his receiving the award, i.e., his ability to keep inflamed the ideas of racial injustice and bigotry as they permeated the South so that, hopefully, some remedy might be effected.

As dedicated as White was to the cause of equality and to the Association, there were times, especially in this period of his life, when he almost left his position with the NAACP to venture into a new field. At one point, for example, he tried to interest Cecil B. DeMille in adapting *The Fire and the Flint* to the screen, and he was ready to drop everything to head for Hollywood and a career as a screen writer. Unfortunately, DeMille decided to base his film on Negro life on another novel, *Porgy*. Another time the singer Roland Hayes mentioned at a party that he would like to have White serve as his American agent, and White was quick to offer his services. The idea was probably the result of high spirits rather than serious consideration; at any rate, that possibility never materialized, either.

A more serious opportunity did arise, however, involving the 1928 presidential campaign of Al Smith. Charles Studin cabled White to return from France for an urgent conference on "a very important matter." When he arrived in New York, White learned that Belle Moskowitz, wife of Henry Moskowitz, one of the original organizers of the NAACP, wanted him to take a leave of absence from the Association and work in Smith's campaign to secure a black following for Smith. In his autobiography White implies that his decision not to work for Smith was immediate, but the correspondence tells a different story. In a letter to Bishop John Hurst of Baltimore, a close friend, White indicated his early hopes that Smith might be a man he could support:[20]

Smith is very sore on the South (though as a good politician he can't reveal that) for the vile attacks which they have been making and now are making upon him. He doesn't know a great deal about the Negro's problems—that is part of our job to teach him. But, I am certain that his slant towards us is fundamentally right. His two closest advisers, Dr. and Mrs. Moskowitz, have pretty much the same outlook as you and I—that is one of the chief objections which some of the Tammany politicians have against them.

There were other considerations to be made, as White informed Hurst. The NAACP was (and is) a nonpolitical organization, and the idea of one of its officers, even on a leave of absence, giving support to and managing part of a candidate's campaign did not sit well. W. E. B. Du Bois felt that the Association would be hurt if White were to manage Smith's campaign, and Studin suggested the only way out was for White to resign his position and take a chance on the board's reelecting him after the campaign. What motivated White to consider the position was the chance he saw for the black voter to assert his independence. He told Hurst:

I do feel strongly that here is a chance to do a really big job—a job whose fruits will not be seen so much now as four, eight, twelve years hence. The Republican Party is never going to respect us and shouldn't until we stop permitting ourselves to be lied to, hoodwinked, and made fools of. I feel that if ever we demonstrate that we as a race can be independent that never again will either of the two parties enter a campaign certain that the Negro vote is going to vote all one way. Not being sure, they'll have to make very real concessions to get our support.

In addition to the idea of developing an independent black voter, there was another matter at issue for White in this campaign. Robert Moton, president of Tuskegee, was heading support for Hoover, and White had never had much respect for Moton's aspirations to power through acquiescence. As he told Hurst: "If Hoover is elected Moton will be practically to him what Booker T. Washington was to Roosevelt. If Smith is elected the NAACP will be the power behind the throne. Neither man can win without the Negro vote." In closing this letter to Hurst, White added an important personal note to his consideration: "If I were single I would be willing to take a chance. If Gladys and I had no children we could weather any storm which might arise. But, have I the right to jeopardize the future of Jane and Walter? That is the element which puzzles me so."

The dilemma resolved itself, however, when Smith refused to issue a statement drawn up by Johnson and White indicating that his administration would show no prejudice in hiring or in making appointments to public office; in fact, Smith appeared willing to ignore the racial issue entirely. Another aspect of the situation which helped solve White's problem for him was Smith's choice of Senator Joseph Robinson of Arkansas as his running mate. He wrote Moorefield Storey:[21]

... some Negroes will not vote for Smith, however much they admire him, when they reflect that should Smith be elected and die in office a Negro-hater would succeed him. There are, too, the lynching at Houston just prior to the convention and the caging of Negro spectators—neither of which can logically be held against Smith but which will inevitably be used against him.

As a result of his doubts concerning the strength of Smith's commitment to the black community, White decided not to work for his campaign and to remain in the Association. In *A Man Called White* he relates a conversation with Belle Moskowitz concerning Smith's regret at not following White's suggestion:[22]

Shortly before her death, Mrs. Moskowitz told me that, after his defeat, Al Smith had told her that he wished he had signed the statement and made an all-out bid for the Negro vote. He was convinced that he would thereby have won enough votes in pivotal Northern and border states, which he had lost by narrow margins, to elect him.

Fortunately, for Walter White and for the Association, this chance for White to leave the Association and enter another phase of public life fell through. If he had become active in more orthodox political activities, White might have gained more widespread recognition, but he would not have been able to effect all the positive good he was able to accomplish through the NAACP.

In order to understand the kind of effectiveness Walter White exhibited, it is necessary to know something of the man himself. Writing about White's activities in lobbying for the antilynching bill in Congress in 1938, Stanley High described him as "small, dapper, exceedingly high-strung and serious . . . " and "a prod and a sting for his people—and their shrewdest lobbyist." Concerning White's approach to lobbying, High said: "Walter White did no buttonholing, had no cocktail parties. . . . He had back of him enough of a record in the mass mobilization of Negro opinion to make any such gestures unnecessary. His presence in the Senate gallery every day was lobby-

ing enough."[23] This combination of personal charm and aggressiveness
and public acknowledgment of his influence in the black community made
White a formidable figure indeed.

And behind the public figure lay an interesting personality. For instance,
White was ever fastidious about money matters. When, in 1924, he felt
he was charged an abnormally high fare for a taxicab ride, he wrote to
the Department of Automobile Licenses to complain, having had the fore-
sight to take the name and license number of the driver. John Drenner, the
head of the Division of Licensed Vehicles, responded that the driver had
failed to answer several summonses and that his license had been suspended.
White replied that he wanted the matter pursued, "until some satisfaction
has been secured."[24] If Drenner had known with whom he was dealing,
he undoubtedly would have offered to pay the difference in fare to White
himself.

In all of his affairs, within the Association and without, White was
always a cautious businessman. A glance at one of his expense account
records shows this clearly. His account sheet for attending the 1928
National Interracial Conference in Washington, D. C., for example, item-
izes such things as four cents for a stamp and ten cents for a telephone
call. When members of the Association's staff held a luncheon for James
Weldon Johnson and bought him a gift on the eve of his departure in
1929 for a leave of absence in Japan, White sent each person involved a
list of expenses, including the cost of the gift (forty dollars for a camera)
and the tip to the waitress at the luncheon (one dollar and fifty cents).
He also included a list of how much each person contributed: J. E.
Spingarn gave ten dollars and everyone else gave five, except "Mr. Andrews"
(three dollars) and Du Bois (two dollars and fifty cents), who added in his
note to White, "Wish I could give more." Since the complete cost of the
affair and the gift was fifty cents more than what was contributed, we
might assume White absorbed the difference, although he usually noted
such things explicitly. Before the publication of Alain Locke's *The New
Negro* (1925), in which an article by White appeared, White asked Locke
what his royalty would be as a contributor. Locke responded that it
would be "7 $^1/_3$% out of a 10% royalty, pro-rated and 50% increase over
3000 copies or on translation rights." He added that he "had hoped that
the race project aspect of the thing would be sufficient inducement."
White replied that he liked to do these things "in a businesslike manner."[25]

If Walter White was businesslike in his dealings, he was also a model of
fairness. Lewis Baer of Albert and Charles Boni, publishers, asked White
if he would edit a book based on the Harlem issue of the *Survey Graphic*.
White replied that he would like to, but could not:[26]

... I don't want to be even faintly guilty of doing something unfair to another man. Alain Locke ... is the man more largely responsible for the number than any other individual. He has worked hard and faithfully on it for nearly a year, along with Paul Kellogg of the *Survey* and it wouldn't be fair for me to come along and take advantage of the work which he has done.

White concluded by saying that he would only consider doing the job if he had Locke's approval. The book that grew out of the *Survey Graphic's* Harlem number, of course, was *The New Negro,* considered by many to be the official herald of the Harlem Renaissance. In fact, some critics prefer to call the period the New Negro Renaissance because of the importance of that work to the times.

Another instance of White's sense of fair play, and an indication of his abilities as a diplomat, involved a reference in *The Fire in the Flint* to a product as "Madam Walker Hair Straightener." On September 8, 1924, F. D. Ransom, manager of the Madam C. J. Walker Manufacturing Company, wrote to White to complain about the reference:

Madam Walker has never put a hair straightener of any kind on the market; ... there is nothing in any of our advertisements or booklets that would indicate that we have a preparation of the kind referred to in your article. The late Madam Walker's claim to fame is based largely on the fact that it was she who first saw the importance of the women of our race having care to their personal appearance. ... The late Madam Walker taught them to take care of the hair and scalp and where the hair was short to grow it by constant care and cultivation. To that end she put a Hair Grower on the market, following it up subsequently with other preparations.

Ransom added that he liked White's novel tremendously and congratulated him on "giving to the world and to the Race a real novel. ..." White replied immediately, apologizing for the mistake and assuring Ransom "that the phrase was not in any sense intended to be derogatory." He continued:

On the contrary, I used it to show that the Madam Walker Company has reached all classes of colored people and has done a great deal in inculcating in the minds of Negroes greater personal pride in their appearance. ... My reference was to the hair grower and the comb which is sold to be used with the hair grower. ... I not only have the greatest respect and admiration for the late Madam Walker but ... that respect and admiration extends to those responsible for the building of that institution during her life time and its continuance since her death. Among those, there is none who is more highly esteemed by me than yourself.

White closed by informing Ransom that he had requested that Knopf change the word "straightener" to "grower" in the second edition of the novel, which was about to go to press. A'Lelia Walker, heiress to the Walker fortune and a celebrity in her own right, wrote to thank White for the change she had been assured would be made and to say that she felt his novel would "be placed among other masterpieces written by members of our race." Interestingly, a month later Harry Evans, advertising manager for the Madam Walker Manufacturing Company, wrote to congratulate White on his novel, calling it "a splendid book, interesting from cover to cover," and made no reference to White's use of "straightener" instead of "grower."[27]

The gracious diplomacy with which White handled the Madam Walker problem was typical of his ability to smooth out rough edges and work with people in a way that pleased them, yet served his needs, too. That quality of White's personality is perhaps explained by a statement he made to Mrs. Henrietta Sperry Reipperger regarding what she had called his "detachment" and "sweetness of spirit" in a speech he had made. White told her: "It is a strong conviction of mine that sanity, temperateness and a willingness to try and see the other man's point of view are all as necessary as strong convictions for what seems to be the right. This balance is not always possible in the face of harrowing injustice."[28]

One area in which White's sense of balance was hardest to maintain was that of race relations. As assistant secretary of the NAACP, he was continually confronted with the pleas of men and women who had been mistreated, attacked, or threatened, all because of their race. Try to control it as he might, it was inevitable that at least a trace of bitterness occasionally tainted his discussion of "the problem"; it is to the credit of his tremendous control that the bitterness did not sweep him up entirely. His correspondence with white people often mirrored his frustration. In 1924, for example, a Miss Annie Bridgman of the American Missionary Association wrote White to complain about an article of Du Bois's (in which the latter called white folks "damned fools") and stated that such a comment tempted a person to ask "whether it is worth while to be friendly with the colored people." White replied that some people thought Du Bois bitter, but, he added, "I often wonder what peculiar factor there is in the makeup of the Negro which prevents him from being ten thousand times as bitter as he is." White continued:[29]

Personally, I try to maintain a reasonably even balance. Sometimes I flatter myself that I do succeed and just at the time when I think that, after all, the problem is being worked out, along comes some new specimen of intolerance which sweeps me right back into the same pessimism from which I have just recovered. The result is that every Negro who thinks at all is constantly swinging like a pendulum between hope and despair. The main reason for hope is that there are white people who are wholly free from the blindness of prejudice. If I did not number among my personal friends those whom I pay the highest compliment I know—that I never think of them as being white but only as being human—I think I should have long since left America never to return. Our problem, then, is not to keep from getting mad, it seems to me, but rather that we should try to keep inevitable anger from blinding us to rays of hope.

White went on to explain his reasons for being particularly bitter on the day on which he was writing his letter:

Pray forgive me for appearing cynical. Perhaps I am more pessimistic today than ordinarily due to an experience which I have just had with the Y. W. C. A. where a fine, intelligent colored girl was barred from the Y. W. C. A. Central School of Hygiene and Physical Education after she had been accepted under the impression that she was white. For two months, this so-called Christian organization has evaded the issue and has told a number of deliberate falsehoods in trying to prevent admitting the girl and at the same time wear the mask of Christianity; . . . at one of the numerous conferences held on this case, Mrs. Henry Sloane Coffin, wife of the pastor of one of New York's most fashionable churches, made the remark that she did not see how Christianity had anything to do with the case. It makes one wonder what white souls are going to do when they reach heaven and find that a few Negroes, too, have entered there.

Like other men of the time, White saw the importance of race relations to the country as a whole; if bitter hatred and prejudice were allowed to grow unchecked, the future of the country would be grim. In March, 1925, Julia Peterkin wrote White: "Your 'Color Lines' [in the *Survey Graphic*] is bitter, but you do not realize, I think, that white people are very cruel to other white people too! I know that!" In reply White said:[30]

I am sorry . . . you thought my "Color Lines" bitter. I tried merely to state the facts as I knew them to be in as dispassionate a manner as possible. White people, it is true, are unkind to each other but the wounds to the spirit which this monster, race prejudice, causes are very hard indeed to bear. It isn't so much the conscious and deliberate cruelty as it is the small and vicious petty things which one has to go against every day. For example, I did an anonymous article in the *Century* for February["White but Black"] in which I, without comment, told of some observations on and near the color line. The April issue of the *Century* carries two letters commenting on that article. One of them declares that the only solution is through the deportation of all Negroes to Africa and the other that the only hope lies in giving all Negroes an industrial education.

We have to keep on though for, as I heard a very talented Negro say in his speech a few nights ago, "The race question in America has resolved itself into a question of the black man's body and the white man's soul."

In many of his letters to white correspondents, Walter White showed this same determination to speak the truth without apologizing for the sting it might inflict.

It was, in part at least, because White felt, as did W. E. B. Du Bois, that "the problem of the twentieth century is the problem of the color line,"[31] that he wrote *The Fire in the Flint.* As he told Mary Trafton:[32]

I am firmly convinced that the great problem of the Twentieth Century in America and in the world is the question of race relations. If men are to be judged and exploited because their skins are not white, inevitable hatred and bitterness will be created which in time will lead to terrible wars and other catastrophes. The growth of terrible organizations like the Ku Klux Klan in the United States and other nationalist and racist organizations in other parts of the world . . . seems to indicate that there is a cancer that must be eradicated if ever we are to have peace. I wrote "The Fire in the Flint" first because the story to me seemed to be one which must be told and, second, as a small contribution on my part towards helping fair minded individuals of all races to know the problem and face it without fear or flinching.

The race problem in America, to be more specific, is largely a question of attitude of mind. When men can be judged from their individual merit and not lumped together and judged by racial fallacies and myths, then, and only then, will we be approaching the ideal state where prejudice is at a minimum.

As this last statement indicates, Walter White was no wide-eyed optimist searching for complete human understanding; he recognized the limitations of human nature. But he dedicated his life, through his work with the NAACP, to an assault on racial prejudice and misunderstanding in the hope that some day men might live, if not in harmony, then at least not in complete discord. In his last published writing, *How Far the Promised Land?* (1955), commenting on the new possibilities for destruction made real by the development of atomic weapons and missles, he observed:[33]

All the peoples of the world are in the same boat now. Today that vessel is unseaworthy because we have not yet mastered the science of living together. Through a major leak caused by color prejudice the waters of hate are rushing in. Our survivial may depend on how swiftly and expertly that leak is caulked.

How Far the Promised Land? is essentially a book of hope, perhaps too idealized by today's standards; as Sterling Brown recently noted, White "saw symbols as being a little more powerful" than one might see them today.[34] But, Brown added, "I really think he believed" that times were getting better.

This note of optimism is, perhaps, finally more indicative of the nature of Walter White than is the bitterness expressed in other places. Most people who speak of him remember him as a warm, utterly charming man who had a way of making everyone feel comfortable and at ease. He also enjoyed a rather active sense of humor, which he often directed, in the tradition of his friend H. L. Mencken, at the foibles of white folks, especially the white southerner. In a letter to L. A. Hamilton, for instance, he indicated that he had done the article "White but Black" for the *Century* anonymously because "I wanted to get under the skins of some of the Nordic brethren and I felt I could do a little more effective work if it were not known that the article was done by a 'professional propagandist.' " When the white administration of the United States Veterans' Bureau Hospital in Tuskegee, Alabama refused to purchase a copy of *The Fire in the Flint* for the hospital library because the book lacked "therapeutic value," White, after trying to place the book through many channels, offered to donate a copy of the novel to the hospital. The exasperated administration finally consented, emphasizing the understanding that the book was to be sent without charge. In his brief study of Walter White in *Thirteen against the Odds* (1944), Edwin Embree cites a story that typifies White's sense of humor:[35]

He [White] likes stories, especially those with an ironic thrust. His wife quotes as his idea of humor the story of a pompous southern gentleman visiting a night club in Hollywood. On seeing Hazel Scott and a dark escort enter, the proud gentleman exclaimed, "Do you allow Negroes here?" And the doorman blandly answered, "Yes, sir. Come right in."

White's wit, though, was not directed solely at white folks. In a letter to Robert Minor, editor of the *Liberator,* White offered this observation on Marcus Garvey and his Universal Negro Improvement Association: ". . . Garvey and his crowd have a most amazing gift at being delightfully indefinite. As a matter of fact, this seems to be their strongest and most valuable characteristic."[36]

No matter who or what his target, White's humor reflected his association with the more sophisticated crowd in New York, men and women of letters and culture. Arthur P. Davis said of White that he was "a typical New Yorker, in many respects."[37] Through parties, at his home and at the homes of others, he came into contact with some of the brightest names of the time. In January 1925, he wrote Roland Hayes: "We wished you for Saturday evening. We had a few folks at the house—Jules Bledsoe, Paul Robeson, James Weldon and Grace Johnson, Carl Van Vechten and Fania Marinoff, Covarrubias, the caricaturist, and George Gershwin, who wrote the 'Rhapsody in Blue.' " A month later he asked L. M. Hussey to a gathering he was planning: "Sherwood Anderson and Konrad Bercovici are coming. . . . If he is able to break an engagement, Ignacio Zuloaga is coming along too. Paul Robeson, James Weldon Johnson, Jules Bledsoe, the Negro baritone, and one or two other Aframericans will be there too."[38] In letters, in conversation, and in many of his writings, White often dropped the names of the famous men and women he knew. As Arthur Davis noted, however, White "knew everybody. . . . He was always willing to drop that name, but in his case, he knew the person about whom he talked." One possible reason for White's infatuation with the famous people he met was offered by Sterling Brown, who observed that, for all his own fame and success, Walter White in many ways remained "the small-town Southern boy making it in the big world."[39] Whatever the motivating factor in White's cultivation of relationships with men like Carl Van Vechten and Carl Van Doren, those relationships often proved invaluable, not only for White but also for the young men and women whom he was able to help because of his contacts.

Walter White was very much a part of the Harlem Renaissance, in spirit and in temperament as well as in actual work. Most studies of White have focused on his later work in the legal battles of the NAACP and on his abilities as a leader in that organization.[40] His obituaries inevitably stressed those roles in his life. In paying tribute to White, for instance, Adam Clayton Powell said: "Without Walter White, civil rights would have been sleeping in the laps of the forgotten past. He magnified civil rights to such a degree that the walls of prejudice, segregation and discrimination came tumbling down. . . ." Arthur B. Spingarn, president of the NAACP at the time of White's death in 1955, said: "Guided in its course by his leadership, the NAACP won for Negroes of the nation the recognition which established for all time their birthright and dignity as American citizens." Finally President Eisenhower, in a telegram to Mrs. White, paid this tribute: "In the death of your husband, Walter White, there has passed from the contemporary scene a vigorous champion of justice and equality for all our citizens. His devoted service to his race over a period of forty years was tireless and effective."[41]

The present study will examine the roles played by Walter White in an earlier phase of his career, a phase that has until now been largely overlooked, except for mention of his investigations of lynchings, perhaps, and passing references to his books. But in many ways White's activities in the twenties helped make possible his later career. More importantly, though, in his contacts with famous personalities, in his own writing, and in his aid to others, Walter White effectively serves as an example of the Harlem Renaissance figure: witty, worldly, and eager to seize the possibilities he saw for expanding his world.

2

THE HARLEM RENAISSANCE:
A Time of Opportunities

> Walter [White] belongs in [a study of the Harlem
> Renaissance] as a friend of the writers and as an
> intermediary and as a writer himself. . . . Among the
> novels, *The Fire in the Flint* is an important novel *of
> that period.* . . . It should be read to understand the
> period.
>
> —Sterling Brown
> *Interview, July 17, 1974*

As Sterling Brown's statement and the discoveries offered in this study
indicate, Walter White, as an influential participant in many of the activities
of the Harlem Renaissance, belongs in a study of that period. Before
placing White and his achievements in perspective with that movement,
however, we might profitably examine, briefly, the period itself.

The term "Harlem Renaissance" has been used to refer to a period of
time roughly between 1919 and 1929 when black American artists were
active, in numbers and intensity, as never before. As the label implies,
Harlem itself played a part in the movement, but more important than
any one place was the attitude of the people during the twenties toward
the black man and his culture. To some he was merely the exotic primitive,
modernized in his Harlem cabaret setting. To more serious scholars and
writers, however, the American black person was, in the 1920s, coming to a
realization of his own possibilities, especially in terms of his work in the
arts, and was therefore the object of sincere study. There was a renewed
interest in the folk culture, as exemplified by Langston Hughes's use of
the blues form in poetry and Zora Neal Hurston's interest in folktales.

James Weldon and J. Rosamond Johnson, among others, published books of spirituals so that they might be preserved.

Along with the interest in black culture on the part of blacks and whites alike, there was also a lively debate regarding the proper treatment of black characters and black life. Some of the younger black writers celebrated in their works the free-wheeling lifestyle of the cabaret-going Harlemites, while some of the older or more staid black writers sought to present the less exotic, more conservative lifestyle of the black middle class. The important fact, however, is that for the first time black American writers were being published in substantial numbers. A few decades earlier Charles Chesnutt and Paul Lawrence Dunbar had dominated the black literary scene; in the twenties the list of names swelled, so that one might indeed talk of a movement instead of a few individual achievements. The works of black writers appeared in prominent national magazines like the *Nation* and the *Smart Set* on a regular basis. Between 1922 and 1933, according to Darwin Turner's bibliography *Afro-American Writers* (New York: Appleton-Century-Crofts, 1970), some twenty-three novels and twelve volumes of verse by black American writers, not including anthologies, were published in the United States. There were also a number of novels, stories, and plays about the black American experience written by white authors during that period, including DuBose Heyward's *Porgy* (1925) and Eugene O'Neill's *All God's Chillun Got Wings* (1924). The success of the all-black musical *Shuffle Along* in 1921 spurred production of similar shows during the decade: *Dixie to Broadway* (1924), *Runnin' Wild* (1924), and *Blackbirds* (1926). A mixture of the old minstrel shows and the more urbane musical comedy, these shows were themselves part of a heated controversy concerning the image which should be projected of the black American.

There was, then, in the twenties an aroused interest in the black American lifestyle, at least in the intellectual circles of New York. While some of the interest may have been simply the result of a romantic intrigue with the sensational world of the Harlem cabarets, much of it was also the result of a sincere effort to understand a percentage of the American population which had systematically been derided and abused for centuries. The center of both kinds of interest was, almost inevitably, Harlem. For a variety of reasons, cultural as well as economic, New York has been a focal point of creative activity in America for at least a century. Within the larger confines of New York, Harlem became the cultural and social center for black America, again for many reasons, some of which are made clear by Langston Hughes:[1]

. . . Harlem was like a great magnet for the Negro intellectual, pulling him from everywhere. Or perhaps the magnet was New York—but once in New

York, he had to live in Harlem for rooms were hardly to be found elsewhere unless one could pass for white, or Mexican, or Eurasian and perhaps live in the Village. . . . Only a few of the New Negroes lived in the Village, Harlem being their real stamping ground.

The pressures of segregation were not the only forces pushing artists to Harlem, of course, and the mere fact that artists lived in a particular place does not explain why they happened to find that place a creative stimulus. Historians such as John Hope Franklin credit much of the surge of artistic activity in Harlem to the newly formed sense of community and self-confidence experienced by those who had migrated from the traditionally stifling influence of the rural South to the freer, although in other ways just as frustrating centers of the urban North.[2] This sense of community was especially felt by the young artists who were coming to New York and to an awareness of race consciousness at about the same time. In an essay published in Alain Locke's *The New Negro,* James Weldon Johnson made this hopeful prediction for Harlem and its influence:[3]

I believe that the Negro's advantages and opportunities are greater in Harlem than in any other place in the country, and that Harlem will become the intellectual, the cultural and the financial center for Negroes in the United States, and will exert a vital influence upon all Negro peoples.

In a review of Locke's anthology Carl Van Doren put his critical perception to a remarkably accurate analysis of the dual phenomena of the "New Negro" and the Harlem Renaissance:[4]

It is probable that the historian of the episode will trace its root to Harlem. So long as the negroes continued to be in the main a peasant race, they had little opportunity to make themselves heard. . . . Then suddenly a greater number of negroes than had ever before been gathered into any city found themselves in Harlem. They had to struggle against serious difficulties still, but New York was at least cosmopolitan enough to leave them more or less to themselves and to permit them to form as complete a community as they could. A generation before, and the thing might have come too early. Oppressively aware of being freed men, they might have made a successful effort to lose the traits which could remind them of their former slavery, and might have sunk into a drab, limping uniformity. . . . The new generation had outgrown the earlier habit of self-depreciation, and some of them were outgrowing the later, and healthier, habit of self-assertion. They had the courage to cherish certain picturesque racial elements in their natures and customs. They moved from the point at which they were bound together by a common condition, in Mr. Locke's phrase, to the point at which they were bound together by a common consciousness.

While Van Doren's assessment of the reasons behind the artistic activity developing within the black community contains faint echoes of the "primitive" mystique,[5] he did rather accurately hit upon the basic elements operating in the formation of that activity, as given by Franklin and others. In concluding his article Van Doren noted that if the black artist preserved his sense of the folk arts and "certain inherited sentiments . . . 1925 will be marked in the history of the nation . . . as the beginning of a new epoch for the African race."

Whatever the sociological explanation for the surge of black art in the 1920s, and there is some controversy, the search for factors always has to end with Harlem itself and the people who created its atmosphere. As Arna Bontemps reminds us:[6]

What made the decade memorable, of course, was not simply an influx of black migrants from the South and the West Indies in that post-World War I era, as some have concluded; . . . an upsurge of Negro creativity, such as New York's Harlem was beginning to detect, to produce, and to foster, required more than a single source. It demanded an array of factors, a favorable conjunction.

Some of those factors were the newly awakened interest within the white community in the "primitive Negro" and the array of night spots that catered, exclusively for the most part, to a white clientele gathered to watch professional entertainers represent themselves as "typical" Harlemites. This interest also brought with it, however, the interest of white writers and publishers about a topic that was coming into vogue. Many of the autobiographies of the Harlem Renaissance writers dwell almost lovingly on the memory of parties and "gatherings" where a young poet or novelist might meet Carl Van Doren, Heywood Broun or any of a number of famous personages of the theater and literary worlds, and Walter White was almost invariably involved in these affairs. Crediting James Weldon Johnson and his wife Grace with bringing together "many who were later to do much in wiping out the color line," White lists several of the people who used to meet frequently at the Johnsons' or the Whites' "or at the homes of one or another" of that circle, including[7]

Heywood Broun, Claude McKay, and Carl Van Vechten, . . . Langston Hughes, Evy and Norman Levy, . . . Countee Cullen, Carl and Irita Van Doren, . . . Edna St. Vincent Millay, Sinclair Lewis, George Gershwin, . . . Willa Cather, Blanche and Alfred Knopf, . . . and many others who then enjoyed fame or were destined to achieve distinction in the arts, letters, or human relations. . . .

In fact, according to Nathan Huggins, it was White who introduced Carl Van Vechten into the Harlem social circle:[8]

It was in 1922, after the publication of *Peter Whiffle,* that Van Vechten, to use his words, became "violently interested in Negroes." . . . Walter White had just published *Fire in the Flint,* and Van Vechten got to know him through Alfred Knopf. Walter White took him everywhere—parties, lunches, dinners—introducing him to everyone who mattered in Harlem.

Recalling those days in his autobiography, Langston Hughes reflects:[9]

It was a period when, at almost every Harlem upper-crust dance or party, one would be introduced to various distinguished white celebrities there as guests. It was a period when almost any Harlem Negro of any social importance at all would be likely to say casually: "As I was remarking the other day to Heywood," meaning Heywood Broun. Or: "As I said to George," referring to George Gershwin.

There was, then, a very important meeting of personalities taking place in Harlem (and in the homes of some of the whites involved); and although the writers' recollections might occasionally seem tinged with the marveling innocence of the humble in contact with the great and near-great, some important relationships did emerge from the contacts thus established. Certainly, Van Vechten's *Nigger Heaven* (1926), for all the controversy surrounding it, was an important work that whetted the appetite of a large reading audience, and it might never have been written without the contact with Harlem that Van Vechten enjoyed thanks to Walter White.

At least as crucial as the meetings with important people in the literary world, however, was the general air of excitement generated at the time. It was a time when, for the young black artists who came to Harlem, almost anything seemed possible. People *were* interested in them, for whatever reason, and they were in the limelight that illuminated Harlem:[10]

It was a period when Charleston preachers opened up shouting churches as sideshows for white tourists. . . . It was a period when every season there was at least one hit play on Broadway acted by a Negro cast. And when books by Negro authors were being published with much greater frequency and much more publicity than ever before or since in history. . . . It was the period when the Negro was in vogue.

No wonder young writers like Hughes and Cullen and even somewhat older writers like White felt swept away by a tide of possibilities.

Yet not all those young writers who showed promise fulfilled their dreams; in fact, those who did succeed were most likely the exceptions, not the rule. In reference to Bruce Nugent, a protégé of Alain Locke, Arthur Davis notes that "the works that Locke got from [Nugent] for *The New Negro* show a potential never realized." Davis then adds:[11]

This was the case, unfortunately, with too many New Negro creative artists.

Too many were one-good-poem or one-good-book writers. One of the most gifted of the latter group was a young West Indian . . . named Eric Walrond. His *Tropic Death* (1926) was in its way as significant a first work as were *Color* by Countee Cullen and *The Weary Blues* by Langston Hughes. But Walrond . . . never seemed to recover from his first success.

Why Walrond and other writers, some well known (e.g., Jean Toomer) and some never really known, failed when others succeeded is a question too broad for consideration here. Perhaps some of them really did have only one book in them, as Davis suggests, or perhaps, like Toomer, some of them felt drawn into different areas of their lives and abandoned writing "race" literature altogether. Whatever the reasons for the failures, there were at least some forces of motivation in the times that helped propel the writers who did succeed.

Those writers who produced on a regular basis during this period primarily focused on the black experience in America. Comparing this interest to an earlier call for a national focus on things American, a "cultural autonomy," by Emerson, Robert Bone says:[12]

The Negro Renaissance was essentially a period of self-discovery, marked by a sudden growth of interest in things Negro. The Renaissance thus reversed the assimilationist trend of the pre-war period, with its conscious imitation of white norms and its deliberate suppression of "racial" elements. The motivation for this sudden reversal was not primarily literary but sociological.

Quoting E. Franklin Frazier, Bone goes on to explain that whenever minorities within the United States have been unable to blend in with the larger society, they have inevitably begun to glorify the very characteristics which caused their exclusion, i.e., those characteristics that are in some way distinctly their own. For the Harlem Renaissance writers this took the form of a celebration of the strength and the positive attitude toward life that enabled the black community to survive centuries of enslavement and deprivation. To these young writers it seemed that Harlem offered the best contemporary source from which to draw their images and characters; or, as Bone notes, perhaps it was more specifically a "Harlemesque *quality*"[1] of strength and vitality which gave their works distinction.

Something definitely was in the air, and it was sensed by many people who were in positions to feel it. In a 1924 letter to Claude McKay, Walter White, then assistant secretary of the NAACP, wrote:[14]

I know you will be delighted to hear of the many changes that have come in America since you left. The marvelous success of Roland Hayes and Paul

Robeson in "The Emperor Jones" and "All God's Chillun Got Wings," coupled with the various novels, poems and other signs of an awakening artistic sense and articulacy on the part of the Negro have caused what seems to be a new day to set in.

A few months later White wrote to Mordecai Johnson concerning the widening opportunities for black writers:[15]

As never before in the history of the Negro is there opportunity today for him to have his say. Within the last few months, I have been asked by five publishers, every one of them of the first rank, to keep my eye open for any promising writer among us.

As we shall see later, White was very active in helping some of the young writers meet the publishing contacts he mentioned in the letter above.

Significantly, this lively interest in black art was mainly emanating from the white community, not Harlem itself,[16] an interesting contrast to our contemporary situation. As Langston Hughes tells us: "The ordinary Negroes hadn't heard of the Negro Renaissance. And if they had, it hadn't raised their wages any."[17] In their introduction to "The New Negro Renaissance and Beyond" in *Cavalcade* (1971), Arthur Davis and Saunders Redding support Hughes's observation:[18]

The great outpouring of serious creative effort did not attract a sizeable Negro audience or patronage, and most blacks were ignorant of the novels, the poems, the plays, the essays. The measure of success for Negro artists and writers was still the degree of white interest and approval. The New Negro Renaissance was sustained by a white audience. . . .

A measure of this lack of interest can be seen in the fact that Jean Toomer's *Cane* (1923), one of the most significant works of the period, sold fewer than 500 copies during its first year.[19]

The people of Harlem, then, were not particularly involved with the literary movement that drew its name from their community. An examination of the nature of the Harlem community at the time might help explain why it was not involved. Harlem was not just a lively collection of cabarets and the night people who inhabited them; it was a community. This fact is brought home nicely by Arthur Davis:[20]

In spite of the bohemian interests which the New Negro Renaissance cultivated, . . . Harlem was basically a lower middle class community with strong middle class attitudes and prejudice. The average Harlemite possessed what James Weldon Johnson has called "second generation respectability." He took pride in himself and his home. He would not appear on the avenue improperly dressed or wearing a "headrag." He seldom went downtown to *work,* but to *business,* carrying not a lunch pail but his overalls and lunch in a *brief case.* Perhaps, he tended to overdo this respectability, but he was of a generation and class which felt that the whole race was judged by individual conduct, and he was determined to hold up his end. Although the majority of Harlemites were Southerners who had migrated North for economic reasons, many others belonged to solid well-established Negro families who had come north to seek freedom.

In later years, of course, the respectable middle class families in Harlem fled from the ghetto jungle it was becoming; in the 1920s, however, Harlem still functioned, at least on one level, like any other middle class community.

The values of the middle class obviously had to clash at some point with the treatment of Harlem life by Hughes, McKay, and others as a special kind of exotic Americana. These artists chose as their characters and subjects for study the "high livers" of Harlem night life: prostitutes, hustlers, dancers, and free-wheeling young people in general. They celebrated the *life* of Harlem, while the middle class wanted them to demonstrate the "respectable" side of black society, i.e., the side which corresponded more closely to the values of the dominant white society. In effect, the middle class wanted a denial of the idea that there was anything "different" about being black. White's two novels technically fit into the "respectable" mode, since his protagonist in each case is from a middle class family and operates, for the most part, within the black middle class. The themes of the works, however, of lynching and of passing, make his novels something more than mere pleas for the "sameness" of the black community.

The conflict of views between community and artist is quite clearly established by two opposing points of view expressed by George Schuyler and Langston Hughes, published a week apart in the *Nation* in 1926. Schuyler's position was that the idea of a "Negro art 'made in America' is as non-existent as . . . the reported sophistication of New Yorkers." He contended that any group of people suffering the same conditions as blacks in America would have produced the same art, e.g., the blues and spirituals enjoying such admiration at the time. For support, he referred to several Negro artists of different countries—Coleridge-Taylor of England, Latino of Spain, Dumas of France—and contended that their work "shows the impress of nationality rather than race. They all reveal the psychology and culture of their environment—their color is incidental."[21] A corollary to this reasoning would be, then, that "Negro" subjects or themes, as something special or unique, would be "non-existent" as well.

A week after Schuyler's article appeared, the *Nation* printed an opposing view from the promising young poet Langston Hughes. Hughes very carefully focused his attack on the need for black expression in art as a means of developing a pride in the black community which years of white racism had destroyed. He distinguished between the "high-class" Negroes who themselves "draw a color line" and the "low-down folks" who peopled the black community at large. In the latter Hughes saw ". . . a wealth of colorful, distinctive material for any artist because they still hold their own individuality in the face of American standardizations."[22] (This statement sounds remarkably in tune with sentiments being expressed in the mainstream of American letters at that time.)

It is in discussing the artists' attitude, however, that Hughes presented the major difference between the New Negro writers of the twenties and those so-called accommodationist writers who preceded them:[23]

We younger Negro artists who create now intend to express our individual dark-skinned selves without fear or shame. If white people are pleased we are glad. If they are not, it doesn't matter. We know we are beautiful. And ugly too. The tom-tom cries and the tom-tom laughs. If colored people are pleased we are glad. If they are not, their displeasure doesn't matter either. We build our temples for tomorrow, strong as we know how, and stand on top of the [racial] mountain, free within ourselves.

Hughes and his peers were not interested in presenting either what the white public wanted or what the black middle class wanted. Although both groups were obviously important to the writers in terms of support, this declaration of literary independence was a necessary psychological idealization for the young writers of the Renaissance.

This "revolt," though, was not so complete as other literary revolutions. The writers still worked within the framework of traditional literary form, even if their subject matter was not traditional. For example, Claude McKay used the Elizabethan sonnet quite extensively in his poetry; and while the subject matter of poems like "If We Must Die" and "The White House" is hardly in keeping with the traditional subject matter of the sonnet, the form of the poems is very traditional. On the other hand, Countee Cullen tended to follow the form and matter of his idol Keats. This does not mean that there was no experimentation with form by these writers (e.g., Langston Hughes worked with transferring the blues into the medium of written verse), but there was no black Eliot or Pound writing at the time. The impressionistic poetry and prose of Toomer's *Cane,* reminiscent of Sherwood Anderson's *Winesburg, Ohio,* in so many ways, stands alone as a truly creative expression blending subject and form. It was not until Melvin Tolson and the later writers of the sixties that black American writers began to experiment with the language and form of literature.

What was important, however, was not so much what the literature of the Harlem Renaissance did not do, but what it did accomplish. One very important contribution of the Renaissance writers was the creation of *real* black characters. The more traditional characters of Dunbar and Chesnutt, the two most significant accommodationist writers of the earlier generation, gave way to the characters of the Harlem Renaissance. While the new characters were in some ways almost as stereotyped as their predecessors they were not demeaning portraits of the subhuman variety often found in the earlier literature. And although the characters are often expressions of black "primitivism," e.g., Jake in McKay's *Home to Harlem,* they are not the same exotic primitives found in the white fiction of the time. They are the people who make up a significant part of the Harlem "low-life" world of cabarets and rent parties.

What we are offered in the works by black writers that is often missing in works by whites on similar subjects is an examination of the interiors of these characters. Even Walter White's characters, for all their stiffness, have some depth in their experiences at least. In these works from the Harlem Renaissance, we see characters live complete lives, not just flashes of their dancing and drinking the night away. We learn of their dreams and their disappointments. We come to realize, in some of the works, that much of the show of gaiety is just that, a show, and that much of the laughing is done to keep from crying. As S. P. Fullinwider notes:[24]

The literary Renaissance was a release of Negro literature from the mode of reform and special pleading. The subject ceased to be "the Negro's plight" and became "the Negro." Characters began to emerge as individuals. They gradually ceased to represent the Uncle Tom, the militant-young-Negro-in-revolt type, or the ravished-but-virtuous-maiden type and achieved some uniqueness of personality. The Renaissance, in short, broke away from the restrictions imposed by the needs of reform and found the freedom to seek a literary genre.

In essence, the characters of the Harlem Renaissance writers, at least some of them, reflected the general trend in American literature toward realism, a trend that did not involve black writers fully until the twenties.

As indicated earlier, however, not everyone accepted the earthy characters of Hughes and McKay; indeed, there was another "school" of black writers who stressed middle class values and the characters to carry them out. In reaction to this attitude Alain Locke wrote:[25]

Just as with the Irish Renaissance, there were the riots and controversies over Synge's folk plays and other frank realisms of the younger school, so we are having and will have turbulent discussion and dissatisfaction with the stories, plays and poems of the younger Negro group. But writers like Rudolph Fisher, Zora Hurston, Jean Toomer, . . . and Langston Hughes

take their material objectively with detached artistic vision; . . . not merely
for modernity of style, but for vital originality of substance, the young
Negro writers dig deep into the racy peasant undersoil of the race life.

Writers like White, Jessie Fauset, and W. E. B. Du Bois chose educated,
"decent" folk for their characters, preferring to stress the troubles a
"normal" black man faced in the white world instead of the seamy side
of life drawn by the younger writers. In his review of McKay's *Home to
Harlem,* Du Bois said: "*Home to Harlem* for the most part nauseates me,
and after the dirtier parts of its filth I feel distinctly like taking a bath."[26]
"The Rear Guard," as Robert Bone calls them, wanted the world to know
that the average black American was every bit as honest and decent as the
average white American. Unfortunately, as James Weldon Johnson once
noted, "It takes nothing less than supreme genius . . . to make middle-class
society, black or white, interesting—to say nothing of making it dramatic."[27]
The mainstream of American literature had recognized that fact for years,
a point made by Hughes and others in their own defense.

In order to gain a clearer perspective of the conflicting attitudes regarding what the black writer should portray and how black characters should
be drawn, we can examine a unique survey conducted by the *Crisis* in
1926, under W. E. B. Du Bois's direction. In the spring of 1926 Du Bois
had Jessie Fauset send the "writers of the world" a list of seven questions
concerning the use of black characters and the more general problems facing
the black artist.

The questionnaire posed seven questions, some of them quite obviously
loaded to suit Du Bois's own prejudices:[28]

1. When the artist, black or white, portrays Negro characters is he under
   any obligations or limitations as to the sort of character he will portray?
2. Can any author be criticized for painting the worst or the best characters
   of a group?
3. Can publishers be criticized for refusing to handle novels that portray
   Negroes of education and accomplishment, on the ground that these
   characters are no different from white folk and therefore not interesting?
4. What are Negroes to do when they are continually painted at their
   worst and judged by the public as they are painted?
5. Does the situation of the educated Negro in America with its pathos,
   humiliation and tragedy call for artistic treatment at least as sincere
   and sympathetic as "Porgy" received?
6. Is not the continual portrayal of the sordid, foolish and criminal among
   Negroes convincing the world that this and this alone is really and essentially Negroid, and preventing white artists from knowing any other
   types and preventing black artists from daring to paint them?
7. Is there not a real danger that young colored writers will be tempted to
   follow the popular trend in portraying Negro character in the underworld
   rather than seeking the truth about themselves and their own social class?

Quite clearly these questions reflect Du Bois's own concern that the prose and poetry of writers like Hughes and McKay would dominate the black writing market, at the expense of the middle and upper class blacks whom Du Bois represented (his "Talented Tenth").

In response to the question of the type of character to be portrayed in works about black life, Carl Van Vechten, whose *Nigger Heaven* added fuel to the controversy, said: "I am fully aware of the reasons why Negroes are sensitive in regard to fiction which attempts to picture the lower strata of the race. The point is that this is an attitude completely inimical to art."[29] Most of the writers responding concurred with Van Vechten's idea; Vachel Lindsay, another white writer who frequently used the black man as a subject for his works, added:[30]

Neither the black nor the white artist should be under obligations or limitations as to the sort of character he will portray. His own experience and his inmost perceptions of truth and beauty, in its severest interpretations, should be his only criteria.

H. L. Mencken, whose answers to other questions more clearly reflect his famous biting wit, stated simply that "the artist is under no obligations or limitations whatsoever. He should be free to depict things exactly as he sees them."[31] Finally, DuBose Heyward, author of the novel (*Porgy*) to which the questionnaire refers, stated: "If the author's object is the creation of a piece of art I feel he should not be limited as to the sort of character he portrays. He should attempt that which moves him most deeply."[32]

Regarding specifically the treatment of the educated black man as a character, Heyward optimistically predicted that "the educated and artistic Negro, if presented with skill and insight, will find his public waiting for him when the publishers are willing to take the chance."[33] Van Vechten, however, questioned the value of such characters:[34]

The squalor of Negro life, the vice of Negro life, offer a wealth of novel, exotic, picturesque material to the artist. On the other hand, there is very little difference if any between the life of a wealthy or cultured Negro and that of a white man of the same class.

Van Vechten's last statement is one to which many black writers, including Walter White, would take exception, but Mencken's response hits home at the real objection to be made to such characters: "The objection is to Negro characters who are really only white men, i.e., Negro characters who are false."[35] There is still unresolved controversy regarding what makes a character "black"; the issue is one which ultimately the artist and his reader must decide.

Sherwood Anderson's response to the problem of the portrayal of black characters who are representative of the worst elements of the community shows a surprising ignorance of some of the realities of the treatment of black characters in American literature:[36]

> As to Negroes always being painted at their worst I think it isn't true. Suppose I were to grow indignant every time a white man or woman were treated badly or cheaply in the theatre or in books. I might spend my life being indignant.
>
> I have lived a good deal in my youth among common Negro laborers. I have found them about the sweetest people I know. I have said so sometimes in my books.
>
> I do not believe the Negroes have much more to complain of than the whites in this matter of their treatment in the arts.

The obvious response to this assertion, of course, is that with the sheer bulk of material about whites available one would have little trouble finding a counterbalance to any mistakenly drawn character, a luxury not so readily offered in the relatively scant field of Afro-American writing at the time.

More to the point, however, is the fact that too often the black characters presented in literature have been taken as representative of black Americans as a whole, not as types, as they should be. No one would think of asserting that Huck's Pap is representative of white male Americans, or even of white male Missourians; yet how many of Twain's readers readily accept Jim as a clear representative of black Americans? The point is, admittedly, a tricky one. On the one hand rests the artist's right to create as he sees fit; on the other hand is the vaguer obligation to realize moral responsibility for one's creations.

The question is no more clearly resolved in the responses of the black writers to Du Bois's questions about portraying Negro characters. Countee Cullen said that " . . . the Negro has not yet built up a large enough body of sound, healthy race literature to permit him to speculate in abortions and aberrations which other people are all too prone to accept as truly legitimate. . . . What would be taken as a type in other literatures is, where it touches us, seized upon as representative. . . . We must create types that are truly representative of us as a people, nor do I feel that such a move is necessarily a genuflexion away from true art."[37] In the same issue Georgia Douglas Johnson lent support to Cullen's idea: "Let the artist cease to capitalize on the frailties of the struggling or apathetic mass—and portray the best that offers. . . . Depict the best, with or without approbation and renown."[38]

Taking issue with statements such as Van Vechten's that the life of the upper class, educated Negro is no different from the life of a white person from the same class, Walter White further questioned the rationale of publishers who reject books about upper class Negroes for that reason:[39]

Suppose we carry this objection to the utilization of experiences of educated Negroes to its logical conclusion. Would not the result be this: Negro writers should not write, the young Negro is told, of educated Negroes because their lives paralleling white lives are uninteresting. If this be true, then it seems just as reasonable to say that all writers, white or colored, should abandon all sources of material save that of lower class Negro life. Manifestly this is absurd.

On the other hand, White continued, "An artist can rightly be criticized if he portrays only the worst or the best characters of any group. . . . Continual portrayal of any type to the exclusion of all others is not only harmful but bad art." (Ironically, White's handling of white characters in *The Fire in the Flint* was attacked for its myopic presentation of whites as evil.)

The dean of black American letters in the early twentieth century, Charles W. Chesnutt, in response to the question of the treatment of black characters, made an interesting observation:[40]

A true picture of life would include the good, the bad and the indifferent. Most people, of whatever group, belong to the third class, and are therefore not interesting subjects of fiction. A writer who made all Negroes bad and all white people good, or *vice versa,* would not be a true artist, and could justly be criticized.

Regarding the use of the kind of characters that Du Bois wanted to see in the literature, Chesnutt issued this challenge to black writers: "It is perhaps unfortunate that so few of the many Negro or Negroid characters in current novels are admirable types; but they are interesting, and it is the privilege and the opportunity of the colored writer to make characters of a different sort equally interesting." As if in anticipation of John Shaft and Virgil Tibbs, Chesnutt added: "If there are no super-Negroes, make some. . . . Some of the men and women who have had the greatest influence on civilization have been purely creatures of the imagination." In addition to his discussion of black characters, Chesnutt offered this note regarding white characters: "It might not be a bad idea to create a few white men who not only think they are, but who really are entirely unprejudiced in their dealings with colored folk—it is the highest privilege of art to depict the ideal." This parallels a comment by H. L. Mencken, although Mencken's statement is much more sarcastic: "The remedy of a Negro novelist," he said, "is to depict the white man at his worst." He then went on:[41]

His remedy is to make works of art that pay off the white man in his own coin. The white man, it seems to me, is extremely ridiculous. He looks ridiculous even to me, a white man myself. To a Negro he must be an hilarious spectacle. Why isn't that spectacle better described? Let the Negro sculptors spit on their hands! What a chance!

George Schuyler's *Black No More* (1931) did just that, and it managed to include some equally pointed barbs at color consciousness within the black community as well. For the most part, however, the white characters in black writing during the Harlem Renaissance were not skewered with the free-wheeling lance that Mencken suggests above.

While the problem of the treatment of black characters, and by implication at least white characters, dominates the questions presented by Du Bois, another, equally perplexing problem emerges through the responses: *what* should black writers write about? Jessie Fauset, then literary editor of the *Crisis,* said: "They must protest strongly and get their protestations before the public."[42] Although this statement was specifically directed toward the question concerning what Negroes are to do with the constant portrayal of the worst of their members, implicit in it is the idea of mild social protest that permeated much of the literature of the time. Typically, the novels of writers like White, Fauset, Du Bois, and Nella Larsen focused on the unjust treatment constantly faced by the educated black man and woman. Most writers did not see this as propaganda, per se; for example, in reaction to a charge that *The Fire in the Flint* was merely propaganda, White wrote Edgar Webster:[43]

There are some people who say that in writing about the Negro one should leave out the racial and interracial conflict. I most passionately do not believe in that school of thought. If one is going to write realistically about the Negro or Negro characters, he cannot leave out this phase of the Negro's life in America for no Negro, intelligent or non-intelligent, illiterate or educated, rich or poor, ever passes a day but that, directly or indirectly, this thing called the race problem creeps into his life. Thus I feel sure that no writer who is honest with himself can ever ignore so important a factor as this and, if he is honest about it, he is going to present it exactly as his characters would see the situation. If by doing so I am to bear the label of "propagandist," I shall do so cheerfully and with a light heart.

The problem comes, however, as Sinclair Lewis pointed out in his response to Du Bois's questionnaire, when all of the works from a particular group center on a limited number of themes:[44]

All of you, or very nearly all, are primarily absorbed in the economic and social problems of the colored race. Complicated though these problems are in detail, yet inevitably they fall into a few general themes; so that there is the greatest danger that all of your novels will be fundamentally alike. . . . You cannot, all of you, go on repeating the same novel (however important, however poignant, however magnificently dramatic) about the well-bred, literate and delightful Negro intellectual finding himself or herself blocked by the groundless and infuriating manner of superiority assumed by white men frequently less white than people technically known as Negroes.

Commenting on the problems facing the black writer in terms of the subject matter of his writing, Chesnutt was at least in partial agreement with Lewis:[45]

The prevailing weakness of Negro writings, from the viewpoint of art, is that they are too subjective. The colored writer, generally speaking, has not yet passed the point of thinking of himself first as a Negro, burdened with the responsibility of defending and uplifting his race. Such a frame of mind, however praiseworthy from a moral standpoint, is bad for art.

While as White suggests, it may ultimately be impossible for a black American writer totally to dismiss the "race problem" from his material, Chesnutt's point is a good one. No man can effectively serve two masters—in this case a cause and art—at once.

Perhaps the sanest response to the question of what characters and themes the black artists should handle was one phrased by White and echoed in many of the responses:[46]

If young Negro writers can be saved, or better, save themselves from too hostile or too friendly critics, editors, publishers, or public, from spending all their time and energy in restricted areas, they can have the freedom to explore whatever fields to which their fancy or inclination draws them.

In brief, sycophants and weaklings will follow whatever trend is mapped out for them; genuine artists will write or paint or sing or sculpt whatever they please.

Although the first part of White's statement suggests his desire to see young black artists back away from "restricted areas," i.e., the "low-life" elements that intrigued Hughes and others, the second part suggests equally that the artist must finally express his art in his own way. And, while White did not always like the mode of expression chosen by the artists (his review of Hughes's *Fine Clothes to the Jew* complained of the limitations of the blues form for use in poetry), he always encouraged the young artists to seek their own means of expression.

There was, then, in the American artistic community of the 1920s, a fairly broad spectrum of ideas concerning the treatment of black characters and themes. The controversy has never really been resolved, but Langston Hughes did offer a very perceptive observation in his response to Du Bois: "You write about the intelligent Negroes; [Rudolph] Fisher about the unintelligent. Both of you are right. . . . It's the way people look at things, not what they look at, that needs to be changed."[47]

The mood and feeling at work in the black artistic community at the time of the Harlem Renaissance were ones of extreme excitement and anticipation. It was a time of real possibilities, both for the artist who wished only to create his art and for the artist who felt the need to help his people in the art he could create; in some cases, perhaps too rarely, an artist might have done both. No matter what the individual results, however, it was the collective feeling of accomplishment that flamed the spirit of the New Negro. As Locke commented:[48]

. . . whatever the general effect, the present generation will have added the motives of self-expression and spiritual development to the old and still unfinished task of making material headway and progress. No one who understandingly faces the situation with its substantial accomplishment or views the new scene with its still more abundant promise can be entirely without hope. . . . And certainly, if in our lifetime the Negro should not be able to celebrate his full initiation into American democracy, he can at least, on the warrant of these things, celebrate the attainment of a significant and satisfying new phase of group development, and with it a spiritual Coming of Age.

Toward the end of the decade a white critic and scholar, Howard Odum, echoed Locke's sentiments. While doubting that there is "a 'New Negro' except as there is a 'new' South and a 'new' Times," Odum offered these observations about the qualities reflected in black writing of the twenties:[49]

Literary portraits reflecting a new realism. A new frankness and courage to face facts without fear, excitement, or apologies. Pride and artistry in the rediscovery and interpretation of a rich folk background of the race. . . . A new understanding of the challenge to achieve universal, as well as racial, standards of excellence. Race consciousness . . . a mellowed bitterness. A mature vision of racial cooperation, race development, and understanding. A new outlook and with it a new zest, tempered by the twin forces of opportunity and obligation.

Whether this "spiritual Coming of Age" was a new birth or a rebirth, it was a time of beginning, and one of the many people who actively participated in this beginning was Walter White. In his capacity as assistant secretary of the NAACP, White was able to help many of the young writers, through his contacts and his encouragements, fulfill some of the promise he and others saw, and his *The Fire in the Flint* and *Flight* offered their own contributions to the times. As we shall see, Walter White was an important part of the Harlem Renaissance.

3

THE FIRE IN THE FLINT

The fire in the flint never shows until it is struck.

—Old English Proverb

It seems probable to me that "The Fire in the Flint"
and "A Passage to India" will prove much the most
important books of this autumn, and it is a curious
thing that both of them deal with the racial struggles.
"The Fire in the Flint" is splendidly courageous,
rather terrifying, and of the highest significance.

—Sinclair Lewis

When Sinclair Lewis in 1924 had this statement sent to Alfred A. Knopf
for use in promoting Walter White's *The Fire in the Flint,* he was undoubtedly somewhat carried away in his praise of this first novel by his new
friend. Today, of course, Walter White's novel pales in comparison to
Forster's classic, yet *Fire* did cause some controversy when it was published
and was considered an innovative novel by more than one critic. It dealt
openly with the problems of race hatred and, more importantly, lynching
in the South, and had as its hero an educated black man, a doctor, who
refused to compromise his principles in spite of the intense hatred generated
in him by the jim-crow South to which he returned to help his people. And
it was promoted as being written by a man who, in his capacity as assistant
secretary of the NAACP and from his experience as a lynching investigator,
knew his subject intimately. While the novel has many literary shortcomings,
a study of it, its critical reception, and the history of its publication and
promotion offers an insight into publishing experiences common to black
writers during the Harlem Renaissance. In fact, the promotional machinery

employed by Walter White and Knopf, his publisher, especially as it involved the NAACP and its branches, was used often by White to help other black writers of the time.

In his autobiography White stated that his decision to write a novel about the true racial conditions in the South was a response to a challenge by H. L. Mencken. White had met Mencken through James Weldon Johnson and was quickly called upon by the editor of the *Smart Set:*[1]

Shortly after meeting Mencken I received one of his characteristically terse and salty notes asking what I thought of *Birthright,* a novel about the Negro by T. S. Stribling of Tennessee. Flattered, I wrote a lengthy and painfully erudite criticism of the book pointing out that the novel had courage in depicting Negroes as human beings instead of as menials or buffoons, but that it obviously was written from the outside looking in. I said that Stribling's depiction of Negro servants was not too bad, but that he fell down badly in his portrayal of what educated Negroes feel and think. Mencken replied, "Why don't you do the right kind of a novel? You could do it, and it would create a sensation."

With Mencken's encouragement, and Johnson's, White accepted Mary White Ovington's offer to use her cottage in Massachusetts for the summer of 1922 and tackled his project with some excitement.

White began to write with no clear direction in mind and only "a rather misty notion" of his main character: " . . . a Negro doctor, trained in a first-class Northern medical school and returned to his native Georgia small town. . . ."[2] This sounds disturbingly close to Stribling's main character in *Birthright,* Peter Siner, a Harvard-educated Negro who returns to his native Tennessee village of Hooker's Bend, hoping to establish a new Tuskegee; however, the two characters and their fortunes quickly become distinguishable. Peter Siner eventually returns to the North, after being frustrated by both the white and black elements of Hooker's Bend, while Kenneth Harper, the hero of *The Fire in the Flint,* remains in Central City, Georgia, and meets a violent end.

As White was to tell numerous correspondents, *Fire* almost wrote itself. According to his own account in *A Man Called White,* he wrote "feverishly and incessantly for twelve days and parts of twelve nights, stopping only when complete fatigue made it physically and mentally impossible to write another word. On the twelfth day the novel was finished. . . ."[3] A letter to James Weldon Johnson, written September 12, 1922, offers a more precise idea of the speed with which White wrote the novel:[4]

Today we have been here one week. Not counting last Tuesday and as I haven't done my day's stint as yet, in six days I have written slightly more th 35,000 words on my novel. I know you'll say it can't be much, writing at that rate but I have the feeling it has got something in it. It's much easier than I thought—the story is writing itself. Incidents and scenes and characters that I knew years ago and thought I had forgotten crop up in the most unexpected manner and fit quite smoothly into the thread of the story. Of course, there will be lots of revisions necessary, smoothing out awkward constructions, amplifying here and cutting there, and the innumerable details to make it a possible and probable and readable tale. By the time I come back, I hope to have a corrected draft ready for the caustic and devastating criticism of yours and the two Spingarns and Mencken, et al. Ora pro nobis!

Over the course of the following two years, many people were to read the manuscript of *Fire,* including J. E. Spingarn, who suggested that the novel, for all its power, simply was not satisfactorily written. In spite of countless readings and suggestions, the book never quite lost its "twelve-day wonder" gloss.

The plot of *The Fire in the Flint* is relatively simple. Kenneth Harper, after being educated at Atlanta University and a "Northern medical school" and after serving in France during World War I, returns to his home town of Central City, Georgia, intent on becoming the best surgeon in southern Georgia; he even dreams of eventually opening a clinic "something like the Mayo Brothers up in Rochester, Minnesota." On his return he finds his younger brother Bob extremely pessimistic about the possibility of any cooperation from the whites. Kenneth believes, however, that if he leaves the white folks alone, they will leave him alone. In fact, at the beginning of the novel he voices his belief that black people have to make it on their own individual initiative:[5]

Bob's seeing things like a kid in the dark. He thinks I'll not be able to do the things I came back here to accomplish. Thinks the Crackers won't let me! I'm going to solve my own problems, do as much good as I can, make as much money as I can! If every Negro in America did the same thing, there wouldn't be any "race problem."

Fire, then, becomes a study of Kenneth Harper's gradual awakening to the realities of racism and the demands imposed upon the individual by an oppressed people.

Robert Bone's analysis of the novel as "a series of essays, strung on an unconvincing plot. . ."[6] is perhaps too severe a judgment. True, the novel is episodic and melodramatic and frequently ranges into exposition, but there is a change in the central character, however belabored, and there is occasional insight into human nature. The Reverend Mr. Wilson, a black preacher, for example, startles Kenneth when his ordinarily crude speech becomes refined in private conversation. Chuckling, the older man explains a fact of southern black life to his young and racially naive neighbor:

There's a reason—in fact there are two reasons why I talk like that [i.e., crudely]. The first is because of my own folks. Outside of you and your folks . . . and one or two more, all of my congregation is made up of folks with little or no education. They've all got good hard common sense. . . . But they don't want a preacher that's too far above them—they'll feel that they can't come to him with their troubles if he's too highfalutin. I try to get right down to my folks, feel as they feel, suffer when they suffer, laugh with them when they laugh, and talk with them in language they can understand. . . . And then there's the other reason. . . . The white folks here are mighty suspicious of any Negro who has too much learning, according to their standards. They figure he'll be stirring up the Negroes to fight back when any trouble arises. [Pp. 106–8]

Here, in a character many white writers would present as a Bible-banging buffoon, White gives us an insight into the workings of the mind of a man who decided to mask his true capabilities in order to serve his people. And Kenneth Harper soon learns that the Reverend Mr. Wilson's statement about the suspicions white folks have of educated Negroes is accurate.

A series of events directly affecting Kenneth Harper fall together to form the plot of the novel. He incurs the jealous hatred of the other Negro doctor in Central City, old Dr. Williams, by asking him to assist in an operation, and he realizes that he will never be more than a "nigger doctor" to Dr. Bennett, the town's inept white physician. He witnesses the injustice that follows the murder of Bud Ware, who was shot when he found his wife and her white lover together; the lover/murderer is the sheriff's brother, so Kenneth's futile attempt to report his findings as the physician on the scene only results in a threat of Klan retaliation if he does not keep quiet. Later Nancy Ware is brutally beaten by the Klan for "talking too much" about the incident.

It is what happens to his immediate family, however, that finally shocks Kenneth Harper into a realization of the world in which he lives. First, his sister is raped by a gang of white toughs, and then Bob, after he succeeds in killing two of the boys who raped his sister, is hunted down and finally kills himself to prevent being taken by the mob. Furious over being denied its revenge, the mob riddles Bob's corpse with bullets, drags it back into town, and burns it in the public square, after which little children dart among the dying flames for souvenirs. While all this is happening, Kenneth is in Atlanta to operate on a patient and to meet with some white businessmen and community leaders to discuss his plan for a farmers' cooperative society for the sharecroppers living around Central City. When he returns and discovers what has happened, he goes into a tirade of hate against the white world which has all but destroyed his family:

"Superior race"! "Preservers of civilization"! "Superior," indeed! They call Africans inferior! They, with smirking hypocrisy, reviled the Turks! They went to war against the "Huns" because of Belgium! None of these had ever done a thing so bestial as these "preservers of civilization" in Georgia. . . . "White Civilization"! Paugh! Black and brown and yellow hands had built it! The white fed like carrion on the rotting flesh of the darker peoples! And called *their* toil their own! And burned those on whose bodies their vile civilization was built! [P. 271]

Mrs. Ewing, a white woman whose daughter Kenneth had saved earlier, calls late that same night to ask Kenneth's help, as her daughter has suffered a setback because the ignorant Dr. Bennett had not followed Kenneth's advice. His first impulse is to tell her that "if by raising one finger I could save the whole white race from destruction, and by not raising it send them all straight to hell, I'd die before I raised it!" Eventually, though, his training as a doctor and Mrs. Ewing's revelation that her husband has gone to Atlanta to warn Kenneth not to return outweigh his bitterness, and he goes to the Ewings. Meanwhile, some Klansmen (including Sheriff Parker), who have been following Harper's every move, see him enter the house and, knowing that Roy Ewing is out of town, immediately conclude that Kenneth and Mrs. Ewing are having an affair. When Kenneth leaves, the men grab him and, after a fierce struggle, shoot him. The next day a news dispatch headed "ANOTHER NEGRO LYNCHED IN GEORGIA" presents the "official" version of the incident:

"Doc" Harper, a negro, was lynched here to-night, charged with attempted criminal assault on a white woman. . . . Harper evidently became frightened before accomplishing his purpose and was caught as he ran from the house. He is said to have confessed before being put to death by a mob which numbered five thousand. He was burned at the stake. . . . In a telegram to the Governor to-day, Sheriff Parker reported that all was quiet in the city and he anticipated no further trouble. [P. 300]

Deciding to end the novel with this callous and obviously falsified news release was probably the most artistic stroke White accomplished in *The Fire in the Flint*. It serves as its own comment on the climactic events of the novel, and avoids the didacticism which is so characteristic of the rest of the novel.

In addition to the dominant protest against the evils of lynching, White also incorporated other minor themes of protest in *Fire*. A significant subplot is developed concerning the efforts of Kenneth Harper and some of the farmers to form a co-op from which the sharecroppers could buy their supplies at reasonable prices, instead of being gouged by the stores from which they are forced to buy. Hiram Tucker explains how the system works:[7]

... all of us folks out dat way wuks on shares like dis. We makes a 'greemen wif de landlord to wuk one year or mo'. He fu'nishes de lan' and we puts de crap in de soil, wuks it, den gathers it. We's sposed to 'vide it share and share alike wif de landlord but it doan wuk out dat way. If us cullud folks ain't got money enough to buy our seed and fert'lizer and food and the clo'es we needs du'in de year, we is allowed t' take up dese things at de sto'. Den when we goes to settle up after de cott'n and cawn's done laid by, de sto' man who wuks in wif de landlord won't giv' us no bill for whut we done bought but jes' gives us a li'l' piece of paper wif de words on it: "Balance Due."   [P. 113]

His attempts to help these farmers marks Kenneth Harper for Klan action as a "meddlin' nigger." Although the idea of a farmer's cooperative being used to alleviate the suffering of sharecroppers in what has been aptly termed "legalized slavery" is not new in White's novel, the merging of the protest motif with the larger antilynching theme underscores the economic factor in racial oppression that White felt was central to the problem.[8]

The real strength of *The Fire in the Flint* lies, finally, in what it says, not in how well it says it. There are flaws in the story and, as Bone points out, there is too much exposition for narrative fiction. White's treatment of the love story involving Kenneth Harper and Jane Phillips is incredibly naive and more fitting a sentimental novel than a novel of protest. And the characters, with a few exceptions, are flatly drawn types. The Reverend Mr. Wilson is given some depth, but only after a rather stereotyped carica-ture of him as a "pompous, bulbous-eyed" and vain man, "exceedingly fond of long words, especially of Latin derivation." It is almost as if White changed his mind about the good Reverend in the process of writing the story. The treatment of white characters in *Fire* is even more sparse; there are few admirable white representatives in it. Judge Stevenson is one exception, and Roy Ewing is another, although Ewing at first wants nothing to do with the "nigger doctor" who operates on his daughter. Sheriff Park-er and the rest of the white townspeople are presented as ignorant, bovine creatures who mull over murder as other men debate the necessity of re-moving crabgrass.

But we must keep in mind that this is 1924, a time when people were still being lynched with some regularity and when most white Americans' concept of Negroes was based upon the caricatures of the minstrel shows and the beasts haunting the pages of Thomas Dixon and his compatriots. *Fire* not only presented a sympathetic examination of the trials confront-ing an educated black man in a society geared to grind him into submission or a grave, it also presented a look at some of the foibles of that society as seen from a black perspective. For example, at the beginning of the novel Roy Ewing comes to Kenneth Harper for treatment of a "social disease" contracted during a night of abandon in Macon. As White says: "That was Kenneth's introduction to one part of the work of a colored physician in the South. Many phases of life that he as a youth had never known about . . . he now had brought to his attention." Harper was also appalled by the whorehouses thriving in Central City, especially the ones in "Darktown": "Here were coloured women who seemed never to have to work. Here was seldom seen a coloured man. And the children around these houses were usually lighter in colour than in other parts of 'Darktown'" (p. 40). White makes good use of his naive hero in these passages. A seasoned cynic would hardly remark the obvious discrepancies of what the whites preached about segregation and what they practiced; he would simply accept it as a matter of course. Through the eyes of the innocent Kenneth Harper, though, White can let his white reader see a world through eyes that are just as unused to the light as his own. Judging from the reactions of people who wrote White after reading the novel, this is exactly the effect the book had, at least in some quarters.

After White's letter to Johnson in September, 1922, further mention of the book dwindled in the NAACP correspondence for a few months. White did write Clement Wood, whose *Nigger* White reviewed for the *Nation:* "I am particularly interested in your story in view of the fact that I have recently tried my hand at the same task but with different success. It was my first attempt at creative writing in the field of literature. However, I shall rewrite and rewrite—if necessary twenty times—until I have, if possible, made something worth while." And on December 15, 1922, White told Floyd Calvin that "my own book . . . now is very much in the embryonic stage."[9]

White is quite calm about his next experience with the novel when he relates the episode in his autobiography. He mentions running into John Farrar, at that time editor of the *Bookman,* published by George H. Doran and Company, who insisted on seeing White's manuscript. Later, White recalls, Doran asked him to meet with him and Eugene Saxton, then an associate editor for that firm; Doran, obviously embarrassed, told White that they would not be able to use his novel because its Negro characters "are not what readers expect." Irvin S. Cobb, White learned later, had read the manuscript, and it was he who persuaded Doran, a good friend, not to accept the novel for publication.[10] White tells us he was "disheartened and disillusioned," but not much more. In fact, the whole episode involving White and Saxton, and Doran's ultimate rejection of *The Fire in the Flint,* provides a clear portrait of a major problem facing black writers in America, even at a time when interest in their work was beginning to blossom.

On June 8, 1923, Eugene Saxton wrote White a letter which sounded quite hopeful:[11]

As to our final action on the book, I cannot honestly say to you before seeing the revised text that we will take it. But I can say that my reading of the first draft impressed me very much and the possibilities seem strongly in favor of our making you an offer for it. Speaking for myself, I shall be much disappointed if your book is not in our announcements late this year or early in 1924.

White himself was evidently very hopeful about the success of his book with Doran. He sent Saxton a list of people he knew, presumably those who might write blurbs for his book; the list included H. G. Wells (whom he had met in London in 1921), H. L. Mencken, Carl Van Doren, Charles Edward Russell, Stephen Vincent Benet, and Dorothy Canfield (Fisher). In addition White stated that James Weldon Johnson would push sales of the book through the Association's branches. Johnson was going to suggest that each member buy two copies: one for himself and one "for a white friend."[12] The next day White wrote Saxton again, this time adding that "perhaps through Mr. [Joel] Spingarn, I can get some comment from Sinclair Lewis," and noting that Curtis Wheeler of the *Literary Digest* had expressed interest in the book. (Both Lewis and Wheeler later reviewed *Fire,* but only after Alfred A. Knopf had published it.)

At this time Saxton was actively engaged in the editorial process with *Fire.* On July 23 he wrote White that his revisions of the manuscript had improved it, but that there were still some problems:[13]

So far two definite criticisms emerge: the manuscript needs in my opinion another careful and thorough editing to correct minor faults of construction; and then there is the large question which hits me somewhat more forcibly as I read the book this second time—namely, the ultimate effect of the picture you paint on the problem which you and we are facing alike in the race question. On reading your story the second time, there are portions of the manuscript which, it seems to me, are bound to make a bad matter worse. And it is a question how wise a procedure that is for anyone who has the cause of justice honestly at heart.

Whether Cobb had entered the picture by this time or not is unclear; however, it is clear that Saxton, either officially or personally, had some doubts about publishing the novel.

By August 16, 1923, Doran had decided not to accept White's novel for publication, mainly because, as Saxton pointed out, they felt the novel was too one-sided:[14]

We have gone over the question very carefully and I had a talk with Mr. Doran about it this morning. The verdict, I am sorry to say, is against the book. No one here, I can assure you, lacks sympathy for the thesis underlying your work but it is the method of presentation to which we take exception. I spoke of this in our first conference in this office and perhaps my personal and lively interest in the subject matter of your story made me over-confident of the results that could be achieved by re-writing. At any rate, after another careful inspection of the manuscript, I realize now that the thing that I saw as a possible result of re-writing was probably pretty much out of reach in this particular case, even if you had agreed with my own point of view sufficiently to desire it.

It seems to me that the race question is so vital and enters so penetratingly into most of our communities that the publication of a partial statement—especially a statement which tends to inflame one section against the other—would only result in putting off further into the future a decent settlement such as we all desire.

More specifically, Saxton felt that the novel's documentation was "exclusively on one side of the case. Practically speaking," he added, "there is nobody in court but the attorney for the prosecution."

White sent Saxton a three-page reply. After thanking him for all his help and assuring him that "there is no bit of feeling on my part of any sentiment other than deep appreciation, . . ." White presented his defense of *Fire*. To Saxton's comment that the case presented in the novel was all one-sided, White replied:[15]

. . . is it not about time that the prosecution should be heard? For fifty years or more the argument has been all on one side, i.e., for the defense. Thomas Nelson Page, George W. Cable, Thomas Dixon, . . . Octavus Roy Cohen, T. S. Stribling, . . . Irvin Cobb—all have painted the Negro as a vicious brute, a rapist, a "good old nigger," or as a happy-go-lucky, irresponsible and shiftless type with the exception of Stribling who tried to picture what an intelligent, educated Negro feels—*terra incognita* to him—and, since he was not attempting a fantasy in "Birthright," a miserable failure.

White went on to present his strongest defense of the novel, one which he was to use time and again in responding to critics—his expertise on the subject about which he was writing:

. . . here is an attempt, however inept and unfinished, to depict the tragedy of color prejudice as seen by intelligent Negroes of high ideals—of which territory I am not wholly ignorant—and you object because an attempt is made to give the other side of the picture which has never been adequately given. . . . Have you not unconsciously fallen into the error common to a vast majority of Americans . . . that fictional treatment of the Negro must be carefully fitted to "stereotypes"?

Later White offered to supply Saxton with data to support the "truths" of his novel, emphasizing that he had, in fact, held back in his attack:

I consciously held myself in check throughout the writing of my novel, for had I told of some of the cases which I know through personal investigation to be true the result would have been beyond belief to all but those who actually suffer these things. If you would like corroboration of that statement I would be glad to send you one or two statements of actual cases made by Southern white people . . . which would make the things in my book seem weak by comparison.

While this statement seems fair enough in response to the criticisms made by Saxton, White used the same argument, that the things about which he wrote could and did happen, to defend *Fire* against completely different charges involving its artistic merit. White seemed unable, or unwilling, to distinguish between "truth" in life and artistic "truth."

In the same letter to Saxton White argued that works such as his were needed for larger social purposes, and to help save America from self-destruction:

. . . what will be the ultimate effect on white America and civilization by perpetuation of the system of which the Negro is the victim in America? . . . it is relatively unimportant what happens to eleven million Negroes in America if there were not an inevitable reaction on those who either oppress them or acquiesce in that oppression by their silence. The brutalization of the dominant whites of the South has come about through their exploitation and inhuman treatment of the Negro. As Mr. Mencken points out with characteristic force in his "Prejudices II" the South is "as sterile, artistically, intellectually, culturally, as the Sahara Desert" almost solely because its energies have been consumed in "keeping the nigger in his place."

This is strong language from a man who is traditionally thought of as moderate in his statements on race relations. And while these thoughts are certainly not new with White, they are legitimate concerns that are still quite relevant.

Finally White queried Saxton regarding the "artistic treatment of a subject as complex as the race problem." As he was in responding to Du Bois's questionnaire, White again seemed most concerned with the presentation of the exceptional Negro character:

Must we always conform to stereotypes created by those who know little or nothing of what the real facts are? Must we treat fictionally men like Du Bois, Braithwaite, Johnson, McKay, Maran, Dumas, Pushkin, Tanner and a host of others in the same manner set by Irvin S. Cobb or Hugh Wiley or Thomas Dixon? Or are we to be honest with ourselves and stand or fall by the one standard, "Is it true?"

After once more assuring Saxton that he harbored no ill feelings and asking him what portions of the novel "make a bad matter worse," White closed the letter with the following sentiment: "I do hope our pleasant acquaintanceship of the past may continue and that our disagreement on these points of attack on the great problem of race relations in America may not in any way affect our common desire to better those relations." In this last statement White seems much more the NAACP public relations man than author, though we can see how well both purposes are served here. Walter White was an expert at extracting as much use as possible from everything he did.

Saxton replied quickly, saying "We are really much nearer together than you imagine." He then articulated more fully his objection to the novel:[16]

I have no quarrel—or practically none—with what you say in your book. It is what you don't say that I find fault with. Personally I should be entirely willing to have ninety-five per cent of all you say remain in the book if there were some moderately fair presentation of the white man's case. Perhaps you don't think he has a case worth presenting. That, of course, is a matter of personal conviction. Entirely honest people draw such divergent conclusions from any given mass of evidence. But however feeble the case may be, it is not set forth with any circumstance or conviction in your story. You may not believe me, but I assure you the heaviest weapon of offense you have against the existing order is your willingness to give it its just due and show that it is essentially rotten in spite of its accidental merits.

This idea of fairness regarding the treatment of the white world in the novel was also used by Saxton in speaking of the characters in *The Fire in the Flint:*

I am not . . . concerned with "stereotypes," as you say. I don't ask you to paint your people in any other way than as you see them and know them to be. But as you present your characters not merely as individuals in a small town, but rather as exemplars of the modern Negro, it seems unfair, and unworthy, to place against them in the scale the white figures who so palpably stand for the lowest order of white intelligence—with one or two ineffectual exceptions.

That is the real crux of the matter as I see it and it is a question in my mind whether your book as it now stands is likely to accomplish the thing you hope for. That it would make money I do not question. But that is not enough either to satisfy you or us.

An examination of *Fire* verifies Saxton's position regarding the treatment of white characters, as we have noted; with the exception of Judge Stevenson and possibly Roy Ewing, White's Anglo characters are narrow-minded, brutish slobs who visibly drool at the mouth as they contemplate the next evil deed they can perpetrate against the black community of Central City.

As a final gesture of his real concern with the race problem, Saxton suggested to White that the NAACP might "give out in a small pamphlet one hundred fully attested cases for the annals of Southern violence . . . the circulation of such a document in the manner of the official 'white paper' and 'yellow paper' would focus a searchlight of publicity on the race question that would be extremely valuable." What Saxton was saying, in effect, was that White needed to separate propaganda from art, and that he had at his disposal the perfect mechanism for the dissemination of knowledge regarding the atrocities of southern violence.

Ignoring this last suggestion, White replied to Saxton's letter on August 23, once again using the authority with which he wrote the novel as an argument against Saxton's objections:[17]

> I was born in Georgia. For twenty-four years I lived there. Between my junior and senior years in college I sold life insurance in that state, spending nearly four months living in small towns of which Central City is typical. There I talked with and learned to know white and colored people of all classes, particularly of the better type. . . since I have been in my present work I have personally investigated thirty-six lynchings and eight race riots. Because of the peculiar advantage I possess of being able to go either as a white man or a colored man I have talked on terms of intimacy with hundreds of white men *as one of them* and to hundreds, nay thousands, of Negroes *as one of them.* I hope I am not too over confident when I say that this varied and intimate experience in garnering all shades of opinion should qualify me to speak with some degree of authority on this subject.

Certainly, no one would deny White's knowledge of the material treated in *Fire,* and he did enjoy a unique advantage in being able to "pass" whenever he desired. The question is not what White knew, but whether he turned his knowledge into art or propaganda. He was never able to convince the people at Doran that he had done the former.

While the disagreement between White and Saxton concerning the representation of "truth" in the novel is interesting and important, this letter from White also contains other information regarding the background of some of the characters in *Fire* and the author's intent in the story. The central character of the novel, Kenneth Harper, White noted, was "the counterpart of a man [Louis Wright?] who is one of my closest friends— who, an honor graduate of Harvard, is today practicing in New York City after having tried to do in Georgia what I made Kenneth Harper try to do. He failed. The atmosphere of prejudice and ignorance was too much for him." White also referred to a conversation between Harper and Judge Stevenson and noted that "it is almost verbatim one I had two or three years ago with E. L. Wharton, Vice-President of the Greensboro National Bank at Greensboro, N. C. . . . ." While White does not say that Wharton served as his model for Judge Stevenson, we can assume from this statement that Wharton's attitudes, at least, were incorporated into the character of the judge. In a letter to Mrs. Miriam Bishop in 1925, White said that "there is only one character in the book [in] the creation of which I can be accused of dishonesty and that is Judge Stevenson whom I painted in a guise slightly more decent than any person I know."[18]

White's intent in the novel was simple and direct. As he told Saxton:[19]

. . . here is what I tried to accomplish. I took a town in South Georgia which seemed to me typical—a town in which I have spent many months. I mentally put there Kenneth Harper. . . . I tried, with as great objectivity as my naturally strong feelings on the subject would permit, to study dispassionately what would be Harper's reaction to his environment and the reaction to him of that environment. Whatever else it may lack, my enquiry was, as far as I could make it, an honest, sincere and frank one.

From that rather straightforward declaration of honest intent, White proceeded to defend once more his treatment of the white point of view in the book:

It is not that I sought to do injustice to the white man, nor was there any lack of desire to give the white man's side of the case. Certainly, I think he has a case but, by all that is holy, all we've had is his side. Disregarding that circumstance, however, I strove to give the picture exactly as I saw it. In attempting to follow your suggestions I developed the character of Judge Stevenson to the point where I almost idealized him—made him, in fact, a higher type than an environment like Central City would produce. And there lies the tragedy . . . the South has so dehumanized and brutalized itself by its policy of repression of the Negro that my white characters are true to life. They *are* ineffectual. They *are* depraved. They *are* rotten. . . . I am reminded of a wise saying by the late Booker T. Washington, "The only way to keep a man in the ditch is by lying down beside him," and the South with its Central Cities has lain down and the turmoil in America today over the race question is due to two things—one, that debasing of instinct and natural human resources, and second, the refusal of the rest of America to face obvious but unpleasant facts.

This is indeed a strong indictment of the existing order of American society in 1923 and a powerful statement for a hopeful writer to be making to his potential editor, especially when that editor is part of the existing order.

This did not mean, however, that White was unwilling to compromise his principles in order to get his book published. He told Saxton that he realized "the whole truth on the race problem will not be accepted as yet," and asked what he might do to make the novel acceptable to Doran:

If we can find some way of approaching the "five per cent" divergence do you think that Mr. Doran and yourself would be willing to reconsider your decision? . . . as I have told you in conversation, there is no firm that I want as publishers as much as I do Doran.

Then White played what he assumed might be his trump card by reminding Saxton that "Boni and Liveright will bring out in the spring a novel by Miss Jessie Fauset [*There Is Confusion*] " and stating his position that "the first novel in the field giving the reactions of the educated Negro is going to have a tremendous advantage. That is why I want Doran to publish the novel prior to any other of its kind." The reception of White's book in the fall of 1924 does not seem to have been influenced one way or the other by the publication of Jessie Fauset's book, but White, the shrewd businessman, obviously could not pass up an opportunity to pioneer in the field, as much for the money as for the distinction of being a "first."

Not content to let his last arguments work alone, White wrote a second letter to Saxton on August 23 suggesting that Doran might publish *Fire* and include a preface consisting of the correspondence between White and Saxton, thus giving Saxton (and Doran) a chance to express disagreement with the novel's thesis. Noting he got the idea from rereading the *Apologia pro Scriptis Meis* in the American edition of George Moore's *Memoirs of My Dead Life,* White added: "The plan would be a corking hors-d'oeuvre for the critics that couldn't help but arouse their interest—which wouldn't hurt sales. It might prove a tasty morsel for them to roll under their tongues. Unfortunately, Saxton responded that he thought it was not a very good idea.[20]

At this time White was pursuing other avenues to help get his novel accepted by Doran. On August 22, 1923, White wrote to J. E. Spingarn, sending copies of the correspondence with Saxton. He also referred to a meeting with Saxton "and my friend, John Farrar," in which it was agreed that a copy of the manuscript would be sent to Dr. Will W. Alexander, Direc of the Commission on Interracial Cooperation in Atlanta, Georgia, "with the request that he answer two questions: first, is the story true, and second is it wise to publish the truth at this stage." White told Spingarn that "Doran finds no fault with the literary quality of the novel other than minor faults of construction. . . . The deciding factor in their decision was Irvin Cobb who advised against publication. This was given me in confidence. Mr. Cobb is a close friend of Mr. Doran."[21] This letter also contains one of the first references to Knopf as a possible publisher; White said that he had written Mencken "to see if he would submit it to Knopf." Wisely, White was not pinning all his hopes on Doran.

The manuscript of *Fire* was sent to Alexander on September 11, accompanied by a letter from White in which he detailed the objectives of the novel:[22]

(1) to give a frank and adequate picture of the feelings and thoughts of intelligent Negroes on the race problem, (2) to show that the lot of the poor white man in the South is, physically, but little better than that of the Negro and that mentally he is somewhat worse off, and (3) to show the tragic position occupied by the liberal white men and women of the South who are seeking a way out of the situation in which the race problem has enmeshed the South.

These last two points are new and seem especially tailored to appeal to the man to whom the letter was sent. On the whole, Alexander was pleased with the novel, and on October 1 he wrote White: "I have read your manuscript and so has Dr. T. J. Woofter, Jr. We were interested and feel that you have written a good story. There are some details which may possibly be out of proportion—but on the whole represent one angle of the situation which should be made known and I would be very glad if Doran Company decided to publish it." White wrote back to thank Alexander and Woofter and promised to send them "an autographed copy of the novel" when it was published, adding that he was to get final word from Doran within the week.[23]

Unfortunately, the approval of Alexander and Woofter did not affect Doran's position, and on October 8 Eugene Saxton sent his final word on the novel: "I am sorry to say that the chance for your book here is definitely closed. . . ."[24] Saxton offered to help place the book elsewhere, and in fact Saxton and White remained close through the years. Saxton later went to work for Harper and Brothers, and White often helped him in promoting books through the Association's network of branches. But Doran's rejection of *The Fire in the Flint*, while obviously a blow to White's hopes, did not dampen his spirits for long. As noted above, he was already arranging to make contact with Knopf, and by mid-December of 1923 Alfred A. Knopf accepted the book for publication.

While the road to acceptance by Knopf was not nearly so rough as the one which White had just traversed with Doran, it was not entirely smooth either. Joel Spingarn was one influential friend to whom White turned for aid; H. L. Mencken was another. On September 12, 1923, White sent the manuscript of *Fire* to Spingarn with the following note:[25]

I need hardly tell you how much I appreciate your interest in it—you know that already. If in reading it you will indicate its lapses either from good literary form or reasonableness of presentation you will still further make me your debtor.

In early October Spingarn replied, giving his criticism of what he considered the novel's major weakness, characterization:[26]

What an overwhelming story you have made of 'The Fire in the Flint'! I
followed Harper's career breathlessly. . . . There are powerful scenes, and
I do not doubt a single one of your 'facts.' What I doubt is your characters.
They simply do not live; and incident without character is melodrama, not
drama. Until you have learned to create characters you have not learned
to write a novel. . . .

White wrote to Spingarn the following day, thanking him for his criticism
and asking to see him to discuss the problem of characters. Spingarn never
did whole-heartedly approve of the novel, even after it was published,
but he did not openly oppose its publication either.

The real influence in Knopf's acceptance, aside from the strong-willed
Blanche Knopf herself, seems to have been Mencken. White had been
corresponding with Mencken for several years before he asked for his
help in publishing *Fire*. The correspondence between White and Mencken
in the NAACP files begins in 1920, but the two had obviously met before.
The key correspondence, however, centered on an article that Mencken
wanted written for the *Smart Set* satirizing Tuskegee in Mencken's "The
Higher Learning in America" series. On October 27, 1922, Mencken wrote
to ask if White could suggest anyone to write the piece:[27]

The formula is about as follows: First, the author pokes gentle fun at the
absurdities of his college, delivers a few smart knocks upon the skulls of
his personal enemies, and then ends up sentimentally. The fundamental
tone of each article is that of good-humored satire.

White responded that it might be better to do the article on Fisk or Atlanta
University because "Tuskegee is important but being an industrial school
puts it in a different class . . . an institution like Atlanta University has
done more towards shaping the thoughts of Negroes than Tuskegee or
Hampton or any other industrial institution."[28] Of course, White had an
ulterior motive in making his suggestion. As an alumnus of Atlanta University, he undoubtedly had visions of doing the article himself. Although
White suggested that James Weldon Johnson would be the best man to
write the article, he did not hesitate to accept the job when Mencken asked
him to do it a few days later.

In the October 30 letter in which he suggested changing the article
to focus on Atlanta University, White also discussed his progress on the
novel he had mentioned earlier to Mencken:

Led on by your rash advice I spent my vacation this summer doing the roug
outline of that novel. Two critics have pronounced it rotten. *Two have
read it.* However, I am now passing through the painful process of re-writin
it, which I will do forty times, if necessary, until I do something that I

think is worth while. I am not going to burden you with it until I think it is in fairly decent shape.

White apparently did not "burden" Mencken with the manuscript until almost a year later. He kept Mencken informed about Saxton's reservations concerning Doran's acceptance of the novel, and finally, in August, 1923, he asked Mencken to read the manuscript. On August 22 Mencken wrote White that he was having his annual bout with hay fever but would be glad to read the manuscript in a few weeks. He also suggested that White try Liveright, adding: "I doubt that Knopf would take a chance on it."[29] Two days later White replied and stated his doubts about Liveright's interest in the book:[30]

Thank you for your suggestion regarding Liveright. I am afraid he is not going to consider any more novels on the Negro problem, for in addition to Waldo Frank's recently published "Holiday" they are bringing out a book of short stories by a young colored man this year [Jean Toomer's *Cane*] and a novel by a colored woman next spring [Jessie Fauset's *There Is Confusion*].

It seems obvious that White was counting on Mencken's reputation and his close ties to Knopf, publishers of the *American Mercury,* to help win acceptance with that firm.

At this point, though, White had still not given up on Doran. A few days before he received Saxton's final rejection of the novel, White wrote Mencken, explained the process by which Alexander was to read the manuscript and comment on it to Doran, and told him of Alexander's response. He also told Mencken about Cobb's reading of the manuscript and his suggestion that Doran not accept it, and added another bit of information: "Mary Roberts Rinehart also read my script and also felt that Doran should not publish it."[31] White then asked Mencken to read the manuscript and give Saxton his opinion of the novel: "Armed with a strong letter from you . . . I think I can succeed in overcoming the barrier which now confronts me." Mencken agreed to read the manuscript then and added this sarcastic, if a bit off-target, comment regarding the influence of Cobb, and the like:[32]

Certainly I'll be glad to read the novel, either in MS or in proof. I doubt that the possible protests of professional Confederates need be taken seriously. The Ku Kluxers of various wings bawl every time anything is written about the South, especially if it be true, but a great many more civilized Southerners are beginning to be heard from. . . . You will never get anywhere, down there or in the North, if you put on the soft pedal. The pussy-footing Southern novel is dead.

The next day Saxton wrote White to say that Doran would definitely not accept *Fire*. White wrote Mencken the news on October 11, moaning that "Irvin Cobb's influence on Doran was too strong for me!"

Mencken read the manuscript in a few days and, while he did find some flaws in the book, generally was enthusiastic about it, perhaps because it gave him even more ammunition to use against his favorite target, the South. At any rate, he did approve of the novel:[33]

> I can't imagine why any sane man should object to anything in the novel. Even the passages that the anonymous reader [perhaps Spingarn] has queried seem to me to be quite all right. There is not a line in the book that has not been established by the most solemn legal proceedings. It is admittedly a Tendenz piece. But it is certainly fair and accurate enough. The Southern crackers, if anything, are worse than you make them. . . .
> It seems to me that you have done a good job. There are some descents to the obvious in the story, but let them stand. I see nothing that should and must come out. You constantly spell it *alright*—a vice highly offensive to me personally. But so does Dreiser. The English is clear and vigorous, the characters have sufficient reality, and, as I have said, I see nothing improbable in any of the episodes. In truth, the objection to them is that they are too commonplace and typical—that the characters thus become types rather than persons. But here again you are entitled to get your effects in your own way.

So, like Joel Spingarn, Mencken saw a weakness in White's characters; unlike Spingarn, however, Mencken did not try to discourage White from seeking publication of the novel.

One point that disturbed Mencken, although it did not concern the novel itself, is of interest here because it relates to a problem faced by other black writers at the time, namely, that they had little choice but to seek a white publisher for their work. Mencken wrote:

> What I object to is the fact that you should be trying to sell the MS to a white publisher. . . . There should be a Negro publisher to do such books, and he should do them as well as a white publisher. . . . Aren't there some colored publishing firms already in existence? If not, wouldn't it be possible to induce somebody to organize one? What you need, beyond anything else, is freedom to write what you please. Dealing with white publishers, you will inevitably run into such difficulties as you encountered with Doran. I think that your best bet, as things stand, is Harcourt, but even Harcourt may feel that he is doing too many Negro books. A Negro publisher would have no such feeling; he'd want all the good ones he could get.

White's response is interesting in its own right, for he argued that, even if it were possible to publish with a Negro publisher, he would prefer to publish with "as conservative and respectable a white firm as would do it. . . ." His reasons:[34]

Colored people know everything in my book—they live and suffer the same things every day of their lives. It is not the colored reader at whom I am shooting but the white man and woman who do not know the things that you and I know . . . the white person who has never suspected there are men like Kenneth Harper, who believes that every lynching is for rape, who believes the ex-Confederates are right when they use every means, fair or foul, "to keep the nigger in his place." I need not say that such are legion. . . .

He went on to say that he would avoid having his books published by "Boni or Seltzer" because " . . . publication by a firm known to lean towards the bizarre or the sensational would cause the very folks I want to reach to dismiss or discount the story. Publication by a colored firm would emphasize such a tendency because it would be considered special pleading." Although White later stressed just the opposite point in trying to promote his book, i.e., Negro readers would be interested in and support his novel, here he quite clearly has in mind directing the appeal of his book to the larger, more rewarding white audience.

Mencken also corresponded with White about more practical matters of writing. In response to a query from White, Mencken presented the following advice concerning the art of writing:[35]

. . . stick to simplicity, by all means. . . . The hardest sort of writing to do is that which is simplest. A man's thoughts come to him in confusion; they are never quite clear. His first impulse is always to give them a specious clarity by translating them into whatever familiar phrases are handiest— usually phrases that are sonorous, but meaningless. To disentangle them from that web of words and make them direct and crystal-clear: there is the hard job. Worse, one victory does not bring peace; one must keep up the battle all the time. I have spent months, literally, trying to get rid of certain adjectives, or to break myself of certain facile complexities in sentence structure. Young men nearly always write badly because they write ornately; it takes an old fellow, of long experience, to get his thoughts into simple sentences.

Since the style of both *The Fire in the Flint* and *Flight* borders on the ornate, we can assume that White either did not choose to take his mentor's advice or was unable to put that advice to use.

But White was interested in getting Mencken's help in persuading Knopf to accept *Fire*. In the October 17 letter White pressed his point once more: "You wrote me recently you doubted whether Knopf would be interested in my novel. Would you object to my talking the matter over with him?" While White was eager to have his novel accepted, he was also careful not to disturb anyone so influential as Mencken by seeming to go over his head. Mencken had no objections to White's pursuing publication chances at Knopf, although he did repeat his reservations about White's chances there. On October 18 he told White to send the manuscript to Knopf, then added: " . . . but I have a feeling that its chances will be better else- where, say with Harcourt, Houghton-Mifflin or Harper. Knopf is rather scarey of Tendenz novels."[36] Eventually, however, Mencken changed his mind. In another note, undated, he commented to White: "I have already told Knopf that I think it would be good business to publish the novel. So all is set for the reading of the MS. Put your chaplain on his knees and make him pray."

White had already made preliminary contact with Knopf. Blanche Knopf had agreed to have Carl Van Doren read the novel and give his opinion of it, and White had written to Alfred Knopf asking for an appointment "when I can present for your consideration the manuscript of a novel which I have recently done." Perhaps as a ploy or perhaps because he honestly had become suspicious after his episode with Doran, White added: "I am particularly anxious to place it in your hands because it deals with the race problem."[37]

At this point in the career of his first novel, White was not deceived about its lack of artistic merit. As he wrote to Blanche Knopf, "I have no illusions regarding the literary style of my novel. I know it has many gaucheries, many inept and crude phrases. Because of that knowledge I am not only willing but anxious that expert editing be done on it to re- move those faults and to smooth out the English."[38] A few months later, in a letter to Joel Spingarn, White explained, though somewhat vaguely, that he was anxious to publish the novel in spite of its faults:[39]

> Ever since I saw you last and you expressed the hope that Knopf would turn down my book for my own good, I have been thinking of what you said. As you know I had no illusions regarding the literary quality of my novel even before I talked with you and my doubts were more than con- firmed by your statements. What I want to say to you is this. I, too, have a high regard for style. I realize my story is far from being what it should be. But some day I can perhaps tell you the reason why it is necessary for me to try my hardest to get it published now. I am sorry I cannot divulge it now, but when I can you will see the situation which now exists.
>
> The above is, I know, rather cryptic. Nevertheless, it is a situation out of which I am trying to find a way.

White's mysterious reason was never really clarified, either in the corres- pondence or in his autobiography. He may have been in financial trouble, in which case he most probably would not have mentioned it to Spingarn. He did ask Blanche Knopf if he could get an advance of $250 on his royalties, but she replied that such a procedure would be against company policy.[40]

Although no advance was given, *The Fire in the Flint* was rather quickly accepted for publication by Knopf. On December 18, 1923, White wrote to Blanche Knopf asking whether the novel could be brought out in the spring to be promoted at the annual NAACP conference in June, but Mrs. Knopf replied that it would not be possible to publish it until the autumn of 1924.[41]

Meanwhile Carl Van Doren was making suggestions regarding changes in the novel. Van Doren had read the manuscript before Knopf accepted it, so he had approved its publication. On December 24 he wrote to White: "I am pleased to death at the news about your novel. You see not all publishers are idiots. If *The Fire in the Flint* sells really well I shall decide that the public isn't all idiots either." White had already done Van Doren a favor by taking his friend Konrad Bercovici around Harlem to get background for a travel book on New York, so he obviously did not feel that asking Van Doren's help with the editing of his novel was too great an imposition. At any rate, Van Doren did agree to help, and in early January, 1924, their correspondence centered on finer points of style. (Blanche Knopf had already told White that any changes made should be editorial only.[42]) On January 8 White suggested to Van Doren:

What I wanted to get from you is a list of those passages in my novel which seem to you to need touching up or rewriting. I don't want to spoil anything which may perhaps be best left untouched but, at the same time, I want to make it as good a piece of work from a literary standpoint as I am able to write. Do the passages occur to you from memory or would you want me to send the MS to you that you may refresh your memory of it?

A few days later Van Doren responded, saying that the changes he would suggest were of a general, rather than of a specific nature:[43]

The questions I had in mind with regard to your book concerned not so much special passages as the phraseology at large, which I found occasionally a little rough and loose. With some revision, I think you can catch most of them yourself. Whoever read your manuscript before me caught a good many instances of what I mean. If you care to let me go over a chapter with you some afternoon, I can point out the details that seem gritty to my taste.

For the most part, the changes White made were only changes in style, although he did tell Blanche Knopf, when he submitted the manuscript officially, that he had removed "one or two passages which seem to me on reading it over after some time to savor too much of propaganda."[44] For the rest of the spring things went along fairly smoothly for the novel. There was a minor crisis when the *Borzoi Broadside* incorrectly listed White's novel as *The Flint in the Fire.* White asked Mrs. Knopf if the error could be corrected, but she replied that, unfortunately, there was nothing to be done. She apologized for the error and said she was trying to locate its source. (After the novel was published, it was referred to by various titles, including *Flint in the Fire* and *The Fire in the Furnace.* This must have been almost as frustrating to White as the time, several years later, when Charles A. Beard referred to *The Fire in the Flint* by "Stuart White" in *The Rise of American Civilization.*[45])

Even before its publication White received responses to the novel from many sectors of the population, within the literary world and outside it. Some of those responses he actively sought himself, and some of them came unsolicited and were, therefore, perhaps truer indices of public and critical response than the others. One critical opinion White sought hopefully as early as September, 1923, was that of H. G. Wells. White wrote Wells, mentioning his novel and stating basically the same principles as underlying its composition that he had written Alexander; but he also added this self-evaluation regarding the novel: "The novel I have done is not a great piece of writing but it is an honest and sincere attempt to give a picture which has hitherto never been shown."[46] Wells agreed to read the galley proofs of the book, but it was not until almost a year later that White finally received Wells's response: "I have now the proofs of your novel. It is a good second rate novel and expresses a point of view with considerable vigor but I do not feel called upon to write anything for publication about it. I'm sorry to seem disobliging."[47] Understandably disappointed, White replied on August 5, 1924: "I am, of course, sorry you did not like the novel any better than you did. I am afraid I did not achieve (certainly not as far as you are concerned) my prime object which was to present an honest picture of the American scene as I have seen it."

Contact with another famous writer turned out more favorably for White. On July 18, 1924, he wrote J. E. Spingarn to inquire whether he thought Sinclair Lewis "could be induced to read page proofs and either do a review which Knopf could place where it would do the most good or, if he did not wish to do that, to do a paragraph which could be used on the jacket." A few days later Spingarn replied:[48]

Nothing, I think, could induce him to write a puff for a book in which he did not believe, and nothing, I know, could induce me to ask him. . . . If you will send me an advance copy of your book, perhaps inscribed to Lewis, I shall be glad to send it to him. . . . Then something may happen, dependent on the impression your book makes on Lewis or his desire in some way to express his attitude toward the race question in America.

White quickly responded that he had been misunderstood and that "of course, I would not ask him to write a puff regardless of the merit of the book."

Lewis did like the book, however, and sent the paragraph cited at the beginning of this chapter to Spingarn so that he could pass it on to Knopf. In the same letter, "a letter to Walter White quite as much as to [Spingarn]," Lewis included some advice for the author, some of which sounds terribly close to what Eugene Saxton had tried to tell White:[49]

I want White to read "A Passage to India" and learn several lessons from it; particularly these two. (1) He must learn to be more just to his villains— not so much for any abstract justice but in order more successfully to attack them. (This is of course an ancient doctrine; it's the one that the wise Harcourt is always preaching to me.) When the reader finds all the persecutors of Kenneth described as fiends and scoundrels, complete, and Kenneth, his brother, sister, mother and sweetheart described as practically faultless, as superhuman saints, then he feels (often inarticuately) that the case has been rigged, that the whole story has not been told. White must remember that fiendish things are often done by men who are not essentially fiends. . . . The tragedy of Kenneth's death is no greater than the tragedy of some, at least, of his killers. . . . This sort of justice to both sides is beautifully done in Forster, though I can see that White would, very properly, not desire to make his Dr. Harper so weak and wobbly as Forster has made his Dr. Aziz. (2) The beginning of Kenneth's love story is weak. The girl is a little too perfect and for the first pages the whole tone lacks confidence—doesn't make me feel that White perfectly saw and felt their reality and the reality of their love.

On the whole, however, I rejoice immensely in the book both per se and in its promise.

As one can imagine, such attention from one of America's most successful writers elated White. On September 12 he wrote Spingarn, " . . . it will be some days before I come back to earth again! Sinclair Lewis' letter has swept me right off my feet, the only anchor that I have being the last two-thirds of his letter and your warning not to let the letter turn my head." That same day he wrote to Lewis to thank him:[50]

I am now reading "A Passage to India." I wish to God I had read it before I wrote "The Fire in the Flint." The weakness in my novel which you point out is one which I have always preached against in talking to colored friends of mine who have the ambition to write. In fact, I have used a phrase so much that it was almost a part of me which goes something like this: "All white men are not super devils nor all Negroes super angels."

In a third letter that day White wrote to George Oppenheimer of Knopf: "I would like very much . . . if the whole paragraph [by Lewis] could be

used including the reference to 'A Passage to India.' I am afraid Lewis and
Spingarn both would be offended if it were left out but, more importantly
than that, I should be very proud to have my first novel linked with so
magnificent a work as that of Forster." White was always quick to capitalize
on any advantage, and certainly having his novel "linked" with one of the
best books of the year could only help him, especially since the blurb supplied by Lewis stopped with his favorable comparison of the two works.
The relationship between Lewis and White extended over several years and
became a real friendship.

Another prominent writer who gave White's book high praise in a
blurb was Carl Van Vechten. In that statement he said:[51]

This bitter and sensational arraignment of a pseudo-civilization, written by
a Negro, would arouse the latent sense of injustice even in the soul of a
United States Senator. *The Fire in the Flint* is a story of a lynching, but
it is worthy of note that the author has been fair enough to make a white
man the most charming character in his book [Judge Stevenson], while the
hero is betrayed by his own race [old Dr. Williams]. The plot is most ingeniousl
articulated, the characters well-drawn. In certain nervous passages the novel
achieves a power, through the use of a curiously subtle variety of restraint,
that almost lifts it into the realm of art. I defy any one to read it without
emotion.

In the letter to Van Vechten to which this blurb was attached in the files,
White thanked him for his kind words and added: "I had no idea that you
would be so interested in a novel such as mine. . . . You saw exactly what
I was driving at." This apparently was the first contact between the two
men, but it was certainly not the last. As Huggins suggests in *Harlem
Renaissance,* White was instrumental in introducing Van Vechten to Harlem circles; White also seems to have profited in this relationship, as Van
Vechten continued to offer him advice and guidance. In fact, the two
remained close even into the forties when Van Vechten worked to establish the James Weldon Johnson Memorial Library at Yale.

White received a much more detailed reaction to his novel from T. S.
Stribling. While not convinced that the book would be read by enough of
the right people to do as much good as it might, Stribling thought that
with Knopf publishing it, the novel would "get the very best hearing it
could possibly get. . . . " He then elaborated on the problems he saw in the
way *Fire* was written:[52]

I think you have done a fine realistic picture, marred by a good many sentences of slipshod writing. For instance there in the last pages of the book
where you say your heroine was bowed "with grief too deep for tears" I
could very willingly have kicked you all over the shop. The idea of putting

a salted mackerel like that into an emotional scene! In another place while Kenneth was looking at a postage stamp under a microscope you spoke of the "infinite" details of the stamp, instead of the infinitesimal details. Now it is the minutiae of writing that make it writing or cobbling. . . . If your whole picture hadn't been fine and appealed to me strongly, I wouldn't have given a damn how you said it.

Stribling, like Lewis, found fault with White's handling of the love story, mainly because Kenneth is so "poky in his love making. . . . I rather suspect a big healthy passion wouldn't have hurt." In addition, he objected to the lack of humor in the novel and, more importantly, to the ending:

I do object to your ending. It lacked subtlety. It was all right to kill Bob, but to murder both your principal characters was bad art, especially in two scenes. I think your effect would have been much more powerful if you could have killed them both at once, or it could have been more sardonic if you had let Kenneth off. The repeated murder and the repeated burning is what I object to. That may be quite natural, and I admit lynchings are monotonous, but art is the escape of life from monotony.

After chiding White for lacking objectivity in the book, a failing, Stribling added, that he could well understand from "a man who has been an investigator of the Ku Klux Klan," he urged White to "go on to your next book. . . . What we need is a succession of novels and plays written with art and fairness, and perhaps at last the man in the second story below will hear a noise in the attic."

White responded on September 6, the day after *Fire*'s release, saying he agreed with "nearly everything" Stribling had to say about the novel, "particularly the infelicities of style and the cliches into which I fell." After expressing his optimism concerning the chances for sales of *Fire*, spurred mainly by Laurence Stallings's highly favorable review of the book in the *New York World*, White reacted to Stribling's criticism of his ending:[53]

I wrote two final chapters. The one which did not appear had Kenneth Harper rescued by Mrs. Ewing who, on hearing the commotion in the yard, opens the door and tells why he was at her house. He is saved but his spirit has been crushed and he goes away from Central City never to return. I submitted this to a number of people, among them J. E. Spingarn and H. L. Mencken, and all of them were agreed that that ending was false—everything in the book led to the tragic ending in the death of Kenneth. My own opinion is biased, of course, but I do not see how the story could honestly have ended in any other way.

It was to Stribling's query about the absence of humor in the novel that White took the most exception. Obviously very sensitive about this ever-present subject of the "happy darky" stereotype, White in his response seemed to be pleading a case important to him:

My dear Stribling, why in the name of God must every story about the Negro drag in humor, real or alleged, by the scruff of its neck? I realize that, artistically, one must give readers a breathing spell but the way I was feeling when I wrote that novel made it impossible for me to lug in humor any more than was done in one or two places. That is just the problem— we have had so much stuff written about the humor of the Negro that there has been created in the mind of the average reader, and many above the average, that the life of the Negro is one long laugh fest. Kenneth Harper had darned little humor in his life, and Kenneth Harper is not an exception among men of his type.

Stribling, however, did not let White off with this protest. Two days later he wrote again to remind White that "life never comes" as "undiluted passion. . . . Even the unhappy Negroes of Georgia can't possibly get clear chunks of tragedy . . . even Loeb and Leopold are full of jests." Regarding the ending, Stribling said he could see the point made by Mencken and Spingarn, but that his point was also valid: "You waste your strength in two scenes so close together of exactly the same character . . . never repeat a situation." He added this encouragement for White:[54]

Here you are, a young Negro writer with a very fine promise. I insist that you write in the big style, in the unhurried style that shows human beings as they are. . . . Now White, detach yourself, my boy. Cut away, be a camera, not a gatling gun. You think the gun is the most necessary under the circumstances, but so does the K. K. K. think the same thing. You know they're wrong. I know you're wrong.

In a state of "humility" White responded a week later, saying that Lewis had just told him the same thing about his novel, i.e., he had been unjust to his villains, and promised to try to rectify the fault in his next novel (on which he had already begun work), "where undoubtedly I shall be flayed from the other side, that is, colored people will murder me for not making the heroine a Methodist Sunday School teacher. . . ." The correspondence between White and Stribling then subsided, with an occasional query from White concerning Stribling's new novel, *Low Road,* and a bit of rather cynical advice from Stribling:[55]

I wonder that you don't pitch into either short stories or novelettes as you can do them very quickly indeed and the pay is much better than any novel less than a best seller. Heaven knows I am not trying to pervert your talent but business is business and so is writing.

This correspondence between the two authors becomes even more interesting when one considers the comparison sometimes made between *Birthright* and *The Fire in the Flint*. For example, in its Christmas, 1925, number *John O'London's Weekly* offered a comparison in which White was decidedly found the lesser author: "In 'Birthright' the facts were presented calmly, realistically, almost humorously, very convincingly. Mr. Walter F. White adopts a different method. With vituperation verging on hysteria he attacks the Ku-Klux-Klan and the poor whites of Georgia. . . . The violent partisanship of the author defeats its own object."[56]

Not every reviewer thought that *Fire* was unfair. In fact, the review that did so much to lift White's spirits concerning the novel's chances came from a transplanted Georgian, Laurence Stallings, and was the one review to which White undoubtedly would refer when discussing the critical acceptance of his book. In part, Stallings's review, appearing in the *New York World* on September 1, 1924, said:[57]

Georgia will not be proud of its newest novelist. His name is Walter White. If his book, which is called "The Fire in the Flint," were to be read by the shaggy citizenry of South Georgia, I dare say Mr. White would be greeted at the train by a literary committee clad in white robes and red crosses and escorted to a discreet part of the town to be cut down. For Mr. White commits all the crimes against South Georgia morals. He slurs the honor of Southern womanhood, and he was born with Negro blood in him. . . . It [*The Fire in the Flint*] is told with scrupulous attention to detail and carries with it the best portrait of a small Southern town that I know anything of—and I know something of the small Southern town too. . . . As a first novel, "The Fire in the Flint" is a significant book. As any novel it is worth while. It is so timely. Few novels have been needed more.

White was so elated by this review that he wrote Stallings the next day, apologized if he were breaking any rules of "etiquette" by writing a reviewer, and thanked him for his "magnificent review," adding: "If the book has any success whatever, I shall remember that you played a large part in that success."[58]

While this after-the-fact reaction to a review raises no question of impropriety, White often did quite a bit of maneuvering before the fact to elicit a favorable review from a critic. His most frequent method was to encourage a friend to do a review. One reviewer he did not have to coax was Konrad Bercovici, whom White had helped earlier. After his first reading of the manuscript in February, 1924, Bercovici wrote White:[59]

This book is so beautiful and so passionate I haven't anything else to say about it but that I like it from beginning to end. . . . If I were to read the book in print I would read it so breathlessly I wouldn't notice it had any defects, if it at all has any; the tempo is so quick.

Bercovici also cautioned White against too much rewriting, which might "rob it of its most pronounced qualities," adding: "Cool judgment makes a cool book." In September, after the novel's release, he wrote White expressing his desire to find a suitable place to review the book:[60]

I am making arrangements for *The Fire in the Flint.* Unfortunately the *Saturday Review* had already given it away [to Zona Gale] when I asked, and so had the *Literary Review* [to Herschel Brickell]. I have written to Margaret Land of the *Nation,* and talked to Stallings. . . . I wanted to get at least a thousand words to review it in. It is not enough for such a book to say that it is a promising, nice first novel, or any nincompoopish thing of that sort. . . . Shake yourself together and see whether you can make any arrangements for me. Whatever you say will suit me perfectly.

Needless to say, White was quick to help such an eager source find a proper channel for expression. On September 11 White wired Bercovici asking whether he had tried the *New York Times;* by September 16, however, White telegraphed that he had secured space for Bercovici in another source: " Mark Van Doren has just telephoned me he wants you to review my novel in the *Nation.* Is very anxious [to] have your review by Monday at the latest."[61] When the review finally appeared, it was, as might be expected, highly laudatory, but Bercovici also had some interesting things to say about the novel in terms of its connection with the New Negro movement:[62]

As a story-teller White leaves little to be desired. He knows the colored race as only a colored man could know it. And he knows the attitude of the Southern white as only a Negro could know it. . . . All through the novel one hears the voice of the new Negro. . . . In the best creative work of the Negro now there is a certain Slavic tendency, self-searching, analytical; this is revealed superbly here. "The Fire in the Flint" may be but the first of Mr. White's novels of Negro life, and more should follow from the pens of others in the interest of a better understanding between the white race and the black—the almost white and the almost black.

The idea that White's novel was a pioneer work, paving the way for other black novels to come, was often voiced in reviews and in letters to White. For example, Clement Wood wrote White:[63]

Your book is magnificent. . . . I shall give it all the publicity I can: it exactly meets what I have long cried for, a first-rate novel by an American Negro. It is magnificent as propaganda, magnificent as truth, never overdone, and, and, I believe, strong as a story. It is not as well written as my *Nigger*, pardon my vanity thus far; but it is a much better constructed novel, and, most of all, is done by the man who has now for the first time found his tongue, your own crescent race.

Of course, there had been a great deal of literature written by black American authors long before White's novel was published; the important thing is that, to a number of white American readers, *The Fire in the Flint* was an initial adventure into the world of the black experience as written from that perspective. White himself saw the novel as a trial balloon for future works by black writers, and he often stated this view. In a letter to Eugene Kinckle Jones, then executive secretary of the National Urban League, written in response to Jones's praise of the novel, White made this observation:[64]

... if a novel as frank as mine sells, I think it is going to have a great effect in opening some of the doors which have hitherto been closed to Negroes who want to write and to white people who would like to write honestly about the Negro problem instead of doing the things that Irvin Cobb and Octavus Roy Cohen have done.

Even a later, and thus perhaps less emotional, evaluation of the impact of *Fire* cited the novel as something of a landmark. In *Black Manhattan* (1930), James Weldon Johnson said:[65]

In 1924 there appeared a novel that struck both the critics and the general public. It was the first piece of fiction written by an American Negro to accomplish this double feat with so large a degree of success. The book created a sensation and was the subject of heated controversy wherever it was discussed. It was *The Fire in the Flint* by Walter White. . . .

One interesting comparison that appeared in several British reviews of the novel paired it with an earlier novel of extreme importance to the black American experience, *Uncle Tom's Cabin*. The *Leeds Mercury,* for instance, called it "a Twentieth Century 'Uncle Tom's Cabin,' " and continued:[66]

What Mrs. Beecher Stowe did for the Negro of the slave days, the writer of this book seeks to do for the Negro of today. His indictment is no less terrible. It will come as a shock to every reader to learn how in the Land of Liberty, the home of self-determination, the Negro is still held in subjection by force and fear. . . .

The *British Weekly*, in a similar vein, noted: "It seems strange that three quarters of a century ago 'Uncle Tom's Cabin' could move the public so

profoundly here and in America, yet these two books ('Birthright' and
'The Fire in the Flint') can be so placidly received. . . . The mental and
spiritual agonies of these educated Negroes must be at least as terrible
as were the physical sufferings of the slaves." Even the *Calcutta Guardian*
made the connection: "The year 1852 saw the publication of one of those
rare books which stir the heart of a nation, 'Uncle Tom's Cabin.' . . . The
year 1925 [the date of English publication] has seen the publication of
another tale of Negro life as it is today in the Southern states of America.
Three-fourths of a century after the 'emancipation' of the Negro."[67]

White received reaction to his book from a variety of people. Eugene
O'Neill called *Fire* "an extraordinary book—a courageous and terrible
indictment—done with fine power and sincerity." Julia Peterkin wrote
White: "Your book moved me with such pity and such terror I could
hardly go on to the end. What a stark picture you have made! What skill
you show with your use of words!"[68] Equally important to the novel's
success, however, was the reaction of the black press. Its support could
greatly enhance the book's sales in black communities across the country.
Generally, the novel was received enthusiastically. James B. Morris, of
the *Bystander* ("The only Negro paper in Iowa"), published in Des
Moines, wrote White:[69]

> I want to congratulate you on this remarkable story. It is destined to
> wake up the slumbering Negroes of the north, who apparently are living
> in ease unaware of the terrible system that engulfs the whole south; to lay
> the Negro question before the white people of the country who have con-
> tinually pleaded ignorance of the conditions and to generally show the
> American people the necessity of going into this problem at the root and
> working through to the extreme end.
>
> I am writing an editorial on "The Fire in the Flint" in our paper this
> week and also carrying an advertisement. I shall do everything possible
> to have the people know about it. . . .

This kind of support from the black press was crucial to White's hopes of
showing the white publishing world that black readers would buy books
by black authors. (The main thrust of his column for the *Pittsburgh
Courier,* which did not begin until 1926, was to encourage his readers to
support works by and about black people, at least if they met with his
approval.)

Of course, not everyone liked *Fire;* in fact, there was some fairly bitter
denunciation of it, especially from the South, as one might expect. In an
interview published in the *Savannah Press,* Irvin Cobb alluded to his having
read the manuscript of the novel for "a certain publisher, whose name he
did not mention," and repeated what he had told that publisher:[70]

I told him . . . that if he wanted to reduce his expenses of publication and relieve himself of any further necessity of sending men into Southern territory, or of ever having an order for books South of the Mason and Dixon line or East of the Mississippi, to proceed with this publication, but if he craved to have his books read in this part of the country as well as every other, never to put his name on the title page of that horrible book. . . . I cannot see any truth in a book which depicts every negro character a hero and a noble creature, and every white man a rape fiend, a coward, or a scoundrel. . . . There are many examples of high-toned colored people to whom this tragedy is brought home, but writing things that are not true in regard to existing conditions, is no solution of a problem whose roots are deep in the history of the people.

In an editorial entitled "A Book of Lies," the same paper said of the novel: "The worst libel we have seen on the South and Southern men and women . . . appears in 'The Fire in the Flint.' It is a book written by Walter White, a Negro, and is undoubtedly published largely for Northern consumption. . . ." All the reaction from the South, however, was not negative, nor was all of the northern reaction totally favorable; Josephus Daniels, Jr., in the *Raleigh News and Observer,* said of White: "This Georgia Negro whatever else he may have done in 'The Fire in the Flint' has written the most significant novel that has come out of the South in a longer time than is pleasant to think about." Many northern reviews were mixed in their reaction to *Fire.* [71]

The violently negative reaction from the South is the one which most pleased White, it seems, mainly because it fitted his idea of how best to generate interest in his novel. This idea appears to have been born in his correspondence with Mencken immediately following Knopf's acceptance of the book and continuing after its publication. When White wrote Mencken to tell him of Knopf's decision to publish *Fire,* Mencken responded with his congratulations and added: [72]

Inasmuch as it is a Knopf book I can't do much for it in the *American Mercury,* but I'll review it for the *Baltimore Sun,* and try to stir up some interest among the Negro Intelligentsia (if any!) there. The best way to get it talked of in the South will be to send it to the worst Negrophobe papers for review, and so try to draw their fire. My own books have been greatly helped in the South by that means. The confederate is always an ass.

The idea obviously appealed to White, as his reply to Mencken indicated: "Your suggestion regarding the stirring up of the Confederate is a great one. I have certain deep and dark plans whereby I hope to get the Klan worked up to an artistic denunciation of my novel as a base slander on that noble band of hundred percenters." [73] In his next letter Mencken elaborated a bit on his "plan": [74]

The main thing is to provoke a discussion of it. The best plan, I think, is to egg on the Ku Kluxers. Can't you get some letters written to the leading Southerner papers when the time comes, denouncing it as subversive and urging them to stir up the police? These imbeciles will then do all your advertising for you.

White did not reply directly to this suggestion until the novel was about to be published. On August 4, 1924, he wrote Mencken:

I am following up your suggestion of lining up a few people who will, when the time comes, write letters to *Vardaman's Weekly,* the *Atlanta Constitution* and the *Memphis Commercial Appeal,* denouncing "The Fire in the Flint" as vicious Ethiopian propaganda. If I can get these upholders of Nordic supremacy to take a few cracks at my head my only worry then will be the income tax collector.

Mencken later made some specific suggestions regarding places to send copies of the novel. Once he reminded White: "Don't overlook the *American Standard* published by a Baptist preacher in New York. It is the hottest Ku Klux paper ever heard of. It specializes in the crimes of the Jesuits, but also keeps an eye on the wops, Huns, Moors, etc." On another occasion he told White to "send a review copy to Ambrose E. Gonzalez of the Columbia (S. C.) State. He is a violent Ethiopicide."[75] Whether this plan had any direct results is hard to determine; there certainly was a bitter reaction to the novel from much of the southern press. At any rate, Mencken and White both took obvious delight in contemplating the imagined reaction of their mutual targets in the South.

Of course, Walter White did not rely solely on the negative response of the South to promote sales of his book. He used every resource available to him as a fairly well-known figure in the New York literary world, both through his business and social contacts with important literary people, and as an official of the NAACP. There are several lists in the NAACP files, most of which were apparently drawn up either for White's own use or as a quick reference he might use in corresponding with the promotional people at Knopf, primarily George Oppenheimer at this stage. One such list was headed: "In America I know personally," and included Carl Van Doren, Mencken, Heywood Broun, Stribling, Oswald Garrison Villard, and Stephen Vincent Benet, among others. There was also a note to the effect that Zona Gale had "agreed to read galley proofs and write her opinion of the novel to be used in advertising." Finally there was a brief list of people in England who had agreed to read the galleys and "write a word of opinio for me," including Wells, Norman Angell, and John A. Hobson.

White was certainly not shy about approaching potential reviewers concerning his novel. When he sent a copy of *Fire* to Irita Van Doren, for example, he added a note: "On reading it, if you feel so disposed, I would deeply appreciate anything you might do towards getting it mentioned in the *Herald-Tribune.*" And to Oswald Garrison Villard he wrote:

I have sent you an autographed copy of "The Fire in the Flint." I shall not feel bad if after reading it you do not feel disposed to review it in the *Nation.* If, however, you should find anything of merit in it which would cause you to want to review it, I need not tell you how happy I would be. . . . I hope you will approve of this, my maiden novel.

While Villard's ties with the NAACP might account for White's bold approach with him, one wonders about his letter to Clifford Smyth in which he stated: "After talking with you last week, I called your office later that day and suggested Eugene O'Neill, Theodore Dreiser or Booth Tarkington to review my novel for the *National Book Review.*"[76]

If a magazine did not review *Fire* within a reasonable period of time, White often wrote to find out why and to encourage a quick resolution of the oversight. When the *New Republic* failed to review the novel, White wrote to Robert Morse Lovett that he had understood from "Mr. Lytell" of that magazine that Stallings was to review the book for them, and he added his persuasive plea:[77]

Probably there have been other authors who have made similar complaints for I know every author thinks his book is of paramount importance—that being one of the natural complaints of scribblers. I do claim, however, for "The Fire in the Flint" one virtue. It is an honest presentation of the Georgia scene and it seems to me that the readers of the *New Republic* would be interested in the book. Won't you let me know why it has not been reviewed? I do wish that you would do it yourself.

Lovett responded a week later that he had been on vacation and had only been contributing occasional reviews to the magazine. He, too, had thought that Stallings was to review the novel for them, and he promised to write Littell "with the request that if he is not committed to some one else he send me 'The Fire in the Flint.'"[78]

White did not depend completely on reviews of the novel—favorable or vicious—to advance sales of *Fire;* he also made use of the fairly wide-reaching machinery of the NAACP—with the help of James Weldon Johnson, William Pickens, and others—to promote the book in the black community. One natural place to get information about his novel to Association members was the annual conference, held in 1924 between June 25 and July 1 in Philadelphia. On April 21, 1924, White wrote to Blanche Knopf to tell her of the meeting and to offer a suggestion:[79]

If it is satisfactory to you, we can take orders at this meeting for a number of copies of "The Fire in the Flint." What do you think of the idea of your printing, say, a leaflet announcing the forthcoming publication of the novel, giving a synopsis somewhat like "The Blurb," to be used later, with the price, and having on the bottom an order blank? We have at these conferences a literature table with a responsible person in charge who could take orders from those who wish to pay at that time for a copy. An attractive leaflet will bring the novel to the attention of these delegates each of whom represents a branch of this organization in his city.

Whether this plan was actually carried through is not clear from the correspondence, although similar pamphlet/order blanks were used to promote other works at NAACP meetings. Knopf did compose a two-page publicity letter to send to members of the Association, to "call attention to 'The Fire in the Flint.' " The letter referred to the novel as "a story that will thrill colored leaders and will cause white readers to stop and think," and included excerpts from reviews by Van Vechten, Zona Gale, and James Weldon Johnson. The last paragraph of the letter contained Johnson's idea about purchasing two copies, "one for yourself and one for some white person. . . ."[80]

From within the Association, Willaim Pickens offered a series of notes to White "about reaching colored book buyers." In a memorandum of June 10, 1924, Pickens presented the following list of suggestions:

1. Note from your publisher to enclose in letters.
2. Reviews by Negro papers, as well as by others.
3. Have we a list of Negro Book Dealers here, and of dealers in Negro Books? We ought to have a list of this sort. Let's compile one.
4. Wherever you speak in meeting, book can be sold after meeting, without interference with the interests of the meeting.
5. Paid ads in widely read papers may pay, but sometimes it does not seem to pay.

Most of these ideas were implemented by White, some before he received the memorandum and some after, so it is difficult to determine how influential Pickens's list might have been on White's sales techniques. However the list might have affected White's approach to promoting books, his own and those of others, it still contains an obviously logical strategy for attack.

White also worked on a personal level, writing friends in various parts of the country to ask whether they could tell him how they thought *Fire* would sell in their area. To E. R. Merrick of the North Carolina Mutual Life Insurance Company in Durham, White wrote a letter explaining his goals in the novel and emphasizing his hope that sales of the book would show white publishers that "colored people would buy books if publishers

ared to bring out those which tell the truth." Then he asked Merrick's
elp:[81]

> What I want you to do for me is to sound out sentiment in Durham, where,
> flatter myself, I have some friends, and give me an estimate of just how
> many copies could be reasonably expected to be sold in Durham and in
> North Carolina among both white and colored people. I will deeply appreci-
> te your doing this and making any suggestions which I might pass on to
> my publishers regarding the pushing of the book in Durham.

A list in the files headed "INFLUENTIAL COLORED PERSONS TO WHOM
LETTERS HAVE BEEN WRITTEN ASKING THEM TO GIVE CONSERVATIVE
ESTIMATE OF COPIES THAT COULD BE SOLD IN THEIR CITIES" included
Merrick's name, along with Carl Murphy (Baltimore), Morris Lewis (Chi-
ago), J. E. Mitchell (St. Louis), and F. E. DeFrantz (Indianapolis). White
eceived a note from C. F. Hilts, Knopf's "personal representative," on
une 29, 1924, telling him that DeFrantz had bought 100 copies of *Fire*
nd asking for the names of others in the Midwest he might approach.

Some of the branches of the Association seemed less than totally en-
husiastic about promoting and purchasing the novel. When the St. Louis
branch voted against handling sales of the novel, James Tanter, a member
of that branch, wrote White that he was going to handle the sales personally,
o which White replied:[82]

> This may sound strange but I am rather glad that the St. Louis branch did
> not take up the matter of the novel. I do not want any branch to feel under
> ny obligations to handle the novel because of my personal connection
> with the Association—in brief, I would prefer it not being done for some
> persons might get the idea that I was using the Association which is far
> rom being the case.

Since White did in fact use the same machinery to help promote the work
of other writers too, one might reasonably accept that last statement at face
alue. But it is often difficult in dealing with Walter White to know what is
aid for appearance and what is truly an expression of personal conviction.

For all the work done to get the novel read by influential people, re-
iewed, and publicized, it was not a very huge success by normal standards,
lthough it did far outsell Toomer's *Cane,* and White himself referred to it
s "a modest best-seller. . . ."[83] On August 28, 1924, White received a note
rom someone at Knopf indicating that of the first printing of 3,000 copies
of *Fire,* about 700 had been sold at that time (a few weeks before its re-
ease). White was hopeful, though, that post-publication attention would
boost sales of the book. He wrote James Weldon Johnson on September 5,
924, the day the novel was released:[84]

Knopf tells me that sales are going along pretty well though nothing to boast of as yet. I did not expect them to for if the novel is a success at all, it will be because of discussion it kicks up after it is published. . . . It looks as though it is going to attract a good deal of attention through the public press.

The novel was in its third edition by November 26, 1924, and by December 26, 1924, it had, according to White, sold between five and ten thousand copies (a strangely wide gap!).[85] And interest in the novel did not die quickly. On October 7, 1926, White wrote Harry Hansen of the *New York World* to ask permission to quote something Hansen had said earlier in praise of *Fire* on the jacket of the planned Borzoi Pocket Classics edition of the novel. Over the years White continued to hear from people who were reading the novel for the first time and were impressed by it, including a letter from W. Somerset Maugham written January 1, 1927. In 1929 White received a letter from Delia Bascom of the University of Wisconsin in which she explained that she examined *Fire* (and *Flight*) in a Y. M. C. A. extension course on "Some Social Problems in Present-day Fiction," in preference to Du Bois's *The Quest of the Silver Fleece,* "because it seemed to me more nearly to show actual conditions. . . ."[86]

The Fire in the Flint also drew the interest, although limited apparently, of readers in other countries. It was published in England in 1925 by Williams and Norgate after a number of other firms had turned it down. While White expressed optimism about the English sales in a letter to Blanche Knopf in October of 1925, on December 10 he received a rather discouraging note from Laurence Pollinger of Curtis-Brown Ltd., the firm that handled Knopf's books in England, saying that a packer's strike had put the book trade "in a very sad way," and that British sales of the novel were probably "in the neighborhood of 300 copies."[87] In addition to its English edition, *Fire* was translated into French, Norwegian, German, Russian, and Japanese, and White received inquiries from potential translators in Brazil and Czechoslovakia.[88]

The novel was also serialized in the *Pittsburgh Courier* in 1926, after White had earlier asked Blanche Knopf to discourage serialization of the novel by the (Baltimore) *Afro-American.* In March, 1925, White explained his initial reluctance:[89]

Knowing something of the psychology of colored people, there are two things that would arise in their minds if "Fire in the Flint" were published in the *Afro-American.* The first would be that the novel was a back number and that sales had stopped and, second, there would arise the definite feeling, "Why should I buy a copy when I can read it in the *Afro-American* in homeopathic doses." The vast majority of the ordinary class of colored people are just beginning to hear about the novel and I for one expect small but steady sales for some time from this class.

By December of that year, however, White had evidently changed his mind regarding the threat serialization would present to sales, because he approved "whole-heartedly" of Blanche Knopf's agreeing to let Floyd Calvin serialize the novel in the *Courier,* for fifty dollars and "any display advertising" the *Courier* might be able to give.[90] From other correspondence in the files, and from the fact that White wrote a column for Calvin's paper and was turned down later for a similar column in the *Afro-American,* one could surmise that the real issue involved personalities and not necessarily the effect serialization might have had on sales of the novel.

Another episode following the publication of *Fire* involved White's attempts to create a play from his novel. People were constantly referring to the dramatic nature of his novel, and no less a figure of the theater than Eugene O'Neill encouraged White to attempt a dramatization of it. As early as September 8, 1924, only three days after the novel was published, White wrote Mrs. Knopf that he wanted to talk to her about "some developments regarding the possibilities of my doing 'The Fire in the Flint' as a play," and the next day he wrote his brother George, was who then at Burrell Normal School in Florence, Alabama, to ask him for some suggestions of humor to help "lighten the play, . . ." adding, "I intend to put most of this humor in the mouths of Mrs. Amos and Hiram Tucker."[91] The dramatization was done in collaboration with George Widder and was first submitted to Edwin Knopf and Horace Liveright for consideration; it was rejected by them on February 28, 1925. White next tried Courtnay Lemon of the Theatre Guild, who also rejected the play.[92] An attempt to interest Arthur Hopkins in the property apparently met a similar fate, and this first version of the play was dropped. In 1928, however, Peter Mason of Charles Frohman, Inc., wrote White to ask whether anyone held the dramatization rights to *The Fire in the Flint.* This was the beginning of an effort that extended into 1932, with Mason still hopeful at that point that the play might be produced.[93] It never was. Ironically, the main problem with the play was that it lacked dramatic action; because the real violence in the novel was so brutal, it obviously could not be produced on the stage, not in 1925. As a result, the bulk of the play became a series of sermons on the issues developed in the novel, and sermons do not make for effective drama. At one point Jim Tully tried to get White's novel accepted by Cecil B. DeMille for a film "on Negro life" the latter wanted to do; unfortunately for White, DeMille decided to buy *Porgy* instead.[94]

The total story of the publication of *The Fire in the Flint,* then, offers an interesting glimpse at some of the problems and rewards for black writers in the twenties. As the rejection of *Fire* by Doran and the call for humor by Stribling indicate, the black writer was still under pressure to meet the expectations of white readers in his works. Once these barriers were overcome, however, the black writer often found doors opened to him that had previously been tightly shut. If Walter White had been white and written the same book, he might not have had the problems he initially faced, but he might never have had the book accepted either. It was indeed a rather bizarre time.

In the course of White's experiences with the publication of *Fire,* he made use of many of his old contacts; more importantly, he made new friends among men of prominence, e.g., Sinclair Lewis and Carl Van Vechte There were, to be sure, black writers whose works were more artistic than White's and men who had more influence with publishers than White, but the total effect of the publication of *Fire* should not be minimized. It helped open doors for works on subjects that before had been taboo by showing that such works could sell, and it broadened the base of associations Walter White had with people in the arts and in society, which in turn enabled him to help other black artists make the contacts they needed to bring their work to the public eye. For these reasons, *The Fire in the Flint* plays an important historic role in the Harlem Renaissance.

4

THE SECOND NOVEL
Flight

The success of *The Fire in the Flint* spurred Walter White into other writing ventures. In fact, even before that novel was published in September, 1924, White had begun work on his second novel. He clearly liked the role of author and was determined to develop in that direction. In a letter to Leo Wolfson dated September 23, 1924, White indicated that he was going away from New York to start his next novel. To Wolfson's objection that *Fire* was "too restrained," White stated: "With each succeeding [novel], perhaps I can more and more gain through what I hope will be an ever more deeply entrenched reputation, the freedom from restraint and the painting of the scene as it actually exists."[1] If the "restraint" to which White was referring was a restraint from violence, then *Flight* marked a clear improvement over *Fire;* if the restraint referred to was a restraint from uncovering the "truths" of black life, however, the change in *Flight* is probably for the worse. While the subject of discovering one's identity through a series of crises is certainly as valid a subject as lynching and is even more closely related to the daily experiences of the black community, White's development of that subject in *Flight* was finally too romanticized to be as appealing to a wide reading audience as the cruder but more exciting *Fire.* Most of the reviewers of White's second novel found it superior in style to his first, but they also noted that, lacking the built-in tensions of *Fire, Flight* was a much less successful book.

As early as August, 1924, White was discussing his second novel with his friends. He wrote James Weldon Johnson:[2]

I have drafted a complete outline of a second novel which Carl Van Vechten thinks will be even more interesting than "The Fire in the Flint." While it is to be a novel about colored people, it will have very little of the Messianic delusion about it. I want to talk it over with you when you come back to see what you think of it.

At this time White was also considering a dramatization of *Fire;* he indicated in his letter to Johnson that Van Vechten was to talk to a friend of his, "a very well known playwright whose name I do not know as yet," about the possibility of collaborating with White on the project. The novel, however, was White's prime concern at this point, and by the first of October he had already contacted Blanche Knopf about publication of the new work. In response to White's inquiry, Mrs. Knopf wrote:[3]

Regarding your new manuscript, I should say that the very earliest it should be published would be Fall 1925 which means that we would not need to have it here until the middle of February or the beginning of March . . . the date of publication will depend entirely on the sales of *The Fire in the Flint* —I mean how these will be keeping up and how the interest will be sustained.

A few days later White responded, "I am going to work steadily and faithfully on the new MS. and, if I can do so, I shall try to let you have it around the first of March." His enthusiasm was high at this point. He told Joel Spingarn later that month: "I have already started to work on my next novel—you see the disease has become chronic. Knopf has been good enough to tell me upon hearing the plot that he is going to publish it."[4]

That enthusiasm waned somewhat in the ensuing months, and by February, 1925, White was apologizing to Blanche Knopf for not having met the intended schedule and explaining his delay:

. . . I have been doing as much work as I could on the new novel which I discussed some time ago with you. I could finish a novel of a sort by the first of March, I suppose, but the margin between what I could do on paper and the concept in my mind would be so great that I don't think you would like it. I have decided, therefore, not to rush it but to take a good deal of time this summer and do the job right. This will mean, of course, that it will be the spring or more likely the fall of 1926 before it can be published. . . . If the play goes well, I don't think this lapse of two years between the first and second novels will hurt, do you?

Blanche Knopf agreed that the novel had come along "just a little too late for the Fall" of 1925, but that they would probably publish it the following spring. After thanking White for the publicity work he was doing for them on behalf of Langston Hughes, she added, concerning his own book: "I am delighted to have the book and I know we shall do something with it."[5]

As this correspondence makes clear, White was not repeating his mistakes of writing *Fire,* specifically the rapid-fire composition which had, in the eyes of most of his critics, marred the work. In fact, *Flight* was still far from finished in the spring of 1925. But in the late summer of that year White was hard at work on the book. He told Claude McKay that the manuscript "is moving along very well and I have as yet hit no 'dead spots' though they are inevitable." He was so engrossed in his project that he was not able to find the time to revise his *Survey* article for Locke's *The New Negro.* He told Locke that he was working from four to sixteen hours a day on *Flight:*

Frankly, I am puzzled about what to do. I am not completely satisfied with the form in which the article appeared in the *Survey.* On the other hand, I know you will realize the predicament in which I now am. I am so immersed in the story that I would hate to leave it but more important than that is the fact that I took my vacation to write the story and the time is nearly gone and I yet have a third of the novel to do.

He offered two alternatives to Locke: to include the article as it stood, with the chance of making "absolutely necessary" changes in the galley proofs or, "and this is the one which I hope you won't accept," to exclude the article from *The New Negro.*[6] Locke did, of course, use White's article in the anthology, but we can see in White's letter to Locke a serious commitment to his new novel, a commitment that was lacking in his earlier effort.

From comments made to various correspondents, White was obviously laboring over his second novel, struggling to achieve his vision of it. In addition to his comment in the February 24 letter to Blanche Knopf, White included this statement in response to a questionnaire from Harold Butcher of the *Liverpool Echo* concerning his writing projects and philosophy:[7]

I am . . . at work on a new novel which will treat of white and colored characters but from a totally different angle from that in "Fire in the Flint." . . . This novel may be published in the spring of 1926 though I intend to refrain from publication until I am able to close appreciably the gap which now exists between the story I have in mind and the one as it now is being placed on paper.

White was even doing a fair amount of research for his new book, or at least intended to. Perhaps too late to help, White finally received from Grace Morris Nail a letter of introduction (dated August 12, 1925) to a "Madame Francis." The letter introduced White as "a young novelist, who is just now writing a book around a dressmaking establishment," and noted that White wished to spend some time around Madame Francis's shop, "a few hours each day for perhaps a week and most possibly less," to gather material.[8] Since the woman for whom Mimi goes to work in *Flight* is named Madame Francine, perhaps White did make use of this opportunity and offered the name as a tribute to Madame Francis.

By early September, 1925, White had completed the manuscript of *Flight*. On September 4 he sent the manuscript to Blanche Knopf, noting that Sinclair Lewis was looking it over: "Perhaps between you and him, some of the grosser faults may be eliminated." Lewis liked the new work, or at least saw it as an improvement over *Fire* in some areas. For one thing, as White told J. E. Spingarn, Lewis felt that White's "tendency" to propagandize in the first novel was "to a certain extent . . . overcome in this second book."[9] In a letter written to Carl Van Vechten that same day, White was even more elated in discussing Lewis's reaction:[10]

Sinclair Lewis insisted on reading the MS. and, with appropriate gestures of modesty, I transmit to you his opinion that "Flight" is three hundred per cent better than "Fire in the Flint." I am afraid that Hal's opinion, however, is biased in my favor.

Blanche Knopf also indicated that she was pleased with the new work and definitely wanted to have it: "We are keen about *Flight* and want certainly to publish it. That is understood . . . I think there will undoubtedly be a few small changes that we will want to suggest. However, we are very keen and glad to have it." By January, 1926, White wrote Robert Toms of Detroit: "Right now, to borrow a phrase from Mencken, I am sweating through galley proofs of the new novel."[11] *Flight* was almost ready.

On several occasions in his correspondence White indicated his intentions in the new novel. In a March 10, 1925, letter to Mordecai Johnson, White said:[12]

I am now at work on a novel dealing with white and colored characters but from as different an angle from "Fire in the Flint" as may well be imagined. It will be considerably less dramatic (or melodramatic) than "Fire in the Flint" but I think it will go very much deeper beneath the surface particularly in the spiritual foundation in which we as a race have our root so firmly fixed and, while it will not, of course, point or preach, it will, I believe, answer, at least in so far as I see it, the question whither— that is, if my ability to tell the story can anywhere approximate the idea that I have in my mind.

In his September 9, 1925, letter to J. E. Spingarn cited above, White was more specific about his goal in writing *Flight:*

I have taken the story of a girl born in New Orleans of Creole and Negro blood and have caused her to go through certain experiences in the city of her birth, in Atlanta, in Philadelphia, and in New York. About the first half of the book is laid wholly within the race. At only one point do white people enter the story at all and then only because certain experiences which this girl has in connection with white people influence her life afterwards. I sought to give a dispassionate, objective picture. How well I succeeded I do not know. At any rate, the girl herself is not perfect and there are no one hundred per cent villains either white or black. The story is not at all to my satisfaction but I hope that when you read it, you will feel that I have learned something since writing "Fire in the Flint."

Clearly, White was hoping his second novel would be an improvement over his first effort; he sought to overcome the propaganda label and to treat his characters more realistically. While he achieved his first goal, whether he achieved the second became the subject of some critical debate.

Flight centers on the life of Mimi Daquin (Annette Angela Daquin) as she experiences the pressures of Negro life, in the South and in the North, and the further pressures she faces when she decides to pass. The novel opens with Mimi, her father (Jean), and her stepmother (Mary) moving to Atlanta from New Orleans. Through flashbacks we learn that Jean did not want to leave his native city but that he finally acquiesced to Mary's badgering to move to Atlanta where, with her father's help, Jean could enter the insurance business and make a success of himself. Although Jean is never really happy in Atlanta, caught up in the faster pace of the business life there, Mimi and Mary adapt fairly quickly.

One of the first pressures Mimi and Jean must face in their new home is the tremendous prejudice against their Catholic religion. Since there are no black Catholic churches to attend and they cannot attend the white Catholic church, they reluctantly agree to attend the "right" church for them, the Congregational church. Other prejudices are encountered from within the black community, especially concerning color and class. The Daquins' light complexion and their relatively secure status, however, allow them to move quite freely into the proper circles of black Atlanta. Soon Mimi has a fast friend in Hilda Adams, and Jean settles in to his work at the Lincoln Mutual Life Insurance Company. Immediately before Mimi first meets Hilda and her mother, she overhears a conversation which introduces the idea of passing for the first time in the novel. The ladies' Fleur-de-Lis Club is meeting, and the gossip centers on Mrs. Adams, who has not yet arrived:[13]

" . . . it seems Mrs. Adams has been going to the Grand Opera House and buying seats in the orchestra, 'passing' for white. . . . Well, the other day, as she was going in, some coloured person saw her and went and told the manager.

She tried to bluff it out but it didn't work—they made her get out."

The petty jealousy illustrated in this particular bit of gossip is what eventually drives Mimi out of her race in disgust.

The time spent in Atlanta is frustrating for Jean and Mimi, until Mimi meets Carl Hunter. In an all too familiar pattern, Mimi at first despises Carl, who has a reputation for being "fast," but finally falls in love with him. Their relationship is a strained one, however, because Hilda Adams also loves Carl and becomes extremely jealous. After Carl returns from school a failure, Mimi is finally pressured by Mary to break off with Carl, who then takes to drinking and staying out all night. One evening when Jean and Mary are out dining, Carl walks by, Mimi invites him in, and soon they are locked in a passionate embrace. From this point, Mimi encounters difficulty after difficulty. Jean becomes ill and dies, and in a few weeks Mimi discovers that she is pregnant. Her reaction is one of joy, but Carl, fearing his father's response to the news, wants Mimi to get "fixed up." The Hunters want Carl to marry Mimi and "do the right thing," but Mimi, fiercely independent and unable to forgive Carl's initial reaction, decides to head for Philadelphia, because "Philadelphia was large, she knew no one there and she was sure she could lose herself in its vastness" (p. 154).

Her life in Philadelphia is a constant struggle. Soon after her son (*Petit* Jean) is born, Mimi's money runs out and she begins sewing for a living. While she is working in the home of one client, the woman's husband makes a pass at Mimi, and she quits the job. Little Jean becomes ill, and a kind doctor saves his life and generously offers to forfeit his fee. Mimi is too proud to accept, however, and vows to pay him somehow. Reluctantly Mimi decides to put Jean in a Baltimore orphanage (white), and she goes to New York to stay with her Aunt Sophie and look for work so that she can once again have her son with her.

When Mimi arrives in Harlem, she is awed by what she sees and marvels at the distinction between white New York and black Harlem:

She was thrilled by the new scene. Gone was the morbid, morose, worried air of the people she had encountered at the other end of the subway. Here was spontaneous laughter, shrewd observations which brought loud and free laughter from listeners. There was an exhilarating sense here that these people knew the secret of enjoying life. Black and brown and yellow faces flitted by, some carefree, some careworn. Mimi sensed again the essential rhythm, the oneness of these variegated colours and moods. It was all vivid, colourful of a pattern distinctive and apart, and she warmed to the friendliness of it all. . . . [P. 186]

Mimi takes a course in design and begins to blossom; she is determined to succeed and get her son back. The friendliness she sensed initially in Harlem soon turns sour, however, and Mimi becomes the victim of a local gossip rag, the *Blabber,* which exposes, courtesy of an old Atlanta gossip visiting Harlem, Mimi's affair with Carl. Humiliated and beaten, Mimi decides to leave her race and pass. She explains to her Aunt Sophie:

"I never thought I'd want to leave my own people. I wouldn't leave them now but they've driven me away—driven me to the point where I've either got to drop out of sight where I won't be hounded again or else I'll do something terrible. . . . My name is French, I speak French—at least well enough to fool anybody who isn't French—I can sew, and they'll never think me anything else but French. . . . I'm leaving Harlem, leaving coloured people for good." [Pp. 207–8]

With that declaration, Mimi crosses over the racial line to start her life as a white person.

In her new life Mimi begins working as a finisher in an exclusive dress-making establishment, Madame Francine's. There she is befriended by Sylvia Smith, a Jew who is passing, and she later discovers that Madame Francine is really Irish. As the years go by, Mimi advances at Madam Francine's, finally coming to the attention of Francine herself. Impressed by Mimi's designs, Madam Francine asks her to accompany her to Paris "to get the new styles." While in Paris, Mimi learns the "inside" of the dressmaking business. Francine is so taken with Mimi's keen eye and quick judgment that she begins to think of the young woman as a possible successor.

More years pass. *Petit* John is now twelve and living with a French family in Westchester County. Mimi has adjusted somewhat to her new lifestyle, but she never completely feels a part of it:

She was lonely, for despite her success she had no intimates [Sylvia had long since left], none she could call friend, though she might have had them had she chosen. She missed the warm colourfulness of life among her own, she had never been able to shake off the chill she felt even when her present-day associates sought to be the most cordial. . . . Frequently when she heard contemptuous remarks about "niggers," "coons," "darkies," from those who showed by their words their complete ignorance of Negroes, she felt like reminding them that to her there are two ways of achieving and maintaining superiority: one, by being superior; the other, by keeping somebody else inferior. [P. 241]

Her defense of Negroes, however, only gives her the lable of "nigger-lover."

On a later trip to Paris, in the process of entertaining a noisy, demand-ing American named Mrs. Crosby, Mimi meets Jimmie Forrester. Mimi is drawn to Jimmie, but she is fearful of getting romantically involved again.

After a long and painful chase by Jimmie, during which both lovers become the stereotyped portraits of unrequited love, Mimi agrees to marry Jimmie. She attempts to tell him of her true race, but he will not let her talk. Mimi soon becomes discontented with her new life; once again she feels the pull of her own race. At a party one evening she joins with Professor Henry Meekins in an attack on the white world's attempt to "civilize" the darker nations, and at a later party she meets Wu Hseh-Chuan, a Chinese whose discussion of his country's view of Western civilization reawakens Mimi's sense of emptiness.

Completely restless in the world of the machine-like whites, Mimi visits a Harlem cabaret with a friend and marvels at the contrast. Entranced by the jazz music, Mimi reflects on its effect on her:

Mimi knew that for her this wild music held its greatest charm in its freedom from rules, its complete disregard of set forms. It refused to be tied down, its creators wove harmonies out of thin air and transferred to their notes the ecstasy of a wild, unharnessed, free thing. . . . Every conceived creature of freedom came to her mind as she sat and listened and felt the ecstasy the music made her feel. . . .   [P. 294]

Finally, after attending a concert at Carnegie Hall by a Negro singer closely resembling Roland Hayes, an experience which deeply moves her and which calls up visions of Africa and slavery and faith, "a faith strong and immovable . . . a faith which made a people great," Mimi decides to leave Jimmie and return to her people. Confidently she heads back into the life she had abandoned years ago:

"Free! Free! Free!" she whispered exultantly as with firm tread she went down the steps. "*Petit* Jean—my own people—and happiness!" was the song in her heart as she happily strode through the dawn, the rays of the morning sun dancing lightly upon the more brilliant gold of her hair. . . . [P. 300]

As this closing passage makes clear, Walter White's style did not improve much in his second effort. In *Flight,* as in *The Fire in the Flint,* White depended heavily on melodramatic clichés in phrasing and in plot. Whenever Mimi leaves one life situation for another, inevitably she feels as if she were "opening a new book" or closing an old one. The following description of Jimmie Forrester after he has pined for months for Mimi is an almost classic stereotype of the rejected suitor:

Mimi felt sick at heart as she saw the changes that had taken place in him. He was no longer the laughing, debonair, assured individual he had been that day they met in Paris. His eyes burned with a blazing intensity from the deep sockets in which they were sunk, his hands twitched as he alternately closed and opened them, he kept his lips pressed tightly together, and his words came short and crisp from the emotion that lay behind them. [P. 258]

On many occasions White's use of figurative language is awkward and, at the very least, questionable. He used this simile, for example, in describing the Atlanta gossips: "Like a great orchestra beginning *pianissimo* upon a symphony, the tongues started clacking in soft and cryptic whisperings" (p. 120).

There are, however, moments of some beauty or impact in *Flight*, especially centering around Jean's love of New Orleans or Mimi's fascination with Harlem. Consider this description of St. Louis cemetery, for example:

. . . in silence they wandered through the confused, close-packed *vieux carré* of the dead, past tombs piled one upon the other, their walls lined with row upon row of ghostly store houses, "the ovens" like those of a baker-shop, each large enough only to hold a coffin. Crumbling bricks, covered with vines within which scampered in the dazzling, warming sunlight lizards of green or gold. Here and there the *Ci-gît* and the *Ici Repos* and the names, birth and death dates of those buried within had been eaten away by countless storms of rain and sunlight until none could tell who had been buried there. [Pp. 35–36]

In addition to the descriptions of Harlem already quoted, White also offered this observation by Mimi on the kaleidoscope of colors within the black community. Mimi is attending a dance at the Manhattan Casino when she observes

faces of all colours, peeping from gowns of all shades. . . . There were faces of a mahogany brownness which shaded into the blackness of crisply curled hair. There were some of a blackness that shone like rich bits of velvet. There were others whose skins seemed as though made of expertly tanned leather with the creaminess of old vellum, topped by shining hair, blacker than "a thousand midnights, down in a cypress swamp." And there were those with ivory-white complexions, rare old ivory that time had mellowed with a gentle touch. To Mimi the most alluring of all were the women who were neither dark nor light, as many of them were, but those of that indefinable blend of brown and red, giving a richness that was reminiscent of the Creoles of her own New Orleans. [P. 199]

In moments like these White is closer to the Harlem school of Hughes and McKay than to the "rear guard" of Du Bois and Fauset.

Perhaps the best description in the novel comes at the climactic scene in Carnegie Hall when Mimi is transported by the singer into a fantastic world of vision. Here White develops the impressions the spirituals create within Mimi:

A vast impenetrable tangle of huge trees appeared, their pithy bulk rising in ebon beauty to prodigious heights. As she gazed, half afraid of the wild stillness, the trees became less and less blackly solid, shading off into ever lighter grays. Then the trees were white, then there were none at all. In their stead an immense circular clearing in which moved at first slowly, then with increasing speed, a ring of graceful, rounded, lithe women and stalward, magnificently muscled men, all with skins of midnight blackness. To music of barbaric sweetness and rhythm they danced with sinuous grace and abandon. Soft little gurgling cries punctuated the music, cries which came more sharply, like little darting arrows, as the ecstatic surrender of the figures to the dance increased.   [Pp. 297–98]

From this vision Mimi enters another, where "weird creatures" burst upon the scene; with their "black reeds which spurted lead and flame," these invaders overpowered the dancers and took them across the ocean:

. . . she saw a ship wallowing in the trough of immense waves. Aboard there strode up and down unshaven, deep-eyed, fierce-looking sailors who sought with oath and blow and kick to still the clamorous outcries of their black passengers. These were close packed in ill-smelling, inadequate quarters where each day stalked the specter whose visit meant one less mouth to feed. Black bodies were tossed carelessly overboard. No sooner did one of them touch the water than came sinister streaks of gray and white which seized the body long before the wails from the ship had died in the distance. [Pp. 298–99]

From that point the vision proceeds naturally to the plantations and fields of the new land, "a world of motion and labour . . . caught up and held immobile in the tenuous, reluctant notes" of the singer. In these passages White transcends the rather laborious prose of most of the novel and reaches a level of description that suggests both the strikingly stark work of Aaron Douglas and the rounded fullness of Hale Woodruff's paintings. Moments like these, unfortunately, are much the exception in White's novels.

As in *The Fire in the Flint*, thematic ideas are much more important in *Flight* than matters of art and style. While the themes of White's second novel are not as dramatically arresting as the dominant lynching theme of his first work, White does consider in *Flight* some essential issues facing the black community. The first of these is the idea of passing, and the forces which operate to drive one to pass out of her race into another. For Mimi the dominant forces which serve to drive her out center on pressures from within the race, specifically color consciousness, religious prejudice, and the petty jealousies of foolish gossips. In New Orleans it is Mimi's stepmother Mary who is confronted by prejudices of the "mellow old families, militantly proud of their Creole and Negro ancestry." In addition to being "an outsider," Mary has skin of "deep brown, in sharp contrast to the ivory tint of Jean and Mimi" (p. 29). In Atlanta color is not so much a factor, at least for the Daquins, as religion. As Catholics, Jean and Mimi are totally out of step with the black community there. But it is the petty gossiping that finally drives Mimi into passing. The Fleur-de-Lis Club's gossip about Mrs. Adams's attempts to pass and the jealous "coloured person" who "turned her in" provide one sample of that gossip; the "story" Mrs. Plummer gives the Harlem gossip rag, the *Blabber*, is another, and the one which finally drives Mimi out. In making her decision Mimi recalls a story told by Booker T. Washington:

. . . he likened Negroes to a basket of crabs—when one of them had with great energy climbed almost to the top of the basket and freedom, the others less progressive than he would reach up with their claws and pull him back down to their level. This had seemed to her then merely an effective story coined for oratorical purposes, but now its applicability was forced upon her with painful truth.   [P. 211]

With a great deal of sadness Mimi concludes that "her passing from the race seemed . . . persecution greater than any white people had ever visited upon her—the very intolerance of her own people had driven her from them."

In her new "white" life Mimi becomes terribly conscious of the distinctions between the two lifestyles, the white and the black. There is a quality to the latter which is completely missing in the former:

. . . in her new life she missed the spontaneity, the ready laughter, the naturalness of her own. She saw morose, worried faces. Here there was little of that softness of speech to which she was accustomed. Here there was an obsession with material things that crowded out the naturalness that made life for her tolerable.   [P. 212]

Later, at a Harlem nightclub with her friend Bert Bellamy, a white male counterpart to Mrs. Plummer, Mimi notices the differences between the white dancers and the few black couples there:

She watched the dancers. The floor was crowded mostly with white couples executing all sorts of fancy steps, swaying and bumping the others in their gyrations. Here and there a coloured couple moved with unconscious grace, a rhythmic sweep to their bodies that made the others seem awkward and graceless.   [P. 293]

The contrast White draws between white folks and black folks hinges mostly on those two qualities: the lively, graceful spirit of the black community versus the somber, mechanical life of the white world.

Along with this concept of a difference between the two races goes the idea of racism, a topic which, as White himself suggested, no black writer could really ignore. In *Flight* White makes use of his own experience in the Atlanta riot of 1906 and recreates that riot in the novel, involving Jean and Mimi in some of the experiences he had faced as a young boy. In setting the stage for his fictionalized riot, White establishes the same causes he discussed in *A Man Called White* as the prime factors for the 1906 explosion: a long hot summer which frayed nerves and sharpened tempers "to razor-blade keenness"; a period of unemployment which caused "a marked loafing of whites and Negroes followed by a long series of petty crimes"; a "bitter political campaign, . . . its central issue the disenfranchisement of Negroes and 'Negro domination' "; a presentation of *The Clansman;* and an irresponsible, sensation-seeking press (p. 67). Just as Walter White and his father had been caught out in the midst of the riot, Jean and Mimi are likewise witness to several brutal scenes. Mimi sees a man walking down Marietta Street and wants to warn him of an approaching white mob, but she realizes her voice would not be heard in the din. Suddenly the crowd spies him:

Too late the Negro saw his danger. He turned to flee but before he had gone many yards the pack was upon him. Mimi saw him strike out, dodge, attempt to elude his attackers. It was useless. Down he went and a great bellow of hatred, of passion, of sadistic exultation filled his ears as he died. Mimi covered her eyes with her hands and pressed close to Jean as she saw the flashing jack-knives.   [P. 73]

Mimi and Jean are almost caught by the mob themselves, but when Jean exclaims "Mon Dieu!" the mob member who had approached them apologizes: "Scuse me, brother! I thought you were a nigger!" Their light complexion and Jean's French exclamation save them.

For Mimi, as for Walter White, this riot acts as an agent for racial identity it solidifies the racial ties. After Mimi witnesses the death described above, she thinks:

To her before that dread day, race had been a relative matter, something that did exist but of which one was not conscious except when it was impressed upon one. The death before her very eyes of that unknown man shook from her all the apathy of the past. There flashed through her mind in letters that seared her brain the words, "I too am a Negro!"   [P. 74]

In the next chapter, after the riot had quieted, White states: "Mimi dated thereafter her consciousness of being coloured from September, nineteen hundred and six. For her the old order had passed, she was now definitely

of a race set apart" (p. 77). This sounds very close to White's comment in
A Man Called White, quoted in chapter 1: "I knew then who I was. I was
a Negro, a human being with an invisible pigmentation which marked me
a person to be hunted, hanged, abused, discriminated against, kept in
poverty and ignorance. . . ."

Mimi's race identity and race pride are other important elements in the
novel. Whether in Atlanta, Harlem, or white New York, Mimi constantly
senses the influences that draw her to her people. When they first arrive
in Atlanta, Mimi and her father listen to an unfamiliar sound in a blues
exchange between a man and a woman outside their window. They strain
"to catch every note of this barbaric, melancholy wail as it [dies] in the
distance, a strange thrill filling them" (p. 17). Later Mimi watches a Negro
convict gang at work and is fascinated by their work song:

Mimi's heart beat faster and faster as she watched and listened. She sensed
that the song carried the toilers far above their miserable lot. For them
the toil and sweat, the louring guards who shouted staccato commands
or flung crisp oaths when one of the convicts slackened or appeared to
slacken in his labour, did not exist. She began to comprehend the thing
Carl had said to her of the "over-soul" the Negro possessed. . . .   [P. 93]

While White's conception of the effect of a work song on the men working
is terribly romanticized, at least he has his character in contact with the
basic musical elements that make up her heritage as a black American. In
fact, within a few pages White covers the work song, the spiritual, and
jazz, and the effect each has on Mimi's developing race consciousness. Her
reaction to the spiritual "Were You There When They Crucified My Lord?"
in this section anticipates the effect of the Carnegie Hall concert at the
end of the novel:

Afterwards she felt as though she had been the victim of some peculiar
metempsychosis—that during the minutes of the song her soul had taken
flight from her own body to that of some other rarer, more sentient,
more delicately strung being of infinite beauty and understanding, to
return only when the spell had been broken.   [P. 95]

Mimi's joy in the black lifestyle continues when she reaches New York.
After she and her aunt arrive in Harlem, Mimi's excitement increases as
she observes the life around her:

. . here was a new life, teeming , exotic, individual. Hurrying along the
streets, coming out of restaurants, standing in doorways and on street
corners were groups of Negroes, well dressed, jubilant, cheerful. Here and
there hurried coloured men in twos and threes, clad in smartly fitting dinner

jackets, snow-white bosoms peeping from heavy overcoats, musical instruments . . . in cases clutched in their hands. They hastened into the subway kiosk Mimi and her aunt had just quitted and were swallowed up. From near by there came to them the bewitching odours of frying corn and chicken, of pig's-feet. They came from a stand where a middleaged coloure woman was serving her wares to passers-by. [Pp. 186–87]

At a dance attended by Mimi and Mrs. Rodgers, Mimi marvels at the "easy grace," the variety of color, and the spontaneity that mark the people of Harlem as something special. After she passes over into the white world, she becomes increasingly aware of an emptiness within her, and her trip to Harlem with Bert Bellamy and her experience at Carnegie Hall convince her that she can never be whole, can never be completely satisfied until she rejoins her people and submerges herself once more in the soothing world she left behind.

The emptiness Mimi feels during her life in the white world stems, in large part, from the mechanization of that world. The role of the machine in the (white) Western world is the last of the thematic concerns of *Flight,* and one which puts it in tune with much of the literature of White's contemporaries. Reacting to the more frantic pace of life in Atlanta, Jean Daquin tells his daughter:

The whole world's gone mad over power and wealth. The strongest man wins, not the most decent or the most intelligent or the best. All the old virtues of comradeship and art and literature and philosophy, in short, all the refinements of life, are being swallowed up in this monster, the Machin we are creating which is slowly but surely making us mere automatons, dancing like marionettes when the machine pulls the strings and bids us prance. [P. 54]

Years later, after her marriage to Jimmie Forrester, Mimi echoes Jean's observation as she reflects upon the white faces in the street:

There was always that strained, unhappy expression on the countenances of these people who, like scurrying insects, rushed madly here and there, each as though upon his efforts depended the future of civilization and life and everything else. Like cogs in a machine, she said of them one day, and thereafter she always thought of them as cogs. Here they have created a machine of which they are intensely proud and of which they think they are the masters. Instead, ironically enough, the machine has mastered them and they must do its bidding. [Pp. 267–68]

If we overlook the mixture of metaphors in this passage, we see White playing on an important theme of early twentieth-century literature: the real possibility that man might become subordinate to his mechanical creations, and ultimately become the servant rather than the served.

Echoing another set of sentiments of the time, White offers American Negroes as a group of people who have managed to escape the trap of mechanization and who are all the better for having escaped. After listening to the black chain gang, Mimi considers with admiration the strength shown by those men in the face of terrible adversity:

She marvelled at their toughness of fiber which seemed to be a racial characteristic, which made them able to live in the midst of a highly mechanized civilization, enjoy its undoubted advantages, and yet keep free that individual and racial distinctiveness which did not permit the surrender of individuality to the machine.

. . . .

In slavery it had kept them from being crushed and exterminated as oppression had done to the Indian. In freedom it had kept them from becoming mere cogs in an elaborately organized machine. Some people called it shiftlessness, laziness, inherent racial inferiority. Mimi herself had heard these charges made and . . . had been ashamed of them. . . . The forced growth of her race-conscious attitude had accelerated this shamedness of her people's apparent lack of assimilation by industrialism—now she began to feel glad that this was so. [P. 94]

This idea is repeated later, in New York, by Wu Hseh-Chuan, the Chinese visitor whose conversation sparks Mimi's yearning to return to her race. In response to Mimi's question of whether the Western world was heading toward "greater wisdom or destruction," he replies:

"Who can tell? The great nation or people or civilization is not that one which has the greatest brute strength but the one which can serve mankind best. The machine has been created—and in turn is mastering its creators. I have been in your country many times and I feel that only your Negroes have successfully resisted mechanization—they yet can laugh and they yet can enjoy the benefits of the machine without being crushed by it. . . ." [P. 282]

Shortly after this confirmation of her own secret thoughts, Mimi makes her decision to return to her people.

Perhaps White's most noticeable improvement in *Flight* was in the area of characterization, at least in terms of fairer treatment of whites and blacks. While there are still more stereotypes than real people in the novel, there are some "bad" black characters and some "good" white ones. The almost perfect Jean and Mimi are balanced by the gossipy Mrs. Plummer and her cohorts, and the myopic Jimmie Forrester, who spouts his disgust at blacks, Jews, "Chinks," and all other people who do not share his color and beliefs, is balanced by the sympathetic Francine and Sylvia Smith.

White's greatest pride, however, was the creation of Mimi; in her, he felt, he had created what F. E. DeFrantz called "a magnificent character." In his April 1, 1926, letter, DeFrantz continued:

I thought of Tolstoi's "Anna Karenina" and I reflected on the "Mimis" I know and you know and all of us know, but are sadly unknown, or better, unrecognized by our white compatriots. It is a beautiful tragedy, and I use the word beautiful advisedly. Mimi will never die—such characters perdure.

White presented his attitude toward his creation quite clearly in a letter responding to John Haynes Holmes's praise of *Flight.* White's comment reveals the importance of Mimi to her creator:[14]

Mimi is, so far as I consciously know, wholly a creation. She is modelled upon no person I have ever known. . . . In telling her story, I sought to solve no problem, to write no treatise upon race or any other question. I sought simply to create a character or, better, to put down on paper a character who had been created within me. To me, Mimi's whole outlook on life in her pathetic quest after happiness and truth is a story as I saw it of all of us who have ideals and try to live up to them. In telling of Mimi, I revealed, I now realize, a great deal more of myself than I knew at the time of writing.

This intensely personal view of his heroine made White particularly vulnerable to criticism of his character. Most of the critics found Mimi's motivation completely undeveloped. The reviewer for the *New York Times Book Review,* for example, said Mimi was "inadequately humanized. . . . Mimi is not a living human being and must be judged from type."[15] As in *The Fire in the Flint,* White demonstrated in *Flight* a flair for incident, although frequently strained and contrived, but he could not create "real" characters or go beyond the stereotyped patterns of the sentimental novel.

In promoting his second novel, however, Walter White demonstrated the same energy that he used in promoting *Fire.* One of the first avenues White pursued was getting a blurb from Sinclair Lewis in support of *Flight.* On September 26, 1925, White wrote Blanche Knopf that he had spoken to Lewis about doing a blurb, but he added that Lewis had "promised to do a number of paragraphs for several other books and he is apprehensive about appearing too often." Lewis did want Mrs. Knopf to write him, though, to tell him what was wanted. Mrs. Knopf replied to White a few days later, saying: "The Sinclair Lewis business is serious and I hope that he is going to be willing to give us what blurbs he can. I'll write him at once."[16] Unfortunately, Lewis declined to write the blurbs, for reasons he stated in a letter to Blanche Knopf:[17]

There is nothing I should like better than to do a blurb for Walter White's new novel, but it is inadvisable for three reasons:

First, I boosted his first novel and people would begin to believe that this was entirely a matter of friendship, which would be of advantage neither to him nor to me.

Second, Walter is known by all of the people who are in the game to be a very great friend of mine and the disadvantages would be as great as I have suggested in the first paragraph.

Third, I have done, for one reason or another, too many books the last year or two and if I keep that up my name will become as common in the book advertising columns as that of William Lyon Phelps, which would be a disadvantage to every one concerned.

Lewis asked Mrs. Knopf to show White the letter and to express his regrets for being unable to help: " . . . it is quite as much on his behalf as on my own. . . ." White was very understanding in his reply to Lewis. He told his friend that he thought he was "absolutely right" in responding as he did to Mrs. Knopf's request. In fact, White said he had been "reluctant" about asking Lewis in the first place: " . . . I never like to appear to be trading on friendship—the friendship with you is far too precious to me. I am awfully glad you wrote [Mrs. Knopf] as you did."[18]

A few months after losing Lewis as a source of promotion for his novel, White was trying to secure a place for another friend, Clarence Darrow, to review *Flight*. On February 19, 1926, two months before the novel's publication, White wrote Johan Smertenko of Knopf:

The other day I was talking with Clarence Darrow who had just read "Fire in the Flint" and who was rather keen about it. He said he would like to do an article on it perhaps for the *New York World*. I suggested that since "Fire in the Flint" had been out a year and a half and inasmuch as my new novel was coming along soon, it might be well for him to do an article on the two books, emphasizing, of course, "Flight." What do you think of the suggestion being made to the *Times* or the *World* or some other place as seems best, letting them know that Mr. Darrow would be willing to do such an article or review.

Evidently, Smertenko thought highly of the idea, for a few days later he wrote to Harry Salpeter of the *New York World* that "Darrow is just now very much interested in the problems of the Negro in America and White's book will furnish him with enough ammunition to do a corking article." In closing, Smertenko reminded Salpeter of Stallings's response in the *World* to White's first novel:[19]

You probably recall that Stallings was extraordinarily enthusiastic about *The Fire in the Flint*. *Flight* is a much better book and it would be good journalism as well as a "lift" to good literature to give some sort of prominence to this new and honest expression of the future of the Negro race.

Smertenko's last comment prompts one to wonder whether he had read the novel he was so energetically supporting. At any rate, no response from Salpeter is in the NAACP correspondence files.

In addition to seeking reviews and blurbs from his important friends, White also pursued other means of promotion. He suggested to Blanche Knopf, for instance, that she have her publicity department do "a fairly lengthy story on the new novel announcing its publication date and whooping it up." White would then have Knopf envelopes addressed at his office to be sent to the 250 newspapers and magazines on the NAACP's service list; he thought "it would look a good deal less like self-advertisement" if the literature went out on Knopf letterhead. The letter, sent out March 16, 1926, announced the publication of *Flight* on April 19 and summarized the plot: "The story presents without bias an angle of the Negro situation which has so far been neglected in fiction, and it is told with such feeling and skill that it will have a profound effect." The letter also included excerpts from favorable reviews of *The Fire in the Flint*.[20] Within the organization of the NAACP White was also considering a plan to combine subscriptions to the *Crisis* with a copy of *Flight*. In a memorandum to a Mr. Dill, White noted that he already discussed the idea with Du Bois and had gotten his tentative approval; Dill was to talk to Smertenko about devising a plan which would be "mutually beneficial" to Knopf and the NAACP, and about advertising *Flight* in the *Crisis*.[21]

As the date of publication of the novel drew nearer, prospects for its success seemed good. Writing to send White a list of "White and colored people" who read books in the Lincoln University area, Langston Hughes told White, " . . . everybody seems to be waiting for 'Flight.' " White wrote his friend Aaron Bernd in Macon, Georgia, on March 19 that Knopf had told him the first edition of *Flight* was already nearly exhausted and that they might have to reprint before the publication date of April 19. Always ready to take advantage of a situation, White wrote R. K. Wood at Knopf that Wood should write a lady with whom White had corresponded about a speaking engagement in Charleston, West Virginia, and tell her that White's novel would be brought out the very day he was to speak there and suggest her organization might want to order copies of the novel to sell at the meeting—and White would autograph them.[22]

After the publication of *Flight*, when the sales of the novel did not meet his expectations, White wrote to Wood to ask if Knopf could not expend more monies advertising his book:

Authors, I realize, have insatiable appetites for advertising but, after all, they can hardly be blamed for a sort of selfish interest in the sale of their books. I wonder if I might make the suggestion that "Flight" might very well stand a little more pushing. For example, Llewellyn Jones gave the feature review of the *Chicago Evening Post* Literary Review of June 25th to "Flight" and in that same section there is a very interesting editorial on the contributions of certain Negro writers; in the *Detroit Free Press* of July 4th, there appears the cheerful news that "Flight" has achieved best-sellerdom in that city . . . and there have been excellent reviews from papers ranging from Boston to Miami.

White included with his letter a press release which noted that *Flight* was "one of the six best sellers in Detroit," a first for a Negro novelist's work. Responding on behalf of Knopf, George Stevens agreed that *Flight* needed pushing but questioned whether advertising it "at this stage of the game" was the "best way to push it":

In the first place, our advertising expenditures on *Flight* have already exceeded the normal appropriations for a second novel. In the second place, if we are trying to squeeze the juice out of the Llewellyn Jones review and the Detroit episode, we shall lose too much time in the process of inserting ads. Both Mr. Wood and I feel that more can be done just now in the way of letters to the salesmen and the trade, and that further advertising should perhaps wait until the sales advance further.

Somewhat mollified, White wrote Stevens: "I entirely agree with you and Mr. Wood."[23]

From all indications, the sales of *Flight* did not fare so well, not even as well as the sales for White's first novel. Another hopeful scheme to make money from *Flight*, through its serialization by Loren Palmer (*Everybody's*, the *Delineator*, the *Designer*), also fell through. Sinclair Lewis encouraged White to submit his manuscript to Palmer and went so far as to call Palmer to tell him he would "be a damn fool if he did not accept" White's novel. In a letter to L. M. Hussey on September 5, 1925, White wrote:[24]

I am to see Loren Palmer next week at which time I shall place in his hands the MS. of "Flight." God or Buddha or Mohammed alone know what will be his decision. The odds are probably ninety-nine to one that he will suffer an attack of chilliness in his pedal extremities. Though I am just selfish enough to want most eagerly the money which serialization of the novel would mean for it would enable me to do some of the things which I have been wanting to do for a long time.

Hussey's reply to White contains an interesting observation concerning the bias of popular magazines:[25]

I pray God Palmer has the courage to serialize your tale. But to print a novel about negroes in a popular magazine seems to me an act beyond the enterprise of the customary editor. . . . I hope my fears prove utterly groundless. You could get enough out of the magazine to liberate you for several years. And God knows we literary gents plead with Fortune for just such a liberation.

The pessimism voiced by both White and Hussey proved valid in this case, and there is no further mention of this particular plan.

The critical reaction to *Flight* was mixed. One of the most common complaints, aside from technical considerations, was that the novel was "too white." After praising *Flight* as a "much better novel than *Fire in the Flint,* and subtler criticism of the white and Negro relations in the United States," the reviewer for *Survey* took White to task, in essence, for not being Negro enough in his novel. The reviewer found the novel "more sophisticated, better designed, more artful in craftmanship, but in white, not Negro craftmanship," than *Fire:* "It contains no elemental emotion, no broad sunlit Rabelaisian humor, no folklore, no rhapsody of style or naive splendor of language."[26] It was, the reviewer concludes, "less Negro" than *Fire!* The review by Emma B. Holden in the *New Republic* struck a similar note and echoed the attitude discussed in Du Bois's survey, i.e., treatment of black characters should somehow be different from the treatment of white characters:[27]

Mr. White seems to feel that he can handle his people from the same angle that one would use in treating a group of whites, and yet create a special interest by assuring us from time to time that they are colored, and by introducing the dramatic episode of Negro persecution. He fails, inevitably. . . . It is neither a very consistent nor a very stirring story. That part of the book which fits the Daquin family into its Louisiana background of radiant sunlight, vivid gardens and Creole indolence is full of charming bits. The rest—the girl's career—is entirely disappointing.

Much of the negative criticism reflected the attitude of J. W. Crawford, writing for the *Literary Digest International Book Review:* " 'Flight' is a disturbingly thoughtful book. In view of its undeniable significance, it is a pity that it has not been completely realized and all the relationships thoroughly exploited. It could be a 'world-beater.' "[28]

Some negative reviews focused more specifically on two related problems in the novel: the abruptness of the ending and, as mentioned earlier, the development of Mimi as a character. The reviewer for the *Times Literary Supplement* complained that White "jerks" Mimi "into an acute realization of her Creole descent" at the end of the novel:[29]

The book ends too abruptly. In the earlier part Mr. White was at pains to trace the influence that Mimi's knowledge she was not a white girl had upon her, but as the book progresses he becomes more and more interested in Mimi for her own sake; and it is only at the finish he remembers he intended his novel to be a study in racial psychology and not the simple history of a girl's life. Mr. White writes carefully and intelligently enough to make his book interesting in both its aspects; but as a result of taking two photographs on one plate, as it were, the portrait of Mimi comes out a little blurred.

Lisle Bell, writing in the *Nation,* found the novel lacking in credibility, as Mimi overcomes all her problems with relative ease:[30]

Any number of difficulties beset the path of Mr. White's heroine, but the flight is theirs, not hers. . . . At each turn of the narrative where one looks for a definite crisis in the antagonisms from which the story is built up the clash is averted. As Mimi Daquin advances her problems melt like snowflakes on a coat sleeve, and—like snowflakes—one quickly forgets their pattern and almost doubts that they existed.

In her review of *Flight* for "Book Chat," the weekly book review sent out by the NAACP, Mary White Ovington found Mimi "a protest against stupidity, conformity, . . . always dissatisfied" and seeking "for something more," but added that, on the whole, there was not the passionate interest in Mimi that White had created in Kenneth and Robert Harper in *The Fire in the Flint.* Miss Ovington also commented upon the way "young modernists" like White and T. S. Stribling (in *Teeftallow*) "treat the heroine to whom is born an illegitimate child." Comparing Mimi to the "carnal sinners" who are placed above hypocrites and traitors in Dante's hell, Miss Ovington contended that " . . . Mimi does not love enough to keep one from having sympathy with the society that condemns her. There are no centuries of home life back of the American Negro, and what the past two generations have laboriously striven to build up, should not be torn down, at least not by such poor lovers as Mimi and Carl."[31] As this last comment makes clear, White was clearly violating some of the "rules" of the rear guard in *Flight;* while he did not perfect his heroine, he did make her earthy enough to offend some of the more staid members of the NAACP.

All the reviews were not negative, of course, and even those reviews which found serious faults in *Flight* sometimes found something to praise in the novel, too. Lisle Bell, for example, wrote: "Woven into the texture of the novel is a study of the development of Negro life in context with American urban civilization, and here the work of the novelist is notably vivid and comprehensive."[32] The reviewer for the *New York Times Book*

Review, who, as mentioned above, thought Mimi "inadequately humanized," found the thesis of the novel "convincing":[33]

Perhaps in the long run the thesis here is more important than the creation of character. And Mr. White, painting pictures, driving home truths, suggesting indictments, draws that thesis with an admirable objectivity. Whatever his sense of injustice, whatever his temptation toward pathos, he lets his story speak for itself. His picture of an Atlanta riot against the negroes needs no commentary to be convincing.

Once again it is White's ability to recreate an occasional dramatic moment that draws critics' attention; his art is still questioned.

Most of the praise of *Flight* centered on the significant insight it offered into some of the problems of the black man and woman in America. The reviewer for *World Tomorrow* said that *Flight* "is more than a good story written with alert understanding and engaging beauty. It is an excellent picture of modern American life in the crucible of race relationships."[34] Predictably, Carl Van Vechten, reviewing the novel for the *New York Herald Tribune,* called his friend's work[35]

an excellent novel which should be read with increasing wonder by those who are unfamiliar with the less sordid circles of Negro life, and which others may read simply as a story without thought of propaganda. Indeed, with this second book Mr. White takes on quite a new stature. There is little doubt but that he will be heard from further.

Finally Ernest Gruening drew an implied comparison between *Flight* and James Weldon Johnson's *The Autobiography of an Ex-Colored Man* (1912):

Besides hurling an additional brickbat at modern Western civilization from a new angle, "Flight" invades the intriguing realm treated in book form but once before and then as a special and unique case in "The Autobiography of an Ex-Colored Man," that of colored Americans who "go white." . . . Throughout Mr. White's latest book one glimpses the profound stirring among American Negroes. . . . "Flight" is an enlightening reflection of their growing race pride, race potentiality, and race achievement.

After conceding that at times the propagandist "over-shadows" the novelist in the book, Gruening concluded that, "despite its flaws, 'Flight' contains much that is moving, and presents an idea not without significance in contemporary America." In his second novel, as in his first, Walter White was again a source of revelation for many (white) readers.

By far the most interesting critical commentary on *Flight* centers on a negative review by Frank Horne in the July, 1926, issue of *Opportunity* and White's subsequent maneuvering to get a response to Horne's review published in the same journal. In addition to Horne and White, two other people play important roles in the scenario: Charles S. Johnson, editor of *Opportunity,* and Nella Larsen Imes, a friend of White's and soon to be a novelist herself (*Quicksand* [1928] and *Passing* [1929]). In his review Horne attacked three areas of the novel: character development (especially concerning Mimi), the novel's ending, and its style. Concerning the characters, Horne wrote:[37]

Mimi Daquin is a character worthy of a novel; she deserves treatment of a kind to place her beside Maria Chapdelaine, Mattie Frome and Salammbo. There is in her travail the lonely vicissitudes of a lost race and it irks no little to see her treated in a manner far inferior to her possibilities. It is in the failure of this central character to diffuse anything of glowing life and reality that the novel suffers its death blow. Mimi sees and acts and does but never becomes activated by the warm breath of life. This glaring fault in the development of the major character descends in proportionate measure upon the subsidiary actors. They are always either villainous or divine; either blatantly white or dastardly black, with the necromantic ability to change abruptly and unreasonably from the one extreme to the other.... Such manipulation smacks of the puppet show and not of creation. And a very creaky, awkward puppet show at that; you can actually see the strings and hear the squeaking of rusty jointed marionettes.

Horne's attack on the "hollow" ending of *Flight* echoed the sentiments of other reviewers:

Suddenly becoming conscious of the essential artistry and beauty of her own "race," as expressed in the voice of Roland Hayes, she overthrows the superstructure of her existence and goes flying back to "her people." One can imagine the possibility of such an happening to such a person, but Mr. White fails to convince us that his particular Mimi in her particular environment could have so acted. And so the climax meant to be so intense and sweeping, strikes a hollow, blatant note.... He has left this girl at the most critical stage of her career. She leaves a white world, with all its advantages of body and spirit, a position of eminence which she has developed out of the soul-sweat of her spirit, to go back to "her people." How then to be received?—how to adjust on a lower, cramped scale a life that had become so full?—how to compensate for the intense freedom of "being white?" Truly, has Mimi been left in the lurch.

It was about the style of the novel, however, that Horne sounded his harshest notes. Although he found the description of the Atlanta riot and parts of the closing scene "alive" and saw some "psychological sidelight" in Hilda Adams's jealousy, for the most part Horne found White's style wanting:

Mr. White's style suffers mainly from a woeful lack of clarity. Such elementary matters as faulty sentence structure often rise to affront one. . . . I was far into the second chapter before I was certain of the identity and relationships of the main characters of the story. These things should not be. "The Fire in the Flint" was at least clear-cut, simple and clearly defined. That story swept along by its very powerful simplicity; "Flight" seldom gets on the wing. . . . There is insight here which is no little blighted by inadequate expressions and puerile vocabulary. As further example of . . . inept writing, his similes are often ludicrously overdrawn and quaintly inapt.

Horne also deplored the lack of "color and poetry" in White's novel, " the very contributions that Negroes are expected to make to the literature of America. . . . His Harlem is a flat, colorless assemblage of brick and black faces."

As one might expect, White did not appreciate this evaluation of his work, and he wrote Charles Johnson immediately to protest what he termed Horne's "mere exposition of smartness." Indicating that he was writing Johnson "solely for [his] private consumption," White said:[38]

I do not object to adverse criticism. I believe, however, that an author has the right to expect that his books be reviewed in reputable journals by persons whose experience and learning are broad enough to enable these critics to comprehend what an author sets out to do. In the review in *Opportunity*, I feel that such is not the case. Mr. Horne is a likeable and intelligent young man but his review, it seems to me, indicates clearly that he has no conception of the broad aspects of my novel. . . . It is a bit discouraging when one of the few reputable journals published by Negroes permits a story which has taken many months of hard work to create to be reviewed by one who failed to understand it. There is an unfortunate tendency among some of those who call themselves new Negroes to use criticism as a means of demonstrating how "brave" and "unfettered" they are. Mr. Horne's strictures on "Flight" would be more bearable, too, if there were fewer split infinitives in his piece.

With the letter White enclosed a copy of Llewellyn Jones's favorable review of *Flight* in the June 25th *Chicago Evening Post Literary Review*. In closing, White asked Johnson to return the letter to him after the latter had read it and added that he hoped Johnson understood "the spirit" in which the letter was written: "It would be an unfortunate thing, if criticism by colored critics of stories written by colored writers should descend into a mere exposition of smartness."

Charles Johnson's reply to White indicated his regret that White had been displeased with the review of *Flight* and added:

. . . it would be unfortunate, I think, if you continue to feel justified in regarding an estimate that appeared in *Opportunity* as disparaging to your effort. Really, we have so few novels and novelists, that one wishes to be most careful in getting honest, as well as stimulating appraisals.

After thanking White for sending him Jones's review, Johnson wrote: "It is remarkable, I think, that you are able with your official duties and travelling to have produced in such a short time two acceptable novels." White's reply repeated the notion that he was not objecting to "adverse criticism" as such, but that he had been "more than ever confirmed" in the belief that Horne's review indicated that he had "failed to comprehend even the more obvious aspects of the theme" of the novel by "numerous unsolicited comments . . . from people who felt that the review was inadequate and unfair." White closed by saying: "I realize that nothing can be done about it now, but I trust that in future my, and in fact all books will be given for review to persons who are capable of doing intelligent appraisals of them."[39]

In a display of fairness that transcended his duties as editor, Johnson wrote back to White to tell him that, "contrary to the feeling expressed in your letter of July 28th, there is more that can be done" about what White considered an unjust review:[40]

I have solicited already from one person a rather full expression of the point of view which I think you would regard as being fully in sympathy with the spirit of the book, and I intend to publish this as a letter apropos of the review and in our Book Section. This person is Mrs. Nella Imes, who writes well and has a most extraordinarily wide acquaintance with past and current literature.

Another person may occur to me and I shall have no hesitancy about making a similar request of him. The discussion should whet interest in the book. Really, I am inclined to go to the extreme in this instance—to be certain of being fair in a situation which can so easily be misunderstood.

It seems a rather curious coincidence that Johnson should have chosen Nella Larsen Imes to write the reply to Horne's review, although he indicates in this letter that he did solicit the reply from Mrs. Imes. While there is no concrete evidence to support the notion, one senses Walter White's hand in this matter, a circumstance that certainly would be in keeping with his approach to solving problems.

This suspicion is heightened somewhat by a mysterious letter in the NAACP files. The letter is a carbon copy of a letter to Charles S. Johnson, with the typed signature "Albert L. Semi," and is basically the same letter Johnson published in the September, 1926, issue of *Opportunity* from Nella Imes. There is no date on the letter, which is a very rough copy, but a letter dated "Tuesday, Twelfth," presumably the twelfth of August, from "Nella" is attached to the carbon in the files. In her note to White Mrs. Imes apologized for the "messy" carbon and added: "I have not said everything I wanted to, nor what I have said as effectively as I would like.' Since Johnson had solicited a reply from Mrs. Imes directly and since the letter was published under her name, with some deletion from the original text by someone, one wonders about the typed signature on the carbon; there is no logical explanation for its being there. The fact that Mrs. Imes sent White a copy of the letter, however, suggests that she was seeking at least tacit approval from White for what she had written.

As published in *Opportunity,* Mrs. Imes's letter was a defense of *Flight* against Horne's "ununderstanding" review. Mrs. Imes began her letter saying she felt "surprise, anger, pity" after reading the review and she then attacked specific statements made by Horne. First she questioned the choice of heroines Horne used for comparison to Mimi, stating that they were, "for their own environment and times, excellent characters," and suggesting that Mimi would be better compared to more contemporary heroines, such as "Galsworthy's unsurpassable Irene Forsyte. . . ." Horne's statements about race, however, were the ones which drew the most of Mrs. Imes's fire:[42]

"There is in her travail the lonely vicissitudes of a lost race. . . ." Which "lost" race? It is here that your reviewer stumbles and falls. It is here that we detect his blindness. It is here that we become aware that he fails to realize that this is the heart of the tale. A lost race. Yes. But I suspect that he refers to the black race, while Mr. White obviously means that it is the white race which is lost, doomed to destruction by its own mechanical god How *could* your reviewer have missed this dominant note, this thing which permeates the whole book? It was this that made Mimi turn from it. Surely the thesis of "Flight" is "What shall it profit a man if he gain the whole world and lose his own soul?"

To Horne's complaint that White has Mimi leave the white world "with all its advantages of body and spirit," Mrs. Imes argued that Horne failed to understand "the fact that Mimi Daquin came to realize that, for her, there were no advantages of the spirit in the white world. . . ." Mrs. Imes also argued that Horne failed to grasp the intent of White's ending:

"Then, too, we must conjecture that he leaves this girl at the most crucial stage of her career." We do *not* conjecture anything of the kind. We know it. And we were meant to know it. Authors do not supply imaginations, they expect their readers to have their own, and to use them. Judging by present day standards of fiction, the ending of "Flight" is the perfect one, perfect in its aesthetic coloring, perfect in its subtle simplicity. For others of this type, I refer your reviewer to Sherwood Anderson's "Dark Laughte to Carl Van Vechten's "Firecrackers," to Joseph Hergesheimer's "Tubal Cane."

After calling *Flight* "a far better piece of work than *The Fire in the Flint,*" Mrs. Imes's letter closed with a final jab at Horne's competence: "It may be that your reviewer read the book hastily, superficially, and so missed both its meaning and its charm."

The material from the "Semi" letter which was deleted from the letter published under Mrs. Imes's name consisted mainly of even more personal attacks concerning Horne's "blindness" in reading *Flight* and his lack of race pride. Of the former, the "Semi" letter said:

It is the blindness, not the abuse which annoys me. I doubt if even Mr. Stuart Sherman or Mr. Carl Van Doren, supposing they had shared your reviewer's feelings, would have treated "Flight" so roughly. My quarrel with this very interesting piece of literary criticism is that seemingly your reviewer lacked the ability or the range of reading to understand the book which he attacked with so much assurance.

The letter's attack on Horne's lack of racial "feeling" is perhaps its lowest point, settling into *argumentum ad hominem,* rather than honest argument against Horne's critical stand:

"How," asks your reviewer, will she "adjust on a lower cramped scale a life that had become so full, how compensate for the intense freedom of being white?" Again, I point out that her life had *not* been full, it had, perhaps been novel, but not full. And I resent that word "lower," and in a lesser degree the word "cramped." I maintain that neither is applicable to Negro life, especially among people of Mimi's class. Inner peace compensated her for the "intense freedom of being white." Some people "feel" their race, (even some Negroes). Your reviewer may not, hence his lack of comprehension. Mr. White evidently does, and so, has given us Mimi Daquin.

Johnson, or someone, also deleted the "Semi" letter's counter-attack against Horne's analysis of White's style; the deleted material ended by defending White's opening sentence, to which Horne had alluded as an example of White's clumsy style, as "all right," comparing it to the opening of Galsworthy's latest novel, "a sentence of some thirty-odd words."

Everything considered, Nella Imes's defense of *Flight* was not very substantive, as Frank Horne indicated in his response to her letter, published in the October issue of *Opportunity.* First of all, Horne pointed out the "illogical" nature of Mrs. Imes's letter:[43]

She falls headlong into a similar pathetic fallacy with the novel she so zealously defends, in that she, too, mistakes the *intention* for the accomplishment, the *conception* for the expression. Hardly anyone—just really anyone—could have missed the intention. . . . The conflict of spirituality and materialism was indicated but never *incorporated* into the being of Mimi. The idea was pointed out, but never woven into the warp and woof of the story. I am certain that Mr. White *meant* to, but it is *he* that missed the point.

Horne went on to defend his choice of heroines with whom to compare Mimi, stating that he chose them "as examples of consummate skill in character creation and analysis. . . ." He also protested Mrs. Imes's judging *Flight* "by present day standards," arguing that any novel must be judged as a work of art, not "as last week's best novel by a Negro. . . . My concern is neither with chronology nor pigmentation, but with the eternal verity of art, and in this intense and glaring light, *Flight* is a poor book." Finally, Horne defended his attack on the novel's ending by arguing that White did not provide sufficient material for the reader's imagination to satisfactorily contemplate Mimi's fate:

I agree with Mrs. Imes that "authors do not supply imaginations" but they themselves must be possessed of enough imaginative power to at least indicate the *direction* in which they wish to be followed. After all, the imagination is a bridging function and the author should at least survey the ground, give me some river to cross, indicate a spot here and there that the bridge is to touch, suggest some distant horizon into which my far flung bridge is to disappear. If not that, then Mr. White's novel might just as well have been written in some such manner as this:—
"Mimi—colored—disillusioned—white—disillusioned No. 2—colored No. 2 . . . please use imagination."

In closing, Horne thanked Johnson for "the privilege of reviewing *Flight* and answering Nella Imes," and added: "I firmly attest that Mr. White is a jolly fine fellow, but I as vehemently insist that he has not written a jolly fine book."

The final chapter of this episode is White's, and it comes in the form of a letter from him to *Opportunity,* written in response to Horne's letter. White wrote the letter on October 9, and it was supposed to be published in the November issue; for reasons of space, however, it was not published until December 1926. Johnson told White that he would carry the letter "by way of offering the author's reaction to the discussion precipated by his product. Thus *Flight* projects itself into a fourth issue of *Opportunity*.' White's letter was very bitter and sarcastic and full of *argumentum ad hominem.* He began with a petty attack on Horne's style in the October letter, supposedly as a defense of his style in *Flight,* and then belittled Horne's capacity to understand what he reads:[45]

It is beginning to become apparent that hereafter I must write two versions of any book I want understood—one of them designed for readers of norm telligence or better; the other supplied with maps, charts, graphs and pictures and written in words of not more than two syllables. . . . Even after Mr. Horne's erudite strictures and his profound dicta, I am afraid I am not yet convinced that I "deserted" Mimi. Of course I could have adopted the fairybook formula of ending the story with the line " . . . and she lived happily ever afterwards." If it will make him any happier, I shall be glad to inscribe that line in Mr. Horne's copy of "Flight."

From this White descended lower, to a rather patronizing comment concerning the certainties of youth:

A few years ago, when I was around Mr. Horne's age, I was as certain of the absoluteness of everything in life as he apparently now is. Perhaps age is gently touching me for the older I grow and the more I see of life in its various phases, the less sure am I that everything in life can be definitely classed as white or black. . . . Perhaps in a few years from now Mr. Horne will not speak with quite the assured air of a combination Anatole France and H. L. Mencken.

As this letter indicates, Walter White was as unable to tolerate adverse criticism of his second novel as he was of his first; for him an attack on his skills as a writer was an attack on him personally. Here, as in his responses to criticism of *Fire,* he completely ignores the real issues concerning the faults of style, concept, and execution, and instead, attacks his attacker. This letter, however, presents in a public format a side of the private Walter White which rarely surfaced in public.

While the critical reaction to *Flight* varied, almost all the personal responses White received sang its praises. F. E. DeFrantz, White's friend from Indianapolis, said he would call the novel " . . . a great novel. Certainly no one, white or black, who has attempted to write of our group has come within a 'hundred leagues' of it." After praising the creation of Mimi, DeFrantz continued his praise of the novel as a whole:[46]

Abounding in rare subtleties that bespeak a depth of vision and a comprehensiveness of human values, it moves with a force irresistible, compelling, and overwhelming. There is a fearlessness and deftness in the marshalling of facts, and this in a novel that cannot but claim the author a master. Well, you have done it, my boy,—you have done it again.

As with the response to *The Fire in the Flint,* some of the most rewarding reactions to *Flight* came from the "common folk." J. Winston Smith, a would-be dramatist from Des Moines, Iowa, wrote White:

I have just finished your "Flight." Just as a common everyday Negro allow me to congratulate you upon the fine work. I pretend to be no judge or critic of literature but I have done quite a bit of reading. And it appears to me that your second novel is more of a success from an artistic view than your first. You seem in "Flight" to get away from your sometime editorial and newspaper handling of situations and make your characters breathe! Surely this is the test of a true author!

In replying to Smith, White wished him luck with his writing (and offered to help), and thanked him for his comments on *Flight:* "I am glad you liked 'Flight' and I am more than glad that you think it is an improvement over my previous novel."[47]

A more elaborate reaction to the novel, but in the same vein as Smith's, came from John Haynes Holmes, at a time when White was depressed over the critical attacks on his second novel. In his letter Holmes noted that he had seen the adverse criticism the novel had received in some quarters and added that he did not agree with them at all:

The book to my mind marks a real advance over your first book in matters that are of the first importance to your new development as a novelist. I have in mind particularly your technical mastery of your art, and "Flight" seems to me to mark a great advance in that regard over "The Fire in the Flint." This first book of yours had a certain power which was irresistible. You wrote it right out of the passion of your heart and it burned its way into the consciousness of every reader. It was a tremendous thing and will always remain in some ways, perhaps, your finest achievement. Its power was primitive in the sense that it sprang from your life without a single element of effort or design, . . . but for this very reason there was a certain roughness or even crudity in that book which marked it as a first work. It was these elements that you had to get rid of by mastering the technique of your task and thus becoming a real artist, and it is just this thing, it seems to me, that you have achieved in "Flight." . . . "Flight" has a beauty about it, an atmosphere, a finish of form and style, an easy flow of incident and characterization, a psychological insight into life, a creation of background and environment, which combine to make the whole thing a finished work in the sense that your earlier book was not. I think that it is this very fact which has taken the dissenting reviewers by surprise and led them to superficial comment. The book perhaps is not so real as your first book. It is perhaps a more deliberate creation than a natural birth, . . . but it marks a stage through which you had to pass if you are to fulfill your great promise and become a literary figure of first importance.

Quite understandably White was delighted to receive Holmes's praise and quickly replied, emphasizing the effect adverse criticism had had on him:[48]

I am too new at the game of writing to be impervious to adverse criticism. I confess that at times I was very depressed when I found that the picture I had created was not seen by the critics but, instead, a wholly distorted viewpoint was taken towards the beauty which I felt was inherent in Mimi

It gave me a sense of defeat. . . . Your letter, therefore, is a tremendous comfort and encouragement to me. I am immodest enough to agree with you that the critics could not understand my doing a story like "Flight" after I had written "Fire in the Flint." A number of them seem to feel that I should have stayed in the same path and merely done a re-writing of "Fire in the Flint." . . . Some of the critics have revealed that they think me unbalanced mentally when I do a picture of a person with Negro blood who can "go white" but who instead chooses voluntarily and not through force of circumstance to go back to being colored.

White closed by telling Holmes: "With your letter and the comfort it brings, I am in a much better position to withstand the criticism of those who cannot see what I sought to picture. I shan't soon forget the comfort you have brought."

Less elaborate bits of praise came from other friends outside the literary circles of New York. Charles Studin, for example, wrote White: "I salute you! You can write and you can tell a story. You have reason to be proud of your achievements, and I want you to know that I have nothing but affectionate admiration for your fine talent." Several months after the publication of *Flight,* Benjamin Brawley, then at Shaw University in Raleigh, North Carolina, wrote White. After apologizing for having taken so long to get to the novel, Brawley added:[49]

. . . I took up the book a night or two ago, and when I did, I did not put it down until I had finished the story. My wife remarked that there must be something to a book that could hold my attention thus; and indeed, especially in the middle portion, I found myself interested in following the fortunes of Mimi. On the whole the production seems to me a highly creditable achievement. I am hoping that it will have abundant success.

These personal observations, from strangers and from friends, helped White accept the critical controversy over the merits of his novel with a little more calm, although he always seemed to bridle when criticism was leveled at his work.

Even before the publication of *Flight* White was hard at work pursuing a possibility that had eluded him with *Fire:* selling the rights to a movie company. On January 5, 1926, White wrote Blanche Knopf about securing an earlier publication date for *Flight* so that he could promote it during a spring speaking tour. The primary purpose of the letter, however, was to ask Mrs. Knopf's reaction concerning another matter: " . . . Sewall Haggard, as you doubtless know, was for ten months with the Famous Players-Lasky people. I know him rather well and I was wondering if at your suggestion or request he might not be able to do something with regard to selling the movie rights of 'Flight.' " Obviously, Mrs. Knopf did not object, for White wrote Haggard a few weeks later. The letter reveals that White was much more the pragmatist than the artist:[50]

> I wonder if you will do me a favor. For perfectly selfish reasons I should like ever so much to have Famous Players–Lasky, Paramount, or some other movie outfit that pays well to consider my new novel, "Flight." . . . From your own period of bondage, can you tell me what is the wisest way to get such consideration and will you advise me how one goes about getting the best figure possible?
>
> As you know, I am looking at this in a perfectly cold-blooded fashion— I am lacking in being an artist enough not to worry so much about what the movies would do with a story of mine as in seeing to it that it brought the best figure possible.

For all his protestations in defense of his novels, White was obviously more interested in the economic effect adverse criticism might have on sales of his books than in the attacks on his art per se.

Haggard's reply, while encouraging in his assessment of the novel, was a disappointment in terms of the book's hopes for movie production. Haggard said he read the manuscript "all in one evening" because he could not put it down and that he was greatly interested in the story. He was not optimistic about the movie possibilities, however:

> As to the motion picture end of it, I am frankly very doubtful. The motion picture companies, as you know, are very timid about attempting anything new and an added objection to this story is that it could not be released in the South. . . . I laid the matter before Mr. Lasky of the Famous Players–Lasky Corporation and he confirmed my verdict. But this does not mean that I think there is no reason to try elsewhere. Some of the companies might be more willing to go in for something that hasn't been done before.

White replied that Haggard's letter was not "so terribly disappointing as it might have been—for my opinion of the movies is just about equal to yours"

The question of racial prejudice raised in Haggard's analysis of the motion picture companies and their probable response to *Flight* serves as a reminder of the formidable obstacles that someone like White had to face in carving a successful career in the arts, all considerations of talent aside. Doran would not accept *The Fire in the Flint* for the same reasons Haggard suggests movie companies would not be interested in *Flight*. And Haggard's analysis is supported by a letter from Oscar Micheaux, the black motion picture producer, to whom Knopf had sent a copy of *Flight* to consider. While expressing his agreeable surprise that *Flight* was not just another work "setting forth vigorously the white man's injustice to our group, . . ." Micheaux said that his experiences with big white production companies had been that they all wanted comedies about Negroes, not drama. He added that he had heard Cecil B. DeMille was to supervise the production of "a Negro film of serious thought," but he doubted that the white man would let even DeMille show such a film.[52] Once again Walter White's hopes for entering the rapidly growing film industry were frustrated.

With the publication of *Flight* in 1926, White's brief career as a novelist ended. Although he continued to write about the NAACP and his activities with that organization for journals and wrote several nonfiction books after this, he did not pursue his role as a novelist. There is mention, however, in the autobiography and other writings, of a third novel, one which he was never to complete. On April 24, 1926, White wrote to Arthur Spingarn:[53]

Some time ago, we were talking about writers who had pointed out the possible harmful effects of a too greatly mechanized civilization. At that time, you gave the names of several writers who had done this, most of which has escaped my mind. I wonder if you would be willing to jot down the names of these writers and their works on a piece of paper and send them to me.

I think I told you that in the novel I am now doing, this factor is going to enter prominently into the story and I want to familiarize myself with all that has been done along this line.

While White does touch on this issue in *Flight,* this letter comes too late to have been intended to produce information for that novel; perhaps White was intrigued enough with the problem to want to continue pursuing it in a third novel. He did mention wanting the Guggenheim Fellowship in 1927 in order to write a novel and a book on lynching, but the latter is all he completed.

As late as September, 1929, he was still at work on the project. In a letter to Eugene Marshall, White indicated that he was ". . . desperately trying to finish a novel." According to his letter, the book was well over half completed: "I did write around twenty-five thousand words which, with the twenty thousand or so that I wrote in France, completes about two-thirds of the book. The prospect for sufficient time to finish it within the next year is not bright."[54] James Weldon Johnson was getting ready to go to Japan on his Rosenwald Fund Fellowship, and White was to assume duties as acting secretary. Johnson did not come back into the NAACP, and White, as the new executive secretary of the organization, never found time to complete the novel. A letter to this writer from the late Poppy Cannon White offers some insight regarding why White did not devote his time in France to the novel. Mrs. White said that White[55]

. . . planned sometime, to write a three generation novel based upon his own childhood and family history. Perhaps you will remember that he mentions in one of his books, that he was given a Guggenheim Fellowship in order to enable him to write this novel. It was only when he got away from America that he felt impelled to devote himself, instead, to the study of lynching which developed into *Rope and Faggot: The Autobiography of Judge Lynch.*

With the decision to develop the antilynching work instead of his third novel, White irrevocably committed himself to his work in the NAACP, and to being remembered as a civil rights leader rather than as a writer.

The two novels that Walter White produced were not to survive as models of excellence from the Harlem Renaissance. *The Fire in the Flint,* as we have noted, did serve as a "trial balloon" in the earlier years of the period, however, and it was a minor sensation for a brief time. While *Flight* did not have as big an impact as the first novel, it was an improvement in some areas of style and control, and it did precede Nella Larsen's *Passing* by three years. And in Mimi's flight from and return to her people, we are given, as White himself stated, an insight into some of the emotional and psychological problems to be confronted by those people light enough to pass for white, people like Walter White. The most important contribution White was to make to the Harlem Renaissance, however, was not his writing, but his aid to artists who were at the core of that movement: Claude McKay, Rudolph Fisher, Langston Hughes, and Countee Cullen.

5

THE LITERARY COUNSELOR
AND FRIEND

Like many other men, black and white, in positions of power and influence during the twenties, Walter White used his personal and professional contacts and prestige to help in the encouragement and promotion of art within the black community. Sometimes this took the form of friendly criticism of material sent to him by both friends and strangers; often it took the form of a direct approach to a publisher or an editor on behalf of one individual or another. On three occasions White even tried to establish either an institute or a general fellowship fund to help new black artists. White helped writers, musicians, artists, and publishers alike, in an attempt to foster the growth of black art in the United States. In 1925 L. M. Hussey wrote White this bit of advice: "You should not go out of your way to invite competition. As it is, there are too damned many literary gents trying to sell their wares. Chemists and pharmacologists are not excessively common—but literary gents are as plentiful as blackberries."[1] White did not heed this advice, however; in fact, he did all he could to help the "competition" reach the marketplace.

In a 1931 letter to Wesley La Violette of Chicago, White emphasized the role played by the NAACP in promoting black art, a role which he paralleled in his own activities. The letter referred to a recent concert in Chicago which featured Louis Gruenberg's musical adaptation of James Weldon Johnson's "The Creation" and noted:[2]

This is but one instance of the manner in which the National Association for the Advancement of Colored People has fostered and stimulated creative and artistic expression by American Negroes. Among its other accomplishments has been the seeking out and encouraging of Negro singers, poets, novelists, painters and actors. Negro writers and illustrators in practically every instance first found publication in the *Crisis* . . . when other magazines were closed to Negro artists. Further stimulation has been given through the Amy E. Spingarn prizes for writing and illustration; and finally, the annual award, for the past seventeen years, of the Spingarn Medal to the American of African descent for the most notable accomplishment during the preceding year.

While this letter refers to specific awards and outlets connected with the Association, the aims of those awards and of the *Crisis* centered upon the idea of encouraging artists in the pursuit of their art, either through monetary reward or through publication. In an accompanying memo to Herbert J. Seligmann, director of publicity for the NAACP, White spoke in more general terms of aid to black artists:[3]

> Will you not take the idea touched upon lightly in the attached letter to patrons of "The Creation" presented recently in Chicago—namely, the part played by the NAACP in the creation and stimulation of artistic expression by the Negro—and see if we cannot get out a piece of literature along this line?
> In addition to the facts given, lay special stress upon the part played by the Association through its press service in calling attention to outstanding artists such as Roland Hayes, Paul Robeson, Countee Cullen, Langston Hughes and others; in the advertising, through circularizing, of concerts between Negro artists on the one hand and critics and other writers, on the other.

The last paragraph of White's memorandum reads like an account of his own procedures for aiding black artists; he made use of the vast publicity and news network of the Association to call attention to specific artists as well as to the state of black art in general, and he helped establish many contacts between black artists and "critics and other writers."

White's awareness of the interest in black art during the emerging decade of the twenties has already been discussed. (See the letters from White to McKay and from White to Mordecai Johnson cited in chapter 2.) One idea he had, to help foster the development of young black artists in response to this interest, was to establish a Negro Art Institute in which such talent could be cultivated. In 1923 Alain Locke wrote to White about the idea:[4]

I am impressed after our very interesting conversation to write you stressing more than I did at the time the extreme timeliness of your effort to have an Art foundation and institute for the expert training and direction of Negro students founded and endowed. Of course as to the merits of the proposition itself as one of the most constructive benefactions possible both from the point of view of the development of the race and of the art-life of America there can be no doubt among well-informed and far-sighted people. It seems rather now a question of how soon and under what auspices.

After referring to the "increasing interest in the artistic possibilities of our race material and of our race temperament" current in Europe, Locke continued:

The demand as far as the artistic material already available in drama, music, painting and decorative arts is even now outstripping the supply of competent interpreters and producers, and the recent success of Roland Hayes shows that country-wide appreciation and recognition awaits the exceptional type of talent. In fact, we may now confidently predicate that recognition and the removal of prejudice can most easily and tactfully be offset by the influence of art, and therefore a benefaction of the character of your plans would in the course of half a generation perform a practical national service in this way, in addition to its intrinsic artistic service.

In closing, Locke offered to help in any way he could in the realization of this idea.

The NAACP files contain an undated, unsigned "Memo for Mr. Walter White on Constitution of AMERICAN (NATIONAL) INSTITUTE OF NEGRO LETTERS, MUSIC AND ART" that seems to have come from Locke. The memo suggested plans for incorporation of the institute, including "a board of directors to be selected according to Charter, with provision, however, for participation of guarantors and life members who might become subsequent contributors." The memo also suggested that such an institute should be located in "a Metropolitan center such as New York or Chicago," because "a great deal of expert service both in criticism and instruction would be available on the basis of voluntary donation of services. . . ." Included was a list of five proposed "departments": Music, Drama, Literature and Folk-Lore, Design and Painting, and Sculpture and African Crafts. The memo concluded with this observation:[5]

. . . no foundation could be more stimulated at the present time in the racial effect or more conducive to the promotion on the part of the general American public of a more sympathetic and revised estimate of the capacities of the Negro race as a group than just such a plan adequately endowed and competently administered.

Locke was not the only one whose advice White sought concerning the establishment of a Negro Art Institute. James Weldon Johnson, in a letter dated April 13, 1923, made the following suggestions concerning the fields that such an institute should offer and the goals it should envision:[6]

These fields should at first be limited to the three in which the Negro has shown the greatest innate ability and in which he gives the greatest promise—Music, Drama, Dancing. These fields could be added to with the development of the Institute.

The Institute should carefully avoid being merely academic or scholastic; the instructors should be persons who look upon the arts as living forces. The final results of the Institute should be, for example, in music, not only the widening and dispensing of knowledge about Negro music, but the producing of composers and performers able to take the great mass of material at their hands and add something original and worthwhile to American music; or in the drama, the producing of playwrights and performers able to take the tragedy and comedy of life among Negroes in the United States and add something new and worthwhile to the American theater.

Echoing the sentiments of White, Locke, and countless others of the day, Johnson added:

It has long been a cherished belief of mine that the development of Negro Art in the United States will not only mean a great deal for the Negro himself, but will provide the easiest and most effective approach to that whole question called the race question. It is the approach that offers the least friction.

Exactly what happened to the plans for a Negro Art Institute is not clear. There is no further mention of it in the correspondence, and neither White nor Johnson refers to it in his autobiography.

There was, however, an apparently related attempt to secure funds for what was called the Negro Foreign Fellowship Fund, designed to offer fellowships to young Negro scholars for study abroad. On April 14, 1924, Alain Locke sent White a revision of a letter of application to the Garland Fund in behalf of the Negro Foreign Fellowship Fund and thanked White for his "large share" in its conception and preparation. A "Memo to the Drafting Committee" (undated) which was attached to the April 14 letter included suggestions for names for the foundation ("The Aframerican Foundation or The Negro Educational Foundation") and a list of people Locke suggested might serve as trustees; the list included White, James Weldon Johnson, Carter Woodson, Du Bois, Benjamin Brawley, Eugene K. Jones, and Locke, among others. On April 8, however, Locke had sent White the following telegram: "The Negro Foreign Fellowship Fund/Use Foundation only in subheadings/ Drive it through/ Sign application in name of incorporators/ Thanks and good luck."[7]

On May 20, 1924, White sent a letter of application on behalf of the Negro Foreign Fellowship Fund to the American Fund for Public Service, Inc., "for aid in the establishment of certain European scholarships for Negro men and women. . . ." Asking for a grant of five thousand dollars for "whatever period [the American Fund] sees fit," the letter outlined the main objective of the proposed fellowship fund:[8]

Our main objective in this effort is to see that a few competent young colored men and women may obtain through study and residence in European countries wider social vision and contact with progressive movements such as is almost impossible for them to obtain under present conditions in America. . . . It is our idea that these students in acquiring these things would also be most serviceable to their people in acquainting foreign intellectual circles with the more representative types and the finer elements of the American Negro, and would therefore be effective agents in combating the further spread of racial prejudice and misunderstanding.

The letter was submitted "on behalf of the following incorporators: Alain Locke, . . . William S. Nelson [of Yale University] , . . . James Weldon Johnson and Walter White," and was signed by White. Unfortunately, this plan, too, failed; the American Fund refused the application. Roger Baldwin wrote White on May 29 that the application was being rejected because ". . . it does not come within the field of activity which the Fund's board has cut out for themselves. I am sure by perusal of our literature this position will be entirely clear to you. We feel that what you propose to do ought to find support in other quarters."[9]

White made one more attempt to secure funds for aiding black artists on a large scale. In 1927 he sent a memorandum to Ethel Bedient Gilbert, a past director of the Harmon Foundation, in which he proposed a fund "for the aiding of Negro artists who show very definite signs of marked ability or genius," and asked her help in securing the interest of a Mr. Burke in the project. White listed two reasons supporting the need for such a fund:[10]

First, the idea of prizes either in the form of cash or medals is an excellent one in recognizing the achievement of Negro artists. Such medals as the Spingarn Medal and the Harmon awards are of great value. These awards, however, come after a man has done a great thing and make no provision for the man of talent who is struggling to perfect himself in his art. My idea is that instead of giving a man a medal or a check after he shall achieve distinction that great good could come from the providing of enough money to a person of recognized merit to enable him to do distinctive work in his chosen field.

White's second reason more concretely reflects his concern with making the current popular interest in black America a more permanent interest, through the development of black art:

. . . the present Negro artistic movement which has brought recognition to such persons of undoubted genius as Roland Hayes, Paul Robeson, Florence Mills, Countee Cullen, Langston Hughes, Aaron Douglas, James Weldon Johnson and others, has led to a glorification of the Negro as an artist which has almost assumed the proportions of becoming a fad. Concrete steps towards furnishing opportunity to hitherto unknown but talented Negroes will serve to perpetuate this recognition and to put it on an even sounder basis than it is at present. It is necessary to prevent diversion of recognition of the Negro into less valuable and productive fields. I am convinced that there is no single factor of greater importance in solving this thing we call the race problem than the work of Negro artists, or in bringing new respect and a new rearrangement of values and opinions concerning the Negro than the work of Negro artists.

White suggested the fund could be based on a gift "of say $250,000 invested in sound securities . . . to bring a return of five or six percent," which would yield an annual income "of around $12,500" to be used for four fellowships and "administrative expenses." After noting the many years of pleasure Mr. Burke would have in seeing his "munificence" at work, White closed the memo with a suggested list of fellowship areas, including:

(a) painting, sculpture, or any work in the field of plastic or pictorial art; (b) music composition, advanced study (singers or instrumentalists), or research in Negro music; (c) writing, whether prose, poetry, drama or history. Fellowships are to be given only to persons who have done work of recognized value or who have shown unmistakable signs of real ability.

While this last statement sounds almost contradictory to his earlier expression of concern about giving "unknown" artists a chance to develop their potential, White's obvious thrust is that the fund would produce quality work and not be a waste of money. Like his earlier efforts at establishing a fund for Negro artists, this one was also unsuccessful. Fortunately, there were other foundations available for this purpose, e.g., the Harmon Foundation, but Walter White clearly thought that more could be done to help young black artists gain the momentum needed to make the interest in black art a sound base on which to build for the future.

Although White's plans for financing black art on a broad scale never materialized, he continually did his best to make people aware of the work being done by black artists. When Ethel Clark of New Bedford, Massachusetts, wrote White to ask his reaction to a pageant she was writing to celebrate Negro achievement, he had this response:[11]

At the present I have only one suggestion to make. Your pageant is an historical one but you end it with Booker T. Washington and Dunbar, both of them extraordinarily gifted individuals who did great good in the cause of the Negro. It seems to me, however, that the progress of the Negro during the last twenty-five years—even during the last ten years—has been so extraordinary that it ought to be brought down to date. This will be evident from a list of the more outstanding men and women of the race.

The list he enclosed included Roland Hayes, Harry Burleigh, James Weldon Johnson, Du Bois, Cullen, Jessie Fauset, and Florence Mills. On another occasion the Reverend George Stewart of the Madison Avenue Presbyterian Church wrote in response to a speech White had made:

I was deeply impressed with your recent talk at the Theta Club. Would you be willing to dictate a note to me at your leisure in which you would point out some of the leading figures in the new birth of artistic creation among the colored people. I am, of course, familiar with Countee Cullen.

White responded in a few days, listing some of the "outstanding figures of the new artistic movement among Negroes," including Hayes, Robeson, Cullen, Hughes, Anne Spencer, Johnson, Rudolph Fisher, Eric Walrond, and Jean Toomer; he also enclosed a list of books by black writers prepared by the New York Public Library, with an added list of his own of books published during 1926.[12] And White did not limit his statements concerning the importance of black writing to those who wrote him seeking advice. When Mark Van Doren's *Anthology of World Poetry* appeared in 1929 without a single poem by a black American, White wrote:[13]

Wasn't there *one* poem by an Aframerican poet from Phyllis Wheatley to Countee Cullen worthy of inclusion in *An Anthology of World Poetry?* You have done a swell job but, frankly, I am just a little bit disappointed and surprised. If no single Negro has fashioned verses worthy of inclusion, is there not in the spirituals native poetry of such merit as to be included, especially as poetry of Indian derivation by Natalie Curtis is there?

In correspondence, in speeches, in private conversation, Walter White kept the fires of the "new artistic movement among Negroes" constantly burning. And, while he was not the only keeper of the fire, he was certainly one of the most dedicated.

Although White was not successful in his attempts to establish a large-scale source of aid to black artists, he was able to help some people on an individual basis. As assistant secretary of the NAACP, he was, of course, highly visible and a natural figure to whom aspiring artists, black and white, might turn for help. Some of the people with whom he corresponded were either already established in their field or were soon to become well known, e.g., Claude McKay and Langston Hughes, but many others were destined to remain lesser lights. In any event, White was inevitably gracious in his correspondence with the hopeful writers, and in some cases helped secure valuable contacts with publishers and editors.

One of the many people White came to know during the Sweet trial in Detroit was Cash Asher of the *Detroit Free Press.* On April 3, 1926, White wrote to Asher regarding a book that the latter was about to complete and included this note of optimism:[14]

I am delighted to know that your book is about finished. I wish you would write me by return mail a brief outline of the plot, indicating the ground you have covered. I tentatively mentioned it to a publisher and he seems interested. I merely told him that I had a friend in Detroit who had done a novel. I did not tell him anything about the story for I did not want him to have any opinion about it in advance, letting its merits burst upon him fresh and unalloyed. You can rely on my promise to do whatever I can to help.

A month later White wrote another letter, this time mentioning the firm that had expressed an interest in Asher's book and offering to serve as "middleman" for him:[15]

Last night I was at a party and talked at length with the two publishers of whom I spoke to you some time ago. They asked me to say that they are quite keen to see the MS, will read it and give you a decision very promptly. How soon will you be ready to let me see it? If you want to send it along to me, I will put it in their hands at once. The firm is the Viking Press. . . . If you would prefer sending it directly to them, you can of course do so saying this is the MS of which Walter White spoke to him. Address it either to George Oppenheimer or Harold Guinsberg.

White knew Oppenheimer and Guinsberg from their association with Knopf, and he did much to help them in their new publishing venture, recruiting books for them and so on, in addition to using his relationship with them to help other writers.

Asher responded to White's letter and said that he was still working on the novel and wanted to get it "as perfect as possible" before asking anyone to read it. He also indicated that he was working on an article about the Sweet case, which he later sent to the *New Republic.* When that magazine rejected his article "Following the Old Trail," he wrote White: "Sometimes I wonder if magazine editors don't do all their own writing—that is, for their magazines—signing pseudonyms, garnered from a biographical dictionary." White wrote back, calling the *New Republic* "a watery *Ladies Home Journal,* . . . " and indicating that Viking was anxious to see Asher's novel.[16]

During a lapse in the correspondence between the two men, Viking rejected Asher's novel, and Asher wrote a review of *Flight.* Worried that he might somehow have offended White, Asher wrote:[17]

Am wondering if you have expired from the shock of my review of *Flight,* or merely have gone on vacation or become lost in the cause of the Negro.

. . . Perhaps you are into the fascination of another novel. If so, take a pot-shot at some of the things I disapprove of, for I haven't reached the enchant-ed field as yet. Am working on another one, however.

White immediately responded that his long silence had been due not to Asher's "understanding and laudatory" review of *Flight,* but rather to his having been on a much needed vacation. In reference to the rejection of Asher's manuscript, he said:[18]

I am sorry about the fate your MS had with the Viking Press. I called them on the telephone after I had no word for several weeks after sending the MS over and found that they had decided against publishing it and had re-turned the MS to you. I had great confidence in the judgment of these pub-lishers and asked them as a special favor that they send you more than the formal note of rejection—that they outline what seemed to them to be the shortcomings in the MS so that you could benefit from their advice. I hope they did this.

In closing, White urged Asher to continue writing him, as he wanted to maintain their friendship.

Some people were more direct in their appeals to White for aid, and they did not always choose to follow his advice. For example, a Miss Lucia M. Pitts of Chicago wrote to ask for White's reaction to some of her poetry; she had been urged to do so by Mary McDowell of the University of Chica-go Settlement. Her initial letter to White gave some of her background in writing poetry and asked for his frank opinion of her work:[19]

For a few years now, I have been doing some things in the line of poetry with a fair amount of success. Some of my scribblings have enjoyed publica-tion in newspapers and other periodicals. Several people have recently sug-gested that I get out a volume and I have been trying to find out lately if such a thing is possible for me. Of course I have faith in my poems, but I make no superior claims for them—that is to say, that I'd appreciate your candid comments and won't feel too badly if you find they aren't just exactly up to par. Then, I understand that it isn't a cinch getting publishers to accept poetry, so I'm prepared for a fight.

In closing she asked whether she might send White some of her poems. A few days later White answered, a bit more curtly than normal: "Suppose you send me some of the best of your poems and I shall see what can be done about publication. Indicate on them the magazine in which the poems which have been published appeared. I shall write you more fully when I shall have had the chance to read them."[20]

It was several months before White sent Miss Pitts his response to the poems. In the meantime James Weldon Johnson had looked at them and, in a note to White, commented that, while some of the poems were "quite well done, . . . I do not feel that the collection [entitled *Dream Dusting*] is sufficiently strong to interest a real publisher." White suggested to Miss Pitts that she might try publishing the poems through a vanity press and repeated his offer to help in any way he could. Miss Pitts, not to be swayed, replied that she was going to submit the poems anyway, to Doubleday, Doran first, and asked White to write them on her behalf. White was firm, saying he thought it would be better for her to wait, replace the weak poems with stronger ones, and then try a publisher: "Because of my own reactions which were amply confirmed by Mr. Johnson I hope you will forgive me for feeling that I would be rendering you a disservice by writing to Doran at this time."[21] Whether White's advice was taken or not, at least he was honest enough to tell an aspiring writer to wait for better material before attacking a publisher.

White's correspondence with hopeful writers often included more practical bits of advice, as well as critical advice and commentary. In 1927, for instance, Cora Jordan White (no relation), who was the executive secretary of the Columbus, Ohio, Y. W. C. A., wrote to Walter White about a book she had written:[22]

The book that you told me I should write is written. Now I want to know what to do with it. I had thought of sending it to the Harmon people, but I thought before I did anything about it, I wanted to hear from you.

Kindly give me a method of procedure. The story in this book is the outgrowth of your trip to South Carolina, also, in a feeble way, it is a challenge to your statement, that we, the middle class, who don't take to cabarets and bootleg parties, and at the same time are not high-brows, are not interesting.

Unsure that he would recall who she was, Ms. White added that they had met at a dinner during White's recent trip to Columbus. In a postscript she asked the number of words in a standard story.

A brief exchange of correspondence then determined that, as Ms. White said, "the thing I have written is a book, I suppose," as it contained around 20,000–25,000 words. White responded that the average length of a novel is between 75,000 and 100,000 words:[23]

After a novelist has established a reputation (say as Willa Cather has done), the public will buy a novel of 30 to 50,000 words in length. Since you say your story runs between 20,000 and 25,000 words it would be classed as a long short story.

He also asked for some idea of the story and how she treated it. Replying that she could easily lengthen sections of the book to make it "standard length," Ms. White offered a summary of her plot:

The book is going to be called "Prejudice," unless you suggest something better. I wish it called that. It is a story of the famous lynching case in South Carolina that you investigated. The story hinges on the fact that there was another Lowman boy at Benedict. This boy, on his way home for a vacation, sees the raid on his house. His friends send him to New York, where he loves and is loved by a girl who is working with young girls in an organization. Their experiences, the experiences of friends and your experiences form the story. The characters are yours, the main ones, the others are mine. The South Carolina locale is mine also. I know the state only too well, you know.

In a reply delayed because he had been out of the city, White told Ms. White that her story sounded "interesting," but added a word of caution: " . . . keep in mind that you are writing a novel and [do] not let it become too much of a thesis or preachment." He offered to look over the manuscript when she completed it and to give her "frank criticism" of her efforts.[24] In addition, he submitted to the *Crisis* a poem she had sent with her March 21 letter. Again there is no final evidence of the effects of White's correspondence with Ms. White, but after reading numerous exchanges of this sort in the NAACP files, one gains an added respect for Walter White's endurance if nothing else.

White also offered more specific criticism of work sent to him, although most of that criticism, unfortunately, is not in the files. In a memorandum to a Mrs. Leland, he apologized for delaying so long in criticizing her play "The Blackman," and made the following observations about it:[25]

There are two fundamental criticisms that I wish to make. In making them, I do not say they are right—they simply are my reactions to the play in considering the possibility of its production.

The first of these criticisms is that John seems slightly too noble a character for truth. So, too, is Roger Carter playing the part of a Southern sheriff a little too erudite for the character he portrays. This leads me to a criticism which may be perhaps surprising. The language you put into a number of your characters, including Ruth, John, and Roger is at times so literary that one has a tendency not to consider them as human beings.

The two criticisms, therefore, can be combined in the one statement that the characters and the conversation of the characters as a whole is more literary than true to life.

The idea that you have is, I think, an excellent one. If it could be drawn little closer to life, I think you would have a strong play.

Some idea about the quality of Mrs. Leland's play might be gleaned from a note from White's secretary which was attached to this letter in the files: "Mrs. Leland asked me to inquire of you your reaction to the working out of the color problem through reincarnation. Did this seem at all logical to you and would it displease the colored people?" There was no response from White.

In another instance Rose Zackem of Detroit sent White a poem which had already been "rejected by several magazines"; she asked him for his opinion of it and for a suggestion of where to try next. Of the poem she said that it was "suggested to me by the Sweet trial, . . . " and she added, "I was wondering if this effort of mine was refused because of the subject matter or because it has no literary value." White's response was typically gentle and included some useful comments:[26]

The spirit of your poem is admirable but it has one or two little technical faults which doubtless led to its return by the magazine to which you submitted it. I have taken the liberty of checking one or two faulty lines and, if I may take a bit more liberty, I would suggest that you work it over again, tighten it up, and then let me see it again.

Exactly what the "one or two little technical faults" in the poem might have been is a mystery, since the poem was returned to Ms. Zackem; given White's native graciousness, they might have been anything from a few awkwardly constructed syllables to chaotic rhythm and meter. But for White to take time to note the weak spots in a poem from a complete stranger (there is no mention of their having met before) is far from taking liberty; it shows a genuine desire to help.

Occasionally White was a bit negligent in efforts to read and comment on material sent to him. George B. Buster wrote an angry letter in December of 1925 complaining about White's losing the manuscript of Buster's play "For the Democracy of the World." Buster wrote:

The loss of the manuscript is bad enough, but what the loss implies is to me infinitely worse. The whole matter implies not only indifference to the production but a gross lack of respect to its author. . . . Suppose you had respected someone enough to turn over to him the manuscript of your recent book to be criticized. Suppose also that after more than eighteen months he should write you saying that he not only had not read your manuscript but did [not] know where it could be found. How would you feel about it?

White's reply was most apologetic, both about not having read the manuscript and about losing it. He had been busy "handling the Sweet case in Detroit and doing a good deal of speaking," but promised to instigate a thorough search at his office and at home for the manuscript: "I am hoping that the lost will be found."[27]

Sometimes White's comments to hopeful writers were more general concerning ideas about literature. In 1926 he wrote to James L. Dameron of Des Moines, Iowa, about a book that Dameron was anxious to publish.

Noting that, since he had not seen the manuscript, he could make no specific comments on it, White offered this observation "in good faith":[28]

You say in your letter that you have injected many of your pet sociological theories into the story. All fiction more or less contains convictions of one sort or another whether sociological or economic. But there is a rather definite dividing line between a novel as a work of art and a sociological treatise. Any novel which demands attention as a work of art cannot therefore be overly burdened with theories. I suggest that you read your MS as objectively as possible and determine in your own mind whether or not your book is a novel. . . .

After assuring Dameron that there would be no need to pay a publisher to print his book, "if you have written a book which is worth publishing," White closed by offering to answer specific questions Dameron might have.

Exactly why some people preferred to send their material to White is made clear in a letter from Carrie L. Shepperson of Little Rock, Arkansas. She had written a novel entitled "Orange and Lemon" which, she said, was set "in Little Rock and its environs" and concerned "the efforts of a white villain and his Negro henchman to get possession by foul means, of a 30-acre farm . . . willed to my leading character." Later Ms. Shepperson explained why she had written to White:[29]

Pardon my continuing to impose on your kindness, Mr. White, but I thought you would be better "up" on the information I seek [i.e., about reaching a publisher] than some of the others associated with you. I feel as if I know well all of the executive officers of our dear NAACP.

This combination of public exposure and accessibility, then, made White a logical source to which a struggling—or perhaps merely curious—novice might turn for help.

Sometimes White's aid came unasked, though not unwelcomed. In 1923 he sent his inscribed copy of Laurence Jones's *Piney Woods and Its Story,* a book about Jones's Piney Woods Country Life School in Braxton, Mississippi ("For Training Colored Boys and Girls in Christianity, Character and Service"), to the Van Dorens, and Dorothy Van Doren wrote a letter in response which White forwarded to Jones. A grateful Jones wrote back to White: "It was surely kind of you to send 'Piney Woods and its Story' along to Mrs. Van Doren and thereby get it into Mr. [Oswald Garrison] Villard's hands. We might not have been so fortunate in getting it to him through other channels."[30] A few years later White received this letter from Willis Richardson:[31]

I am writing to thank you for mentioning my plays to Mr. Frank Shay, who informs me that he hopes to include a Negro play in his next book of contemporary one-act plays. At his request I have sent him "The Chip Woman's Fortune" to read.

Although I have never met you personally, I shall list you among my friends for your kind interest.

As we can see from this examination of White's efforts to help almost anyone who asked him, his position in the Association and his social and professional relationships with editors and publishers enabled him at least to initiate contacts that otherwise might have been impossible for most of these people; or, if he thought the material not good enough, White showed remarkable kindness in trying to dissuade a writer from pursuing a career for which he was not ready. Some of the writers he helped and encouraged, however, did become quite successful or if they already enjoyed success in some measure, were helped in broadening that success through White's efforts at publicizing their work and at promoting an interest in black art in general.

One such writer was Rudolph Fisher. Fisher became an important member of the New Negro movement, through the publication of his short stories in magazines like the *Atlantic Monthly* and the *Crisis* and through the publication of his two novels *The Walls of Jericho* (1928) and *The Conjure Man Dies* (1932). At the time the correspondence between White and Fisher began in 1925, Fisher was involved in his internship at Freedman's Hospital in Washington, D. C. White wrote Fisher on February 3, 1925: "Mr. Bagnall has told me of some of the very interesting things you have written. I blush to confess that I did not know of your work but I am tremendously interested. I am looking forward to reading your article in the Harlem number of the *Survey*." He offered his help and asked if Fisher would "care to let me see some of the work you have done."[32]

Fisher responded immediately, saying how much he appreciated the "generous spirit" shown in White's letter and adding:[33]

It's not very surprising that you knew nothing of my work, since my first story, "The City of Refuge," tho accepted fully a year ago, has only just come out in the February *Atlantic Monthly*. I should be glad, if you find time, to get your reaction to it.

Fisher's letter enclosed a story manuscript, and he asked White if he could present it to Mencken at the *American Mercury*, " . . . only if [he] felt that the story was really worth the effort." The story was "High Yaller."

In replying, White expressed his enthusiasm for Fisher's talent. He had read the stories and said:

They are both gorgeous pieces of work. You have very real ability as a writer, you handle your situation splendidly, and you have not only the ability to express what you see but, what is more important, you have eyes that [can] and do see. I, myself, have just begun to get my feet wet in the field of literature but I am uttering a most cordial welcome to you.

Earlier in the letter White noted his special interest in literature and offered some encouragement for the young writer:[34]

I am tremendously glad to know of your work because I am so deeply interested in literature and particularly things that you and I and the rest of us can do now and will do in the future. To me, there is no more absorbing or worth while way to which to devote one's every effort. . . .

In addition to these words of encouragement, White said that he had sent "High Yaller" to Mencken and that he had mentioned Fisher's story in the *Atlantic Monthly* to Carl Van Vechten, Carl Van Doren, Sinclair Lewis, Zona Gale, and others. To Van Vechten, White wrote:[35]

I think I have discovered a real writer. Read "The City of Refuge" in the February *Atlantic Monthly* by Rudolph Fisher. Fisher has sent me another story which I think even better than the *Atlantic Monthly* one. Its name is "High Yaller" and I am sending it to Mencken today. When next Fisher comes to New York, I am going to see that you meet him if you would like to.

In a similar vein White wrote to Mencken about Fisher, adding that his discovery was from Mencken's "own Baltimore." He enclosed "High Yaller" and asked Mencken to consider it for the *American Mercury*. Mencken rejected the story but was interested in the talent Fisher displayed:[36]

Fisher's story was too long, and the device of the devil seemed to me to be a bad one, but he writes well, and I hope to fetch him soon or late. I suggested an article to him, but have not heard from him.

The article Mencken wanted from Fisher was one on the Negro doctor, and White tried to persuade the somewhat reluctant Fisher to do it: "It is original territory and you ought to be able to do a gorgeous piece of work on it." Fisher explained that he really preferred to write fiction, although the demand seemed to be for articles:

I have not been interested in exposition, but it appears that there is more demand for "articles" than for my preferred medium, fiction. The *Atlantic*, after two story acceptances, has also suggested something of the essay sort. Can I hope to satisfy two so diverse journals as it and the *Mercury?*

After talking to Locke about Fisher and his work and learning that Locke had discouraged Fisher from writing an article such as the one Mencken wanted "at this stage of the game," White simply stated that it would be a decision Fisher would have to make for himself.[37]

Meanwhile, White corresponded with Fisher fairly regularly, attempting to encourage his writing. After the letter of February 6, in which White mentioned his telling several people about Fisher's work, Fisher wrote:[38]

Because I place high value upon your opinion, I am very much pleased with what you say about my two stories. Thank you for your interest and for the contacts which you allow me to anticipate. Mr. J. W. Johnson has already sent a gratifying note.

Fisher added that, because of the pressures of completing his internship and his working to "pass a state board or two, . . . it will be difficult for me to write as much as someday I hope to." He also thanked White for his "attitude" toward "High Yaller" and asked him to send it to *Harper's* if "the *Mercury* can not use it," with this apology: "I had no idea of asking you to 'peddle' it for me."

White's response of February 14 included his philosohpy of helping other writers:[39]

You owe me no thanks for any interest I may show or help that I may give. As I see it, there is such a tremendous field open to those of us who have the urge to write that any of us who refused to do anything he could to help the other would be a small person indeed. As I have said to you before, I think you have very real ability. I will get a deal of satisfaction in seeing you make the name for yourself that I believe you will make.

After mentioning a talk he had had with Van Vechten, who liked "The City of Refuge" and wanted to see "High Yaller," White encouraged Fisher to come to New York, which he described as a mecca for writers:

To me, there is but one place in America for a writer to live and that is Manhattan—that is if he can adjust to the hectic life here and keep out of his life all the external things which prevent one from doing his work. . . . In New York the contacts which are possible so far as I know only here of all places in America, keep one keyed up to such a point that no matter how much work he may do, nevertheless he feels like a loafer when almost everyday he meets someone who is doing two or three times as much as he.

It is very difficult to imagine anyone doing "two or three times" as much work as Walter White, but he tried to instill in others his own enthusiasm for work and development.

Mencken, as mentioned earlier, rejected "High Yaller," and Fisher wrote White the news on February 15; in the same letter he asked White's help again with the story. A Mrs. Deland had recommended the story to Thomas Wells of *Harper's,* and Fisher asked White if he "would care to strengthen its cause by speaking also to Mr. [Frederick] Allen" of the same firm: "It would add to my obligation and gratitude." White replied that he would "be delighted" to speak to Allen.[40] A few weeks later, however, Fisher sent this dejected note to White:[41]

The nuisance has returned. I mean both "High Yaller" has returned to me and I have returned it to you. My only apology is that you once suggested that Mr. Carl Van Doren would like to see it. I wonder if it would be convenient for you to show it to him.

Within two days White sent a letter to Van Doren, along with the story manuscript, and asked him to consider using it for the *Century.* Van Doren's reply came quickly: "Mr. Fisher's story comes pretty soon after "White but Black" [an anonymous essay on color prejudice by White], and I'm afraid I can't use it. Moreover, I think it's a little unorganized." Attempting to buoy up Fisher's sagging spirits, White suggested still another possible source:[42]

What about trying it at *Scribner's?* Unfortunately I know no one there and the odds are probably against its being published in that magazine but one has to keep a thing going until it finally lands. Don't let this discourage you—I have probably a drawer full of rejected manuscripts.

Several days before the rejection of "High Yaller" by Van Doren and White's attempts to ease the blow, White had written to Fisher, discussing more generally his attitudes toward the writing of fiction and its place in the current surge of interest in black art:[43]

Yes, there are very definite signs of limitations in the field of fiction. When I see the great flood of novels pour forth every season, nine-tenths of them at least which never should have been written, I am inclined to feel that the novel is being done to death. On the other hand, I think that you, I, and the rest of us who are writing about Negro life as it really exists are exploring a field which is as yet practically untouched.
. . . I had a long talk with two publishers, that is, two members of a new publishing firm. It was the feeling of all three of us that the present keen interest in the Negro as an artist had its roots firmly fixed and that, instead of being a fad comparable to Couéism, Mah-Jong, and the present crossword puzzle craze, it was a movement that was destined to develop and flower.
By this I don't mean that we should confine our work wholly to fiction. I think we should go into every form of writing and, indeed, of all the arts.

But to those of us who have a particular penchant for fiction, I think it is up to us to develop whatever gifts we may possess and by the very excellence of our work will we gain a hearing. It is not an easy gain. Indeed, to the weak hearted my advice would be to take up something easy like digging ditches.

In closing, White quoted a passage from Havelock Ellis's *The Dance of Life* ("No man, indeed, can write anything that matters who is not a hero at heart"), and told Fisher that he had mentioned his name to the publishers "and suggested that they read 'The City of Refuge' and keep their eye on you for future development."[44]

After this the correspondence between White and Fisher becomes almost negligible. But "High Yaller" was finally published in the *Crisis* and, in fact, won the Amy Spingarn prize for 1925. Fisher's first novel, *The Walls of Jericho,* was published by Knopf in 1928. While nothing in the files indicate that White was in any way involved in the publication of that novel, he did review it (in the *New York World*) and had the Association's office address envelopes to be used by George Campbell of Knopf to send out copies of a promotional letter. And in 1930 White wrote a recommendation for Fisher to the Guggenheim committee. In the recommendation, White said:[45]

> Dr. Fisher has written, in my opinion, the best short stories of Negro life that have been written within recent years by any person, white or Negro. I refer, especially, to his stories "The City of Refuge" and "Blades of Steel."
> He is an exceedingly alert-minded and perceptive individual, blessed with a saving grace of humor.
> I am particularly interested in the novel which he wishes to do under a Guggenheim Fellowship [*The Conjure Man Dies?*]. The . . . idea is one which I have had for some years, but I am sure that Dr. Fisher, if he achieves the idea which is expressed in his outline, will do a most significant and valuable story.

From White's initial letter to Fisher to this letter of recommendation to the Guggenheim Foundation, we can trace the steady encouragement White gave Fisher. While the tangible benefits White achieved for Fisher might not be so evident as those he achieved for Cullen, Hughes, and others, his continuing interest in the work of this radiologist/satirist is indicative of White's untiring effort to keep the spirit of creativity burning in those in whom he found it.

Another young black writer whose career was just beginning to unfold in the mid-twenties was the poet Langston Hughes. Hughes, of course, was to become the most revered of all black American poets; he is often referred to as the "poet laureate" of black America. At this time, however, he was

st beginning to receive some recognition of his talents. The first reference
Hughes in White's correspondence in the NAACP files was in a letter
om White to Blanche Knopf, dated January 4, 1925, in which White
anked Mrs. Knopf for sending him the proofs of *The Weary Blues,* Hughes's
rst book of verse, which White planned to review. He added: "I have fol-
wed Mr. Hughes' writing since he was first published in the *Crisis* and I
ok forward eagerly to reading these poems."[46]

The direct correspondence between White and Hughes began with a
ongratulatory letter from White on the impending publication of *The
eary Blues:*

hasten to extend to you my warmest congratulations on the acceptance
' your book of poems by Knopf. It is certainly great to have a foreword
√ Van Vechten and have Covarrubias to do the jacket. I was delighted when
heard it.

hite also told Hughes about a press release that was to be sent out promot-
g the book and offered to help in any way he could, promising to contact
Mrs. Knopf about the book and find out in what way I can help." Hughes
plied in a brief note, thanking White for his letter and asking advice for
a budding writer."[47]

White answered, rather modestly, "I don't know of any suggestion right
ow which I could make to you and I am always reluctant to offer advice."
e did advise Hughes, however, to read his poetry to "women's clubs and
her meetings," emphasizing that "personal contact" is the best way to
terest people in a book. White added that he was as elated as Hughes,
ooth that you have a first book of poems coming out and because Knopf
bringing it out," and offered to call the attention of various critics to
e book. Writing to thank White for the suggestions made in this letter,
ughes added: "I certainly would appreciate your bringing my book per-
onally to the attention of those very important critics who you know
hen it comes out—but that won't be until next winter." He also noted
e reaction he had seen to the NAACP press release:

uite a number of the Negro papers used the NAACP press notice, and with
e distaste my poem "The Weary Blues" excited in the colored critics I
n getting a good deal of interesting publicity.

hite replied that "you may be sure I am going to do everything I can to
elp get your book known," and indicated that he had placed a note con-
erning the book in the program of an upcoming Association conference in
enver.[48] After this letter the correspondence between the two dropped
ff for a few months.

On October 29, 1925, Hughes wrote his "dear friend" about his efforts to raise enough money to enroll at Lincoln University in February. He was at that time working in a Washington, D.C., hotel and had asked James Weldon Johnson to see "if he and The Garland Fund can't help me. . . . Some big hearted person ought to be interested enough in the development of talent to grant me a loan." *The Weary Blues* had gone to press, and Hughes indicated that he was at work on a "book of prose which will perhaps be called *Scarlet Flowers: The Autobiography of a Young Colored Poet.* You think that's a good title?" White's answer, delayed because of his involvement with the Sweet case in Detroit, had his gentle but sarcastic touch:

I am mighty glad to know you are at work on a book of prose. Frankly, the title, "Scarlet Flowers: The Autobiography of a Young Colored Poet" doesn't exactly hit me between the eyes. Somehow or other it sounds like Louisa M. Alcott. I may be wrong and probably am—but that is the way it strikes me right now.

White also promised to help Hughes try to secure a loan and asked if there was "a particular place" where Hughes wanted him to review *The Weary Blues:* "I will promise to be as gentle as I can. I have just done Countee's book [*Color*] for the *Saturday Review.*" Hughes responded almost immediately and agreed that his title was perhaps unfortunate:

The title for my prose book does sound sort of Louisa Alcottish, doesn't it? Glad you spoke of it. But titles can always be changed. The important thing is to get a book to change them on. And I haven't made much of a start yet on the actual writing of it. Working all day in a hotel didn't leave me much time for anything else. And I'm still a sleepy-head.

Concerning the review White wanted to do, Hughes said, "I would be very much pleased for you to review *The Weary Blues* for the *Saturday Review,* the *Bookman,* or any place you choose. And don't be too gentle: I like knocks."[49]

White's paternal concern for the younger writer is brought out well in his next letter to Hughes:[50]

There are lots of things I want to talk over with you, especially in regards to your forthcoming volume of verse and your prose volume. Don't worry about a title for the latter. I am not saying that "Scarlet Flowers" is not a good one—it just doesn't strike me smack between the eyes. If you like it, disregard utterly any opinion that I or any other person may have. I know the difficulties you are undergoing in writing it.

The same amiable guiding and directing are reflected in White's letters of criticism to other writers who sought his advice, as we have seen; he was always ready to react to the works sent him, but he never demanded that his reactions be accepted as final.

Blanche Knopf sent White the galley proofs of *The Weary Blues* on December 24, 1925, and added: "We are all rooting here for it and I am eager to see what you are going to say—we're publishing January 23." White, anxious to help as always, replied:[51]

I am very enthusiastic about Langston Hughes' poems. I will do a review of it somewhere and anything you want me to do before then you know already you have only to tell me what it is. If you want a blurb, I will write one cheerfully.

In addition to promoting Hughes's poetry through the Association, White tried to make people aware of the young poet whenever occasion arose. For example, when Fay Lewis, a friend of Clarence Darrow, was impressed with Cullen's *Color,* White wrote him:[52]

There is, by the way, another young Negro poet of a different technique but in some respects a superior of Cullen who will have a book out the latter part of the month. He is Langston Hughes and his book is "The Weary Blues." I will have a copy of this for you when you come.

This reference to Hughes as "a superior of Cullen" is particularly interesting; in most of his statements concerning the two poets, White seems to have preferred Cullen. Perhaps he was merely carried away in his more immediate involvement with Hughes's volume at this time.

Correspondence between White and Hughes dwindled again. In February White received an inquiry from W. C. Handy concerning Hughes's "Washington address"; Handy wanted to set some of Hughes's blues poems to music. White sent him the address, and a month later received a letter from Hughes, then at Lincoln University, in which Hughes indicated that he had seen Handy and that "he seemed very pleased with those Blues of mine." Hughes also added that "I like Lincoln and the country out here immensely and am not anxious to leave. . . ." Except for a letter from Harry Bloch at Knopf thanking White "for all the trouble you are taking for Langston," and a letter from White to Jack Stephens of Martinsville, Indiana, noting that Hughes had just been in to see him and told him that he had won "the Witter Bynner undergraduate poetry prize with his poem 'The House in Taos,' " there is not much correspondence between White and Hughes in the correspondence files for 1926.[53]

Their correspondence picked up in 1927, dealing with two main topics:

White's attempts to work out a satisfactory arrangement with Emanuel Haldeman-Julius to publish a Little Blue Book of Hughes's and Cullen's poetry, and White's review of Hughes's *Fine Clothes to the Jew* (1927). White had written an article for Haldeman-Julius entitled "The Negro and His Problems," which was to be brought out as a Little Blue Book after its publication in the *Haldeman-Julius Quarterly*. He wrote Haldeman-Julius (of Girard, Kansas) on January 5, 1927, explaining his delay in sending the manuscript for "the first Blue Book." White went on:

I have taken up personally with Countee Cullen and Langston Hughes the matter of a book of poems with a short foreword by me. Will you let me know what remuneration they will receive so I can give them definite information on this score?

Haldeman-Julius replied that the policy regarding remuneration was "$100 for an original work; $50 for a Little Blue Book of reprints. The book of poems by Cullen and Hughes can be handled this way: Divide $50 among the authors and then we can pay you in addition a fee of $50 for your editorial work." Disturbed over the low figure quoted by Haldeman-Julius, White tried to get more for the two poets:

I am taking up with the publishers of Cullen's and Hughes' books the matter of obtaining permission for printing poems by them. I had already stated to both Mr. Cullen and Mr. Hughes that you had told me that they would receive fifty dollars each for the use of their poems. As their contracts provide that for second publication whatever sums are secured must be divided between them and their publishers, giving them twenty-five dollars each would mean very little return. As Cullen is just out of school and Hughes is still in college, I imagine they must each count their pennies. As I want to be absolutely fair and live up to my word, I don't see how I can explain to them without embarrassment the reason why they should get less than the fifty dollars of which I spoke.

Of course, an obvious solution to this predicament would have been for White to give up his editorial fee; we have already noted, however, that White's own financial standing was not too secure, so that would have been asking too great a sacrifice. At any rate, Haldeman-Julius decided not to publish the book of poetry. He wrote White: "Regarding the poetry of Cullen and Hughes, perhaps we had better pass that up. Poetry has always been a luxury around here. We sell very little of it, but I like to publish it."[54] So, what might have been an almost definitive book of poetry from the New Negro movement was not published; we can only speculate about what the contents of that volume might have been under White's editorial guidance.

Langston Hughes's second book of poetry, *Fine Clothes to the Jew,* was published by Knopf in 1927. The typescript of White's review of *Fine Clothes* (sent to Harry Hansen of the *New York World*) reveals some interesting glimpses of White's critical leanings. In the review White apologized for the poetic limitations of the blues form that Hughes used so extensively in that collection. At one point, for example, White noted: "Inevitably the repetition of a single emotion in time grows monotonous and often triteness cannot be avoided because there are few changes to be rung on the blues theme." He suggested that a reader unfamiliar with the blues listen to Bessie or Clara Smith, "either in the flesh or on phonograph records," in order to understand the form as it is used vocally. His main concern was that Hughes might be limiting himself too much with the blues format in his poetry:[55]

Out of the blues form it is possible and probable that a more inclusive poetic form may develop but that form would not be blues as the term is now interpreted. It will be interesting to watch these changes as they are developed by Mr. Hughes and others who may follow him in the growth of either a more universal medium of expression or a broadening of the scope of the moods themselves. Mr. Hughes' friends and admirers may perhaps have some apprehension that too diligent working of this vein may cramp him or lessen the fine, flowing, ecstatic sense of rhythm which he so undoubtedly possesses.

White praised some of the nonblues poetry in which Hughes "evokes magnificently stirring emotions from the life of Negro porters and prostitutes and others of humble estate." After quoting from "Brass Spittoons" and "Mulatto," a poem which "brought tears to the eyes of Carl Van Vechten and Clarence Darrow" when Hughes read it to them, White concluded with praise for the book as "one that will grow upon its readers in its evocation of beauty and rhythm and color and warmth."

A day after this piece was composed, White wrote to Hughes to thank him for sending him a copy of *Fine Clothes,* "and especially for that lovely inscription." Then, perhaps because he feared his reaction to the collection might upset Hughes, White added: "I haven't had time to go through it as thoroughly as I should like but such peeps into it as I have taken make me think that it is even a finer piece of work than 'The Weary Blues.' " In a later letter, however, White sent Hughes a copy of the review from the *World* and indicated that they had "cut it somewhat," so he sent Hughes carbon of the original review.[56] To White's first letter (February 2), Hughes replied: "I'm hoping you will like 'Fine Clothes.' The [*Chicago*] *Defender* gave it a grand review this week, but I'm expecting the 'razz' from most of the other colored papers. I don't believe they'll understand ."[57]

In the same letter Hughes said he was sending White some poems and asked him to send them to Frederick Allen of *Harper's:* "I'm not sure any of them are suitable to *Harper's,* but you can never tell what an editor will take." White said that he would do what he could at *Harper's* and added: " . . . if I meet with no success there, I will try somewhere else. Perhaps I can do something through Carl Van Doren of the *Century.*" Within a few days White wrote Allen:

Some time ago, I telephoned you regarding Langston Hughes and you said you would like to see some of his poetry for possible use in *Harper's.* He has just sent me the enclosed which I pass along to you. Let me know, won't you, if you can use any of it.

Allen did not accept the poems, however, and Allen's objections to them are not specified. In a related piece of correspondence, White wrote Allen:

There is a sharp division of opinion as to the relative merits of Cullen and Hughes as poets. A number of people whose opinion I respect think Hughes is a better poet, while the majority favor Cullen. Thanks so much, however for the consideration that you gave to Hughes' poems. I hope some time soon he will land in *Harper's.*

White did not return the poems to Hughes until a month later, so he might have tried placing them with Van Doren; there is no correspondence to that effect, but White often carried out such business over the telephone. At any rate, he returned the poems to Hughes on April 13, "with two comments upon them which are self-explanatory." Hughes did not seem too disturbed by the rejection: "Many thanks for what you did with my poems and for the criticism. I know myself that I've done better. I certainly appreciate your sending them around for me."[58] When we consider that while White was trying to get Hughes's poems placed, he was also helping other writers and trying to obtain a Guggenheim Fellowship for himself, we can appreciate the genuine desire to help which motivated him.

Correspondence between Hughes and White in the NAACP files becomes quite sporadic after this point, at least for a number of years. In 1930 White wrote Ruth Raphael (of Harper and Brothers) on Hughes's behalf, trying to secure copies of books by American Negro writers for Hughes to send reviewers in Cuba, where interest in "the work of American Negro writers" was quite high. That year White also corresponded with William Hallock Johnson, president of Lincoln University, about helping sales of "Four Lincoln University Poets," which included poems by Hughes. In fact, Hughes had asked White to do whatever he could to help the other three poets represented in the pamphlet. Johnson sent White fifty copies to distribute, and White replied that "among others . . . I am sending the pamphlet to are a number of the more important critics." Ever the accountant, White also suggested charging a price of twenty-five cents for the pamphlets, if there were enough publicity generated to sell them, an idea Johnson found "a good one." Finally, again in 1930, White wrote Bernard Smith of Knopf concerning the release of Hughes's novel *Not without Laughter:* "I shall read this at once and, if it is as good as I think it is, I will be glad either to do a review or to send you a paragraph on it for whatever use it may be to you." In addition White suggested that Smith send a copy of the novel to Miss Hannah Moriarta, who was "assistant for the William E. Harmon Awards for distinguished achievement among Negroes. By sending a copy to her," White explained, "you will place Mr. Hughes' novel before one who is largely responsible for the Harmon Awards." White went on to note that, since James Weldon Johnson had already received a First Award in Literature from the foundation and could not receive the award a second time, "I am sure that Mr. Hughes' novel, with his previous work, will place him in line for the Harmon Award in Literature for 1930." In closing, White added that Smith should "say to Miss Moriarta that you are sending the book at my suggestion."[59] That is the end of the White-Hughes correspondence for this era. The two men naturally continued their relationship over the succeeding decades, but the most important phase of White's aid to Hughes centers in the 1920s.

White's real attitude toward Hughes is difficult to estimate. He undoubtedly liked Hughes's work, at least part of it, but his enthusiasm for Hughes's poetry in this period was not nearly so emphatic as his enthusiasm for Cullen's poetry or Fisher's prose. Of course, Hughes had a patron, so White might have felt that Hughes did not need his help as much as others did. One has a distinct impression, however, that when White wrote Allen the letter cited above concerning the "relative merits of Cullen and Hughes as poets," he was probably including himself in "the majority" of people who, he said, "favor Cullen."

If White's attitude toward Hughes is unclear, his attitude toward Claude McKay is truly confusing. While White continually did his utmost to help McKay, from raising money for him to trying to help place the manuscript for McKay's first attempt at a novel, in a letter to Hughes he referred to McKay's work at this time as "third-rate." Yet White's correspondence with McKay indicates that he liked immensely McKay's earlier volumes of poetry, *Songs of Jamaica* (1912) and *Spring in New Hampshire and Other Poems* (1920). An examination of the White-McKay correspondence during the twenties establishes White's ambiguity concerning McKay's work.

By 1924 McKay had already established himself as a poet, having published three volumes of poetry. (*Harlem Shadows* was published in 1922).

At this time, however, he was living in France, apparently almost destitute. On January 26, 1924, White wrote McKay and sent him one hundred dollars that he had raised in response to a plea from McKay for funds. Tactfully White added in his letter: "I need hardly say that, knowing your sensitiveness, I approached only those who knew you well that there be no thought of anything other than joy in coming to your aid on the part of those approached." Not so tactfully White included an itemized list of the amounts contributed by each person: Arthur Spingarn contributed fifty dollars, while the others contributed from one to five dollars.[60] This listing was characteristic of White's meticulous concern for exactness in money matters.

The letter McKay wrote asking for help was addressed to "Comrade" Grace Campbell, who forwarded it to White. The tone of McKay's letter was typical of the letters he wrote in those years: pleading, yet tinged with an air of aloof pride and an expectation of service. In asking for money to be raised "to tide me over these bad times," McKay added:[61]

You might show them that I have been working here—not idling and that so far it was impossible for me to sell anything to the bourgeois papers. . . . My life here is unsatisfactory for a propagandist—cadging a meal off people who are not at all sympathetic to my social ideas. There is so much work to be done if I am helped a little, but no one can work against such odds single handed, especially when he is not even guaranteed a little food and a bed!

Several times during their correspondence McKay was to plead his destitute condition to White, who generally seemed quite willing to do what he could to help, whether that meant raising money or securing information for McKay's use.

Actually White and McKay had been corresponding before the episode in 1924. When McKay returned to Germany after his visit to Russia in 1921, "a great triumphant trip," he mentioned meeting some opposition from certain American comrades in the Soviet Union: " . . . although I am a Communist, I am a fearless champion of race rights even when that championship should reflect on the American comrades." Toward the end of 1921 White wrote to Joel Spingarn about the publication of McKay's *Harlem Shadows:*[62]

I had luncheon with Claude McKay yesterday and he seemed to be greatly elated over the fact that Harcourt is to bring out his book of poems. In a review in the *Boston Transcript* of Brawley's revised "The Negro in American Literature and Art," I took the occasion a few days ago to quote McKay at length and to mention the fact that Harcourt is bringing out his book and I hope that it will have some effect on the sales.

At this time Joel Spingarn was at Harcourt, although White also knew him, of course, in connection with the Association.)

A flurry of correspondence was precipitated between McKay and White over a statement attributed to McKay in an article by Hubert Harrison of the *Negro World*. Harrison quoted McKay as saying he had been "lionized at lunch by 'pseudo-intellectuals,' " referring to some officials of the NAACP with whom he had dined. McKay wrote Harrison a letter and sent White a copy, "so that you may know that I was not a party to [Harrison's] nasty little reference" to the NAACP people. In his letter to Harrison, McKay said: "You are very wrong to think that you can praise my work by a personal attack on intelligent minds, that whatever their faults, are working for the common cause in their own way." In response White wrote McKay that "I know you too well and have too high an opinion of you to have believed for a moment that this rather nasty little piece of journalism could have in any way been due to you."[63] He also indicated that he would probably review *Harlem Shadows* in the *Boston Transcript* "and in either the *New Republic* or the *Nation*," and added: "If your forthcoming book is up to the standard of 'Spring in New Hampshire and Other Poems' you need not lose any sleep over the way I shall treat it." White apparently liked the early work McKay was doing, then, and as usual was most eager to help the poet succeed.

In 1924 much of the correspondence between White and McKay focused on their novels, White's *The Fire in the Flint*, which had just been published, and McKay's first novel, which was never satisfactorily completed. In September, 1924, White wrote McKay inquiring after an illness that had hospitalized the latter; he also asked about the status of McKay's manuscript:

I am delighted that you have finished and that you are now revising. In my former letter, I asked for some specific information about the book—its exact nature, who is going to publish it, etc. When you are ready to divulge this information, let me know if there is anything I can do towards helping to get the best presentation.

A few months later, a worried and pessimistic McKay wrote White concerning his novel:[64]

I am afraid it is not good enough to publish as it is. I want to do tons of things to it. And I don't know how I'll ever get the finance to go through with it. If I could convince some publisher—but not bloody likely—not yet.

Meanwhile White had arranged for McKay to meet with Sinclair Lewis in

Paris, because, White said, "he is a dynamic, lovable individual and one who could help you tremendously." Lewis, White added, "went over page by page, line by line, parts of 'The Fire in the Flint' " with him, and he had "learned more about the things that I must correct in my style than from all the treatises that have been written on the novel."[65] In his 1937 autobiography, *A Long Way from Home,* McKay had this to say about his meetings with Lewis:[66]

Sinclair Lewis was in Paris also, and he was very kind. He read some of my stuff. He had been generous to many radically-inclined writers since his first success with *Main Street,* and he hadn't seen any results. . . . In a shrewd American way (chastising me and making me like it), Sinclair Lew gave me a few cardinal and practical points about the writing of a book or a novel. Those points were indicative and sharp like newspaper headlines. I did not forget them when I got down to writing *Home to Harlem.* I reme bered them so well that some critics saw the influence of Sinclair Lewis in my novel. Scott Fitzgerald, in a note, said that the scenes seemed in the Zola-Lewis line.

This account reflects the experience that White had with Lewis; unfortunately, there is no reference in McKay's autobiography to White's being involved in the meeting between Lewis and McKay. McKay was more interested in figures like Lewis, Max Eastman, and Frank Harris than in Walter White in relating his life story. Like many of the black writers of the time, White included, McKay was too dazzled by the literary lights around him to offer a very helpful perspective concerning the lesser figure who might have been involved in his progress.

In this period of correspondence McKay was also writing White concerning *Fire* and offering some criticism. One scene he particularly found wanting was the rape of Mamie, which McKay thought was unnecessarily brutal. White replied, "I don't believe that rape by one is possible. . . . Mir you, I am, of course, diametrically opposed to the Vardaman-Dixon schoc but, to put over this story picturing it in the raw, I had to talk in those terms which could be understood." McKay countered that White should have convinced his readers of the credibility of Mamie's rape. After taking White to task for having the rape occur "in the heart of a pretty populous city" instead of in a more isolated spot outside the city limits, McKay offered this observation about the nature of rape:[67]

After all raping is not an instinctive thing to average men. It arises from special conditions . . . among soldiers and sailors who are starved and som what bestialized in nature . . . sometimes among Southern whites who wa: to assert their savage masculine and race superiority over a reserved and respectable colored girl or among blacks who are tabooed from consortin; with white women.

In spite of faults he found in the novel, McKay wished White well in his sales, royalties, and attempts at securing translations.

In addition to writing White about their own work, McKay included some observations on other black American writers such as Alain Locke, and on the current interest in black art in America. Of Locke, McKay said:

It's so hard to pin down what he's driving at. It's a fault of many colored writers. I don't know if it can be traced to the long years the black race has lived in America without being able to express its own thoughts and feeling. . . . He could really do wonderful things if he would be simple and clear and not confuse the reality of Negro life in the purple patches of mysticism.

McKay also expressed his conviction that black writers would have "to stand good straight-out criticism and not allow ourselves to be patronized as Negro artists of America," and stated that "indiscriminating praise from Negro journals" and critics like William S. Braithwaite could only hurt black artists and their work.[68]

Several months later McKay repeated his conviction that black artists should develop discipline in their art and not be swept up in the tide of popular approval:[69]

I am so happy about the aroused interest in the creative life of the Negro. It is for the Negro aspirants to the creative life themselves to make the best of it—to discipline themselves and do work that will hold ground beside the very highest white standard. Nothing less will help Negro art forward [;] a boom is a splendid thing but if the works are not up to standard people turn aside from them after the novelty has worn off.

Following this general statement McKay added: "I was interested to hear of Cullen's work—I don't care for what I have seen of his poetry but Langston Hughes is a real poet [,] strikingly original if he will only work hard and take his work seriously. . . ."

In the summer of 1925 McKay was getting his novel manuscript in final form and trying to find a publisher. White and others in the States, especially Arthur Schomberg, were doing their best to help. (Among other things, White sent McKay a city map of New York so McKay could check locations for his novel, and two hymnals—one A. M. E. and one from "a colored Baptist church.") White and McKay had very different ideas about where the latter should try to place his manuscript; McKay did not particularly want to submit it to Harcourt, Brace & Company, who had published *Harlem Shadows.* White urged McKay to submit the manuscript to the newly formed Viking Press. "The advantage of a firm just starting out is that they of necessity, for reasons of finance and of reputation, must push every book on their list," he stated, whereas an older firm would not necessarily push every work as hard. White had already been in contact with Oppenheimer and Guinsberg of Viking. In May, 1925, he wrote them that Claude McKay "has about completed a novel," and that he was not going to submit it to Harcourt: " . . . from my own knowledge of him and from his poetry, I am sure his novel must be well worth looking into." An obviously interested Oppenheimer replied:[70]

I cannot thank you enough for your kindness in letting us know about Claude McKay's novel. I am writing him immediately in the hope that we will be able to see his manuscript.

It is awfully good of you to go to this trouble and we deeply appreciate not only this but all you are doing and have done for us.

White first mentioned Viking to McKay in a letter written a few days before the letter to Oppenheimer and Guinsberg. In the letter to McKay, White offered to put McKay in touch with the firm and urged him to "get [his] novel ready for publication as soon as possible" because publishers were searching for material. In addition White asked to see any short stories and poems that McKay had ready: "If you have anything that you really like, I think I could quite easily get it published." McKay, however, rejected the idea of submitting his manuscript to Viking; he preferred a more established firm, such as Knopf or Liveright. Regarding White's request for short material to place, McKay said: "I have a story some place that I might send to you. Poems—I don't care to publish any of what I've got for a while yet. I sent one story to America and never heard tell of it."[71]

In a postcard to White, McKay asked whether he had seen Schomberg about his book. White wrote Schomberg on July 23, 1925, to ask about the manuscript and to reiterate his stand that McKay should try a new publishing firm in order to get the best support for the novel. Schomberg's reply indicated that Knopf had rejected the manuscript:[72]

. . . the MS of novel had been submitted to Knopf's in compliance with [McKay's] wishes. The MS is again in my hands because the literary critic, while he speaks well of it as a whole, the element of prudery or candid references appear too strong for publication. If you wish to submit the MS to a publisher, I will be glad to have you try your hand in keeping with Claude's instructions to me, which no doubt covers both of us, viz. best cash terms and royalty.

Whether White eventually sent the manuscript to Viking is not clear, although he did send George Oppenheimer a note in August, saying, "I wanted to give you some new information I got from Sinclair Lewis about the McKay novel and to give you one or two other leads which might be of some value."[73]

The manuscript which was being considered for publication in 1925 was not *Home to Harlem,* although it may have been a rough prototype of it. This becomes evident in correspondence from McKay in August, 1925. McKay wrote White two letters on August 4, the first of which was highly emotional. In it he berated White for taking so long to answer his letters and said that was why he sent his manuscript to Schomberg, who was "extremely loyal and kind." Then McKay presented his reasons for preferring an older publishing firm:

What you say of the new firm pushing a book is all right, but an old established firm has always a better selling agency—if a book has any chance of selling at all. What's wrong with the older firm is their conservatism from which Knopf is also suffering.

After stressing his dire financial need, he added: "Frankly I don't know if you will like the novel at all. I rather think you won't but I hope that will not prevent your pushing it if you can. . . . I can't apologize for it even though it finds itself up against Mr. Bloch's [of Knopf's] morals, for I don't understand morality in the conventional sense." In closing he noted that he would be willing "to cut out anything that is thought obscene."

In the second letter McKay apologized for the earlier one, which was written "in a hurry when I was feeling quite unwell," and said he wanted to clarify some points, including why he was so anxious to get his novel published quickly:[74]

About the novel itself, my chief regret is that Knopf's reader was allowed to keep it so long. I don't mind the rejection at all but I am hoping that the book gets published for the fall season. I also hear by a roundabout way that your friend Carl Van Vechten is doing a novel on Harlem Negro life and I don't want him to get in ahead of me because he would hurt my chances, being a white man and a popular novelist known to all the gaudy crop of bleating reviewers, who are all log-rollers hoping someday to be kindly reviewed for the novels they intend to write.

Again McKay indicated his willingness to make some changes to accommodate the demands and expectations of publishers, although he was not exactly happy about the idea:

I'm all willing to take out anything illegal that might involve me with the Laws of the Land. In reality I tried hard to avoid anything of that sort but something *may* have slipped up. . . . However, I should not like harmless innuendoes and jokes that flavor the narrative to be touched at all. If people

who can stomach Mrs. Warren's profession . . . can't stand Color Scheme
it would only demonstrate that the white literate cannot stand for a black
author laughing at white folks' foibles. That would be at the bottom of any
objection to the theme of the book. I hope that such a supposition has no
validity that, benighted as America is with all its Great White Ways, there
is yet a silver stream of intelligence that remains unpolluted.

Since McKay gives us a title here, "Color Scheme," and since *Home to Harlem*
does not fit thematically with the book being discussed, we can safely assume that the two works are different entities.[75]

Clearly, the manuscript being sent around in 1925 was in great difficulty.
On August 27 White wrote Arthur Schomberg:

> I had two letters from Claude last week, and I do not know what would
> be the best thing to do. I think the wisest thing, however, would be for
> you to send it to Harrison Smith at Harcourt, Brace and Company. . . .
> Since Knopf turned it down, and since Claude does not want me to submit
> it to the Viking Press, I do not know of any other possible place except
> Harcourt's. As a matter of fact, from what I heard indirectly from Knopf,
> I don't know what the chances are going to be even there.
> I think I understand Claude's viewpoint in wanting it published by an
> old established firm. When I first spoke to the Viking Press I think I could
> have gotten it by there, but now I do not think they would be so interested
> in it.

White also suggested that Schomberg contact H. L. Mencken, "asking his
advice," since McKay had indicated that he himself had written Mencken.
The next day White wrote McKay, apologizing for his delay in responding
by saying that he was "in the throes of rewriting" his new novel (*Flight*).
In the letter he reassured McKay that, after talking with Harry Bloch at
Knopf's, the man who made the decision regarding McKay's novel, he was
convinced that "there was no element of color prejudice or conservatism"
in the rejection of the book, "for Bloch is so great a friend to the Negro
that he would be prejudiced in favor of anything done by a colored writer."
Attempting to encourage McKay, White told him that he had advised Schomberg to send the manuscript to Harcourt and that he would do his best
to get Smith to "react favorably":[76]

> There is a great demand for stuff by Negro writers just now, and if the
> conventionality of Harcourt can be overcome (since you say there are
> points of the story that can be objected to as obscene), I think you can
> do no better than to get published there. Harcourt has nothing by a
> colored writer on its list since Johnson's Anthology, so they are ripe for
> a book by a colored writer now.

McKay, however, was far from cheered by White's letter. In his reply he quoted from Bloch's letter to Schomberg, in which Bloch stated that many passages in the manuscript were "certainly not within the law and . . . we certainly could not publish the book without considerable expurgation." Concerning what White had said about Bloch's attitude toward black writers, McKay noted:

What you say about Bloch is of interest. It may be that he is so prejudiced in favor of the Negro that when he is confronted with a work of art that touches on the life of colored people he immediately approaches it in terms of propaganda and *not* of art and life. That's the great trouble with Jewish art and literature in America (I don't know if Bloch is Jewish), indeed with the whole field of American art and literature. We are made impotent by the fears and misgivings of minorities and by the harsh judgment of majority opinion, and thus we become emasculate in ideas and the expression of them.

McKay then presented a very lucid contrast between art and propaganda, as reflected in the artist's purpose for creating his art:[77]

Every work of art is in reality personal propaganda. It is the way in which the artist sees life and wants to present it[,] but there is a vast chasm between the artist's personal expression of himself and his making himself the instrument of a group or a body of opinion: The first is art, the last is prostitution, and that is the sole difference between art and propaganda whether the field be that of conservative or radical politics, national or racial questions!

In closing, McKay told White that he realized how hard White was working, for himself and for others, and said: "I honor and commend you! But my position is tragic. I am always working under the shadow of insecurity and it paralyzes me."

Exactly how much McKay depended on White to the exclusion of other friends in America is never quite clearly drawn, but it is certain that McKay turned to White for help often. In September, 1925, he sent White the first of "those series of short stories that I'm working furiously at just now to save myself, if I can, from a strange foreign gutter. I am on the edge right now." After asking White to send the story to Eric Walrond if he was unable to handle it himself, McKay added: "I do hope your duties and your own literary work will yet give you time enough to handle this yourself . . . as you can do more for me than anyone else." In October McKay said he was going to send White another story "called Within the Belt," which, he said, was "about an octoroon girl in Harlem" and was somewhat like Fisher's

"High Yaller," but treated the subject "from a different angle." He also mentioned sending poems to several magazines, including the *Century*, the *American Mercury*, and the *Nation*, with instructions to send unwanted poems to White: "Hope you won't be offended by this liberty." Then, almost as a final dig, McKay added: "I am willing to pay an agent to handle it if you can't."[78] Obviously, tact was not one of McKay's prominent traits. There is every indication that White was doing as much as he could for him, especially considering the demands of White's position, his own writing efforts, and his efforts in aiding other people.

On October 27 White received four of McKay's poems; two had been rejected by the *American Mercury* and two by the *Nation*. The *Mercury* sent back "America in Retrospect" and "My House," about which James Weldon Johnson noted, "These are good, but I don't know who will consider them available." The *Nation* rejected "The Shadow-Ring" and "We Who Revolt," with a note from Lewis Garnett indicating that Mark Van Doren had accepted one other poem.[79] White's opinion of these poems is reflected in a comment he made in a letter to Langston Hughes:[80]

Claude has sent me a number of poems and one short story and, I don't like to say it, but they are almost uniformly third rate. The story is too long to go into here but I will tell you all about him when I see you.

As his correspondence with White makes evident, Claude McKay was, for the most part, a very moody man, given to fits of despair. In a letter to White, McKay once presented this poignant self-evaluation:

You're lucky in making friends, you're so altogether charming and fine. I'm a son of a bitch—I like really well so few people, that those I can like, I prize dearly and I always feel happy when I can possibly like some new freak of God.

McKay suffered from constant feelings of abandonment from those "few people" he numbered among his friends. In addition to statements we have already examined, there is this one, written in November, 1925:[81]

I feel as if I was entirely deserted by every one just at a time when I have failed and am down and out. It gives me a terrible, bitter feeling. If you are displeased with me or with my work I wish you would be frank and tell me so. And then I should no longer be hoping you might do something for me.
... I feel so let down by everybody.

The combination of his ill health, his frantic financial status, and his repeated failures to have his recent art accepted weighed heavily on McKay, the same

an who, in that very year, dedicated these lines to those involved in the
orkers' struggle: "Reckless we live, careless of clothes or victuals, / And
l the things that tend to blind and bind."[82] Apparently, McKay suffered
om the revolutionist's predicament of needing physically what he rejected
eoretically.

For the next few years the correspondence between White and McKay,
available in the NAACP files, dropped off almost completely. In July,
927, after *Home to Harlem* had been accepted by Harper and Brothers,
hite wrote McKay: "Yesterday I was at the office of Harper and Brothers,
d was delighted to see the dummy of your novel. Harper has done a
eautiful job and the cover by Aaron Douglas is magnificent." There was
so a note from James Weldon Johnson to White concerning the release
f the novel:

laude McKay's novel, entitled "Home to Harlem" is just out. Harpers sent
e copies yesterday. I do not know how well he has done the book—I have
mply glanced at it. From that glance I can see that he has gone "Nigger
eaven" one or two better. I hope, however, he has used the material
rtistically.

later memo from Johnson repeated the information about the release
f McKay's book and added that "the first edition of 2500 was entirely
xhausted and . . . there was not a single book" left at Harper's.[83]

White's opinion of the book, and of McKay's contribution to the awak-
ning spirit of race pride in America, was presented in a letter of recommenda-
on he wrote to George E. Haynes of the Harmon Foundation in 1928. Con-
erning McKay's contribution to race pride, White said:

r. McKay is possessed of great ability, in my opinion, but I do not feel
at he has yet used that ability to greatest advantage. In his volume of
oetry, *Harlem Shadows*, which was published in 1922, Mr. McKay pro-
uced a number of poems which, I believe, rank high in merit. Especially
this true of certain of his poems which have done so much to awaken
mong Negroes of the United States and the West Indies a sense of the
eauties of Negro life.

Home to Harlem, however, White felt that McKay had not lived up to
is potential:[84]

In his recently published novel, *Home to Harlem*, I do not feel that Mr.
cKay was at his very best. There are passages in this novel where Mr. Mc-
ay forgets himself as a novelist and becomes once again a poet. Those
assages are of to me exceedingly great beauty. The novel as a whole, how-
ver, does not greatly impress me. I have no objection to the choice of his
aterial by an author nor do I quarrel with him in what he considers the

form of a novel. *Home to Harlem* does not impress me as being as fine and as sincere an accomplishment as Mr. McKay is capable of.

I do not mean by this to imply that I believe him guilty of intellectual or artistic dishonesty. I do know that he has suffered greatly within recent years from illness and poverty. It is out of this suffering that I believe the shortcomings of *Home to Harlem* emerged.

In closing, White said he knew "something of a forthcoming book, *Banjo,* upon which Mr. McKay is now working," and that, although he had seen no part of the manuscript, he understood "from one who has that it is a much finer piece of work." In spite of what appears a fairly negative recommendation from White, Claude McKay won the Gold Award from the Harmon Foundation in 1928. There was some controversy over whether McKay had relinquished his British citizenship (if he had not, he would have been ineligible for the prize), but he was given the benefit of the doubt—and the prize, which included four hundred dollars.

The last bit of White's correspondence revolving around McKay concerned the publication of *Banjo* in 1929. On March 15 of that year Eugene Saxton, then at Harper and Brothers, wrote White:

We shall be publishing very shortly Claude McKay's new novel, "Banjo," which, as you probably know, deals with life in the old port of Marseilles. I shall send you advance copies as soon as possible and I shall be very grateful to you if you will do what you can to give the story a good send-off.

Saxton also requested a list of persons to whom he might also send advance copies for review and/or publicity purposes, but White penciled a note on Saxton's letter that he had telephoned Ruth Raphael of Harper's and she already had a list.[85] In April, William Aspenwall Bradley, McKay's agent, wrote to ask White's opinion of *Banjo* and noted that 8,000 advance copies had been sold. White replied that, in general, he found McKay's second novel an improvement:[86]

I like McKay's *Banjo* much better than I did *Home to Harlem.* (Interesting enough I read *Home to Harlem* in the Province and *Banjo* in Harlem.) My chief objection to *Banjo* is that McKay allows too much of his personal feeling on certain matters to peep through. Particularly do I refer to his resentment to the attitude of the Negro press towards *Home to Harlem.* The book, however, shows a distinct artistic advance, it seems to me, and has had superb reviews.

As we noted earlier, White's attitude toward McKay is confusing. It is apparent that he thought much more of McKay's earlier work, and his

oetry in general, than of his later attempts at fiction. Whether this is pri-
narily due to White's distaste for the more "earthy" subject matter of
1cKay's novels is really immaterial. Whatever his attitude toward McKay
s an artist, White obviously tried to help McKay make publishing contacts
n the States. And while McKay does not mention White's efforts on his
>ehalf in his autobiography, he did tell White once that "you can do more
or me than anyone else." This might only have been the plea of a desperate
nan trying to elicit aid from a friend removed from him in distance and
deology, but it is nevertheless a statement we should consider in evaluating
Valter White's efforts to help other writers and in attempting to assess the
attitudes of those writers toward White.

That Walter White held Countee Cullen in the highest esteem is evident
n all phases of their correspondence. Along with Langston Hughes, Cullen
vas one of the most prolific of the Harlem Renaissance poets. Between
1925 and 1929 he published four volumes of his own verse, placed individual
>oems in numerous magazines, and edited an anthology of black American
>oetry. In April, 1924, White, attempting to get some of Cullen's poetry
>ublished, turned to a few of his friends. First White sent Cullen's poems
o Carl Van Doren at the *Century* to ascertain "the wisdom of his seeking
a publisher for them." At the time Cullen was interested in a Rhodes scholarship and, since he was not an athlete, White thought he should do some-
:hing literary to gain consideration:

Two things cause me to go slow: one is that I don't know enough about
poetry, and the other is, I am so fond of much that Cullen has done that my
udgment, such as it is, is biased in his favor.

Van Doren's response, while not totally negative, was not particularly encouraging, either:[87]

I hardly think Countee Cullen has enough verse here for a volume that
would be quite worthy of him. Perhaps ten of his poems are excellent; the
rest are below his best.
If I could, you may be sure I should be more encouraging, but I am too
much interested in him and his future to feel like advising him to hurry. If
there is reason to think a volume would help him to a Rhodes scholarship,
it might be worth while to run the risk. Otherwise I should counsel him to
wait till he has more.

Van Doren added, however, that he would like to see the best of Cullen's
unpublished poems to consider for the *Century*.

Meanwhile White was proceeding to arrange a meeting between Cullen
and Horace Liveright concerning a volume of Cullen's poems. In a rather

secretive note to Cullen on April 14, White said: "I want to have a talk with you soon; I want to look over some of your poetry that you like best Something worth while may come of it because of a statement made to me last night by a certain publisher." The "certain publisher" was Liveright, and on April 25 White, in spite of Van Doren's advice, tried to convince Liveright that Cullen had enough material for a volume of verse:

Following our talk at the Du Bois Dinner, I asked Countee Cullen to let me see some of the best of his poems. I have gone over them very carefully and there are about thirty which seem to me to be well worth publication. . . . Perhaps a volume about the size of Edna Millay's "A Few Figs from Thistles" which Harpers publishes could be brought out if you thought it wise. Cullen tells me that Witter Bynner has agreed to do an introduction.

White tried to convince Liveright that publishing Cullen's poetry would be a sound venture:

My opinion may not be of very great value but, such as it is, I give it to you. Cullen has done enough poems to merit publication and I believe there could be created sales enough to make it worth while. He has a considerable reputation for a young man and many friends who would help push the book.

On the same day as his letter to Liveright, White sent a copy of the letter to Cullen and reminded him: "Remember my word of caution. You are to know nothing of my conversation with Liveright. In talking with him, be sublimely innocent of my connection with it in any way." A few days later Cullen wrote to thank White for the "fine letter" he sent to Liveright: " . . . it ought to impress him; if I were a publisher it would impress me. However, whether or not anything comes of it, I am deeply grateful to you for what you have done for me."[88]

Unfortunately, this effort proved unsuccessful. Liveright wrote White that, although his poetry readers liked Cullen's work, they did not feel it was "distinctly big" and were afraid it would not sell: "It has, of course, an individual poetic note which we'd love to recognize." As an afterthought Liveright suggested that Cullen might want to try publishing on a guarantee sale basis:

Countee Cullen has so frequently said that he was sure he could sell a number of copies that I feel almost like asking him to come across and guarantee a sale of 500. I hate financed books, though, or anything that smacks of them.

White responded that he agreed with Liveright's decision; he acknowledged Liveright's fairmindedness in publishing black authors, and added that he

o felt that Cullen would run "the risk of a set back if he is published too
on." In a reply Liveright said that he believed Cullen would "be very
appy at the end of another year if he decides not to push his present vol-
ne through to publication. I think that he will mature greatly in this
ne." When he wrote Cullen about Liveright's decision, White tried to
onsole the young poet by telling him that Alain Locke had said that he
lt Cullen's best poems would probably hurt more than help in getting a
hodes scholarship from the rather conservative board, and added: "While
ou have done some poems which are of the first rank, I do not feel that
ou have enough to your credit as yet to run the risk of being labeled as
lything less than a poet of the first rank." Understandably disappointed,
ullen said he was sure White had done his "utmost" for him, and that he
as "sincerely grateful"; he rejected completely the idea of a financed
ook, as "a matter of pride," and closed wth a romantic flourish: "I am not
the least discouraged . . . as better poets have waited far longer for pub-
ation."[89] As a matter of fact, Cullen had to wait only a short while; his
rst volume of verse, *Color,* was published by Harper and Brothers in 1925.

In the meantime White was continually on the alert for a chance to
ake people aware of Cullen as well as other contemporary black writers.
n December 23, 1924, White wrote to Mary Trafton, who had given a
lk on Negro writers and had omitted Cullen:

ountee Cullen who had poems in the November *American Mercury, Century,*
arpers, and the *Bookman* and in the December *Harpers,* is beyond doubt
ne of the most talented of the Negro poets. Though he has not as yet
ublished anything in book form, Negro poetry could hardly be considered
lequately with his name omitted.

everal months later White responded to an inquiry from Ruth W. Thomp-
on of the Mentor Personal Service Department concerning information
out Negro poets. After referring Miss Thompson to James Weldon John-
on's *The Book of American Negro Poetry* (1922) as a good source of informa-
on, White added: "There are two Negro poets of real merit who have
ome to the fore since Mr. Johnson's book was published. One of these is
ountee Cullen whose first volume, 'Color,' will be published next month
y Harper; . . . the other poet is Langston Hughes. . . ."[90] While, as this
st reference shows, White was ever ready to keep all of the young writers'
ames in peoples' minds, he clearly demonstrated a fondness for Cullen
lat was not always present in his comments about other writers.

After failing to place Cullen's proposed volume with Liveright, White
irned once again to a favorite source for publication help, Eugene Saxton
f Harper and Brothers. Writing to Saxton on February 13, 1925, White
iid of Cullen:

He has a very well established reputation for a young poet and he has a number of influential friends and well wishers who would do all in their power to see that the book is circulated.

I for one have great admiration for him not only because of the excelle technique of his poetry but because he to me seems to have that indefina thing which stamps him as a poet of very considerable gifts.

The next day White wrote to Frederick Allen of Harper's concerning Cull and his poems: "Eugene Saxton telephoned me the other day about Culle book of verse. I think a volume by him would sell very well and I so infor Mr. Saxton."[91] By the early part of March Harper's had accepted Cullen's book of verse for publication. In congratulating Cullen on the acceptance, White also lent his support to a suggestion by Harper's that Cullen reduce the number of poems in the collection:[92]

If I may offer a bit of advice, I think the recommendation of Harpers to select about seventy-five of the A-1 poems from the one hundred and twe that you submitted is a wise one. First volumes of poetry have a hard tim at best and if one can avoid giving critics just cause for uttering the platitu nous, "The book has merit but is very uneven," it will be much better.

In addition to collaborating with Cullen on a biographical sketch for Harper's use, White also was quite active in promoting the sales of the book. Of course, White used the standard machinery of the Association to send out press releases concerning Cullen's work and to promote interest in the book at the annual convention. In thanking White for the conventic publicity, Cullen noted: "I think either Harper and Bros. or I ought to pay you. If the book has any sale at all, much of it will surely be due to the fine spirit of cooperation you have shown in the matter." White's efforts the 1925 Denver conference of the Association included distributing print postcards with information about *Color,* which, he believed, did "a good deal . . . towards creating interest in the book." Saxton wrote White: "It is very good for you to keep the fire burning under this [i.e., *Color*], and I hope there will be a chance to do some joint effective publicity in the fall."[93]

Even while he was working on publicity for Cullen's book of verse, White was trying to get some poems placed for Cullen elsewhere. On June 19 he sent several of Cullen's poems to Irita Van Doren, editor of the *New York Herald Tribune*'s book section:

. . . I hand you enclosed some of Countee Cullen's poems which you aske him to send you that night at our house. He asked me to say to you that you are at liberty to use any of these. The ones marked "B" will be in Mr. Cullen's book to be published in October so, if they are used, they will ha to be used before that date.

Mrs. Van Doren's secretary replied that Mrs. Van Doren liked Cullen's poetry and had decided to publish three of the poems: "Black Magdalens," "More Than a Fool's Song," and "Atlantic City Waiter." In gratitude Cullen wrote White on July 20 to thank him for his "kind service and all that you are doing for me." He continued: "Irita Van Doren wrote me telling me she had taken three poems, all to be published this summer. She was quite sure, as she was due to be, that she had you to thank for getting them."[94]

When *Color* was published in October, 1925, White went to work again, bringing the book to the attention of as many people as he could. He wrote Carl Sandburg at the *Chicago Daily News:*

You probably know of the work of Countee Cullen, the young poet who has achieved such unusual fame during the past two or three years. . . . I am very much interested in him and in his progress and I am taking the liberty of sending you a copy of his book which I hope you will enjoy reading. If you should like it, I wish that you would use whatever efforts you may choose to help secure for Mr. Cullen's first book the recognition I feel it so richly merits.

There was no response from Sandburg. White also supplied Harper and Brothers with an extensive list of the names of people he felt could "do the book some good," for which he was thanked by Ruth Raphael, who wrote on December 31, just a few months after the release of *Color:*[95]

I'm gratified to tell you that *Color* is enjoying a very good sale. The Sales Department just reported to me the book is in demand from coast to coast —that we are constantly receiving reorders and that it is selling very much better than the average book of poetry. We are certainly grateful to you for your splendid help.

Ms. Raphael also asked White to read some of Cullen's poetry on a special radio show she was producing for Harper's.

A few days later White wrote Cullen about the possibility of his reading some of Cullen's poems on the radio and about a speech he had given recently. White, in a typical moment of false modesty, told Cullen: "I read poetry rather poorly but I am a willing victim if it is going to do the book any good." Then White offered a rather cynical observation regarding the nature of literary patrons:

I spoke at the Plaza last Wednesday and devoted a good deal of time to you, reading a number of your poems. A number of the smug, fur-coated, well-fed ladies wrote down the title. I hope they spend some of their money for copies.

He closed the letter by saying he had sent a review of *Color* to the *Saturday Review,* "which I suppose they will print sometime soon." In his reply

Cullen thanked White for the review ("I'm sure I'll like it") and for mentioning him in the Plaza speech; Cullen recalled a similar experience at a meeting where he read from Langston Hughes's book and "many persons took down the title. . . ." But, he added, "I'm afraid such things mostly end there."[96] Obviously, both men were well aware of the fickle nature of the pseudoliterary crowd upon whom the *real* sales of their works had to depend.

The relationship between White and Cullen extended into more professional areas as well. In January, 1926, Cullen asked White to write an introduction to a special "Negro Poets' number of *Palms,* a poetry magazine published in Mexico," which Cullen was editing:

. . . for this issue I should like to have an introduction of between a thousand and fifteen hundred words, telling of the general trend of modern Negro verse (if there is such a dubious thing) and with a few brief commen on the characteristics of the more important poets. Among those to be included in the number are: Hughes, Ann Spencer, Jessie Fauset, Gwendolyn Bennett, Georgia Johnson, and one or two less known. In the introductior mention would need to be made of McKay and James Weldon Johnson, surely.

White replied that he was busy correcting galley proofs of *Flight,* but that he would try to "do something that may have some merit in it." Within four days White sent the introduction to Cullen. It was, perhaps necessaril a very sketchy survey of poetry from Phyllis Wheatley to the modern poets, including the "newer school" of poets, such people as Hughes and Cullen, "who are writing not only first-rate Negro verse but . . . excellent verse which takes no cognizance of race":

Though on this point I do not expect agreement, yet I am glad that both Mr. Cullen and Mr. Hughes and the others are not going to the other extre —of casting overboard the gifts of their experiences as Negroes in America life. From this springs a passion, a colorfulness, a strength which gives ther most decided advantages over many of their white brothers who are writin verse.

In concluding, White said he looked for even better work from these "flow ers" springing from "the rich and abundant soil of Negro life." When he sent the introduction to Cullen, White apologized for it, saying it was neither "very thorough nor very polished," but that it was the best he could do under the circumstances.[97]

The idea for Cullen's anthology of Negro poetry, *Caroling Dusk* (1927) more than likely sprang from this project. Cullen sent White the manuscript for that book, and White later gave Cullen his reactions to the poem included in the anthology, which White said "could stand a good deal of pruning." Two of White's favorite Cullen poems, "For a Lady I Know" and "Incident," were not included, and White also missed Hughes's "Mulatto" and "Brass Spittoons." (The poems by Cullen were added to the final manuscript, but the Hughes poems were not.) In the rather lengthy letter White went through the poets included in the anthology and gave his views of their works. His final comment expressed a concern for the possible abuse of the current popularity being enjoyed by Negro writers:[98]

You have material for a magnificent anthology if it is thoroughly weeded. A hostile critic could take three or four poems of the present collection and print them as samples and damn the book. Negro poetry has reached the stage where a poem has no distinction simply because it has been written by a Negro.

Although Cullen chose to ignore most of White's suggestions for improving the content of his anthology, we can nonetheless appreciate the effort White took in painstakingly going through the material and offering his reactions to the anthology.

Whatever their professional relationship might have been, and there is every indication that it was extremely cordial, the personal relationship between White and Cullen was always warm, especially in White's praise of the younger poet's achievements. When Cullen was made assistant editor of *Opportunity* in 1926, White wrote to the journal:[99]

May I extend my congratulations to *Opportunity* upon its great good fortune in adding Countee Cullen to its staff. My felicitations are not wholly based upon the fact that Mr. Cullen is a friend of mine though I am proud indeed to have him as a friend. This note instead comes because Mr. Cullen is without doubt one of the most brilliant writers of America and in saying this I do not mean that he is one of the most brilliant *colored* writers. His genius transcends all lines of race or color.

White's true affection and admiration for Cullen's work are probably best summarized in the blurb White wrote for Harper's to use in promoting *Color:*[100]

Countee Cullen belongs to that company of lyricists of which A. E. Housman and Edna St. Vincent Millay are the bright stars. He is no mere versifier, no simple matcher of words that rhyme without meaning or feeling, no trite measurer of lines. His verse has an emotional depth which is extraordinary in one of Mr. Cullen's years [;] he makes his words hum and sing with none of the triteness and verbosity usual in a beginner. He etches his emotions and pictures with acid clearness, while underneath lies a genuine and sympathetic understanding of the joys and sorrows of life itself. All this he does with a magnificent imagery that seldom permits anything he writes to savor of the commonplace. Countee Cullen is a real poet.

And finally there was this tribute to Cullen, written for White's *Pittsburgh Courier* column in 1927:[101]

Perhaps you have gained the impression that I am enthusiastic about Countee Cullen's verse. If so, you are wholly right. His achievements must inevitably be of magnificent encouragement to other Negro poets, who, dismissing racial barriers, or using those barriers as foot stools, [has] sung and made the world listen to those songs.

In echoing Cullen's "Yet Do I Marvel," White pays perhaps the ultimate homage to Cullen: what could be greater than for a poet to be seen as a bright representative of his own poetic creation?

Even while preparing for his Guggenheim year in France, White was helping Cullen and the others. In July, 1927, White wrote Ruth Raphael: "In October I am to deliver some lectures in England and you may be sure I shall speak at length of various Harper authors and particularly of Mr. Cullen." A few days later he sent another of his lists of people "to whom it would be advantageous to send copies of 'Copper Sun' " to Harriete Ashbrook of Harper's.[102] And we have already noted White's attempt to secure publication of a Haldeman-Julius Little Blue Book for Cullen and Hughes. Clearly, White's efforts for Cullen, whom he so greatly admired, were a labor of love for him. Of all the writers of the New Negro movement, White seemed most to admire this soft-spoken poet.

The correspondence between White and Fisher, Hughes, McKay, and Cullen is the most extensive in the NAACP files; however, White also tried to help other writers of the time. For example, in 1926 White attempted to place Georgia Douglas Johnson's *An Autumn Love Cycle,* but with no success. Ms. Johnson wrote White on August 1, informing him that she had completed the manuscript and was anxious to "get it into the hands of someone. . . ." She even offered to pay him for his services, to which White replied: "Under no circumstances would I want any pay for helping to get your manuscript published. I make no promises and do not know how successful I will be, but if you will send the manuscript to me at my home, . . . I will see what can be done." Assuring White that she could place the book in various southern libraries as she had done with her other books of poetry (*The Heart of a Woman and Other Poems* [1918] and *Bronze: A Book of Verse* [1922]), Ms. Johnson, at that time working for the Department of Labor, added: "You cannot imagine how happy I was to receive your most generous response to my letter. However I was not surprised as it was like you and yours." She also noted that she had already inquired into possibilities with Boni and Liveright, "who are not anxious to put out volumes of the love theme solely," and Alfred Knopf, "who has already gone to press with his fall books catalogue."[103]

Within a few weeks White gave Ms. Johnson the unhappy news: "I have submitted 'An Autumn Love Cycle' to several New York publishers and I regret to say that in each instance it has been returned to me." He then summarized some of the criticisms made about the collection:

There are certain of the poems such as "I Want to Die While You Love Me," "Song of the Sinner," "I Closed My Shutters Fast Last Night," and one or two others which are very good lyrics. The only fault that can be found is that they follow a much traveled path—so many others have written of the self same experiences and emotions. It is not that many of these are not well done, but that this style of lyric has been well done so often before.

Publishers and the poetry-buying public have become rather fed up on this particular style of poetry no matter how well it may be done. . . . Publishers today demand freshness of viewpoint and novelty of expression.

Then, in a more conventional editorial tone, he noted: "There is a feeling that 'An Autumn Love Cycle' is not suitable for publication by these firms because it does not exactly fit their needs." Ms. Johnson thanked White for his efforts in trying to place the manuscript and admitted: "I realize it is not modern as things go now."[104] The book of verse was eventually published, however, some six years later.

Another writer with whom White was more personally acquainted in this era was Nella Larsen Imes. White read the manuscript of Mrs. Imes's *Quicksand,* and on October 1, 1926, sent her this preliminary response to it:

Burdened as I am with household duties and the role of both father and mother this week, I have only had a chance to read a part of the MS. There are one or two minor things which I think can be improved but I like the story immensely. In the one incident where your heroine talks with the school principal, you bring her sharply to life. At the same time, I think you have handled beautifully the principal. I vaguely feared that you would make him a wholly unsympathetic character and I was glad that you didn't for you showed understanding and sympathy with both his and the heroine's. More later when I have had a chance to finish reading the script and to digest it.

When the book was completed, White even arranged to have his secretary type the final manuscript for Mrs. Imes: "When I finished painting the picture to Miss Overton of you as a poor, pathetic soul, she almost burst into tears and promised me that she would write you today regarding the

MS." (At this time, too, Nella Imes was engaged in her defense of White's *Flight* against Frank Horne's unfavorable review in *Opportunity*.)[105]

In 1928 White wrote a letter of recommendation for Mrs. Imes to Samuel Craig, president of the Book League of America. Citing Mrs. Imes's experience as a librarian in the New York Public Library system, White continued:

> . . . Mrs. Imes . . . is one of the best known of the younger Negro writers. Mrs. Imes as you possibly know is the author of the novel, *Quicksand,* which Knopf published. Mrs. Imes' novel is in my opinion one of the best written by any Negro author and one of the most distinguished first novels by any American author written within recent years. Mrs. Imes also has written another novel [*Passing*] which has just been submitted to Knopf.

White added the weight of his position in the Association by stressing the social impact, and the financial rewards, that hiring such a person as Mrs. Imes would have for the Book League:

> Aside from the general experiences and ability I feel that it would be a very real advantage to the Book League of America to have a young colored person of ability attached to its staff. There is a large and constantly growing number of book reading and book buying Negroes in the United States and Mrs. Imes is very well known among them. Her connection with the Book League would I am sure commend the Book League instantly and favorably to those persons.

Within a few weeks David Roderick of the Book League, to whom Craig had referred the matter, wrote White to say that he had met Mrs. Imes and was trying to reach her for further discussion. White immediately sent him her address *and* phone number, and wrote Mrs. Imes to suggest that she contact Roderick.[106]

Finally, in 1929, White wrote a letter of recommendation for Mrs. Imes to the Guggenheim Foundation, in which he stressed his "great interest and admiration" for "her development as a writer." He continued:[107]

> It seems to me that she has a gift for prose writing and an objectivity in approaching her material such as no other person possesses who is writing fiction regarding the Negro. In the two novels which she has published— *Quicksand* and *Passing*— I was most pleased at revelation of the technical development shown in her handling of the two stories. She is possessed of an uncanny instinct for divining and depicting those emotions which govern the words and acts of her characters. She writes with an economy and with a lack of verbosity which is characteristic of another woman writer—Willa Cather—whom I greatly admire.

n conclusion White added that he was convinced that granting a year's
ellowship to Mrs. Imes "would give her opportunity for development which
yould make Mrs. Imes an even finer artist than she is today."

Another interesting effort by White concerns Arna Bontemps's first
ovel, originally entitled *The Chariot in the Cloud* and later revised and
ntitled *God Send Sunday*. In April, 1930, White sent the first manuscript
o John Farrar of Farrar and Rinehart. White told Farrar he could either
nform Bontemps directly of his decision or inform White: "I would rather
ot give you my opinion of [the manuscript] until you have had a chance
o read it yourself and form an independent opinion of it." Farrar rejected
he manuscript: "It's an interesting work, but I think terribly difficult to
promote, and I fear that we could have a hard time with it." White returned
he manuscript to Bontemps and told him that Farrar believed he should
ake it to other publishers, which Bontemps did, with no success. So Bon-
emps rewrote his novel. In October, 1930, Bontemps sent White copies
of two letters—one a rejection from Macmillan and the other an acceptance
rom Harcourt. L. H. Titterton, an associate editor at Macmillan, told Bon-
emps why they had rejected *God Send Sunday:*

It has been read by four members of our staff and the opinion is unani-
mous that the first part is admirably done, and a coherent and convincing
piece of writing; but that the second part is distinctly weaker and by its dif-
fuseness and change of emphasis tends to weaken very materially the impression created by the earlier chapters. If you could revise the second part
—which of course we recognize as coming practically unchanged from the
earlier manuscript—"The Chariot in the Cloud" which you sent to us—pre-
serving Augie as the central figure, . . . it would result in a manuscript of
greater power. . . .
    It is not often that we get a manuscript which has so many excellent
qualities, but which we honestly feel it would be a mistake to publish in its
present form.

Alfred Harcourt also found some weakness in the second part of the novel,
but he wanted the novel anyway:

A number of us have read the manuscript of your *God Send Sunday*. It has
impressed us a good deal and we want to publish it. The first half is certainly
amazingly good; the second half has splendid spots in it, but does not come
off quite so well. As a whole, however, it strikes us as an unusual achievement, of which you should be proud and which we shall be happy to publish.

In sending the letters to White, Bontemps reminded him that he had asked
to see them and that White was to consider whether or not he agreed with
the criticism: "I shall be interested to know because I am now at work on

the new version of the second part and, according to the terms of the contract, must finish it by the 15th of December." Bontemps added that he was also anxious to get the manuscript back from White because he wanted to give it to "Doug" (Aaron Douglas), who was to do the jacket for the book. White responded that he was swamped with work, but that he would give Bontemps his reaction to the criticism when he got back to New York and that he would give the manuscript to Douglas so that the work on the dust jacket would not be delayed.[108]

In addition to helping younger writers get started, White also involved himself with encouraging and promoting the efforts of older, more established writers. Charles W. Chesnutt, who, with Paul Laurence Dunbar, was one of the most important writers in black America at the turn of the century, had been in retirement from writing for almost two decades, although he was quite active in his vocation as a court reporter in Cleveland. In 1926 he sent White autographed copies of four of his books (he could not find a copy of *The House behind the Cedars*), and cautioned White: "Don't say anything about that new novel, for it may not materialize. What you say, however, about the reception which a new book by me would receive encourages me to see what I can do." Referring to the tremendous sales of Durant's *Story of Philosophy,* Chesnutt wondered, "Why can't one of us write a book of fiction that will sell like Dr. Durant's 'Story of Philosophy'?" White quickly responded:

I hope you won't let anything keep you from doing that novel. The more I think of it, the more certain I am that you could do a story which would be of tremendous value as well as of great beauty and importance. Perhaps it might not sell quite as widely as the "Story of Philosophy," . . . but it ought and undoubtedly will sell in larger numbers than any of your other books. Even if it should not measure up to the previous ones in merit (this is a contingency of which I have no fear) the market has so greatly increased since your other books were published, I think it would bring you at least a part of the reward which you so richly deserve.

Chesnutt responded that he would go ahead with his plans for the novel, but again stated that he would prefer that White say nothing about it, "lest it might fall by the wayside." Nothing further was said about Chesnutt's novel, and he did not complete it before his death in 1932. White was able to secure a writing assignment for Chesnutt in *Colophon* in 1930, and when Chesnutt wrote to thank him, White replied: "You owe me no thanks; . . . if anyone is in debt to me, it is the *Colophon*."[109] As this correspondence suggests, White had nothing but complete admiration and respect for this elder statesman of Afro-American literature.

Another writer of established reputation to whom White often offered assistance and, occasionally, a defense, was the man who brought him to the NAACP, James Weldon Johnson. White was instrumental in getting Johnson and George Oppenheimer and Harold Guinsburg of the Viking Press together concerning *The Book of American Negro Spirituals* in March of 1925. And after the book was published, White composed a notice to be sent to the Association's branches to encourage their support for the book. When Florence Loeb Kellogg slighted the book in her review for the *Survey Graphic,* White wrote a letter to the editor:

... [Miss Kellogg] says, "It *(The Book of American Negro Spirituals)* is still not the ideal one-volume collection of Negro spirituals in accompaniment and words." Perhaps Miss Kellogg can tell us why this is not the ideal one-volume collection but she doesn't do so in her review. This great body of music is so extensive and, until late years, had been so little understood or studied that to include all of the songs would make a book so huge it could not be handled.

Between the time of publication of the first *Book of American Negro Spirituals,* coedited by J. Rosamond Johnson, and the publication of the second book the following year, White acted as an intermediary between the New York Johnsons and Howard Odum and Guy Johnson of the University of North Carolina, editors of *The Negro and His Songs,* as the four exchanged research, arrangements, and songs to their mutual benefit.[110]

The publication of Johnson's *God's Trombones* in 1927 was another exciting event for White. As he told a friend, "I am frankly of the opinion that this is one of the greatest books of verse that these United States have yet produced." In a letter to the Pulitzer Prize Committee, White recommended *God's Trombones* as "the best book of verse by an American author published during 1927," and went on:

Mr. Johnson has made a distinct and most valuable contribution to American literature in that he has in this volume caught the spirit and imagery of the old time Negro preacher. In doing this he has not descended to mere humor or caricature. Instead his volume is a great addition to American folklore ... awarding the Pulitzer Prize to Mr. Johnson for this volume would not only reward and honor him but would serve to call attention to this valuable source of beauty, strength and rhythmic power which has sprung from American soil.

In addition to promoting interest in *God's Trombones* at home, White also devoted "a good deal" of his talks in England, while in Europe on the Guggenheim fellowship in 1927, to Johnson's book. On October 15, 1928,

White wrote to the editor of the *Bookman,* pointing out what he termed the "striking similarity" between Carl Sandburg's "Is God, Too, Lonely?" which the *Bookman* had recently published, and Johnson's "The Creation," which was "published first in the *Freeman* some ten years ago and included in Mr. Johnson's *God's Trombones.*" And in 1933, when the reviewer for the *Interracial Review* was less than enthusiastic about Johnson's autobiography, *Along This Way,* White wrote to protest that the review was completely out of accord with the widespread praise the book had received. In a note to Johnson he added: "Can you beat this little literary tadpole (or the female whatever-it-is of a tadpole: is it tadpolette?) of the *Interracial Review?* I should like to ask where the hell she gets off at, but writing to an ecclesiastical journal I had to restrain myself."[111] (While White was ever the gentleman in his correspondence, there are occasional glimpses such as this to remind us that the man was quite human after all.)

Walter White was not only interested in the promotion and development of black American literature; as we saw in his attempts to establish a Negro art institute, his interests spread over all the arts, including music and painting. He was a close friend of Paul Robeson and of Roland Hayes. At one point, in fact, he was seriously considering quitting his NAACP position and becoming Hayes's American manager. That proposal, though, along with a proposed biography of Hayes which White was to write for Harper's, fell through. In 1925 White was able to get Clifford Cairns of the Victor Talking Machine Company and Paul Robeson and Lawrence Brown together, resulting in the release, on September 25, 1925, of Robeson's "Steal Away," "Were You There," "Joshua Fit de Battle ob Jerico," and "Bye and Bye," the latter two recorded with Brown.[112] Others White helped in securing recording tests with Victor included the team of J. Rosamond Johnson and Taylor Gordon and the Sabbath Glee Club of Richmond, Virginia, a group first brought to White's attention by Carl Van Vechten. And, when Jules Bledsoe wanted his release from a contract with Sol Hurok an agency he felt was doing nothing for him, it was Walter White who went to work on Bledsoe's behalf.

In the field of art White was particularly interested in helping Hale Woodruff, a young painter from Indianapolis whom White met through his friend F. E. DeFrantz of the colored Y. M. C. A. White tried to secure funds for Woodruff so that the latter could go to France to study. In 1927 White wrote letters of introduction for Woodruff to Carl Van Vechten, Aaron Douglas, and others who might be able to help him in some way. He also got Otto Kahn to agree to give Woodruff $250 a year for two years, provided Woodruff could find others to make up the difference he would need. Woodruff eventually went to France, and in 1930 he sent White some paintings to sell for him: "My work . . . has taken on a remarkable change of conception and execution. I feel that I've made a deal of progress and I wanted to turn over to you some of those more recent paintings." Unfortunately, the recent stock market crash had all but destroyed the art market, and White had little success in selling the paintings. In 1931 White sent letters to Van Vechten, Aaron Douglas, Du Bois, the Spingarns, and others, trying to raise money to send the nearly destitute Woodruff.[113] White's efforts to help Woodruff echoed, in many ways, his earlier attempts to help the struggling Claude McKay.

Walter White also extended his aid to established white writers of the time, especially to Carl Van Vechten. As noted earlier, White was the one who introduced Van Vechten into Harlem society, but his aid did not stop there. In 1925, for example, White wrote to several people trying to secure copies of out-of-print books on Negro folk songs for Van Vechten to use in a number of articles he wanted to do on the subject. More importantly, when *Nigger Heaven* was released in 1926, White defended it against attacks from the black press and from Du Bois in the *Crisis*. The *Pittsburgh Courier* initially refused to carry any advertisement for the book, which prompted this telegram from White to Robert Vann:

Have just been informed by Alfred A. Knopf that *Courier* has refused advertisement for "Nigger Heaven" Carl Van Vechten's new novel. I have read the novel and it is a magnificent picture with amazing sympathy and understanding of Negro point of view. The title which I assume is cause of *Courier's* refusal of advertisement is an ironic one as will be seen upon reading book. May I urge reconsideration of refusal of advertisement by *Courier* especially in view of fact that another colored newspaper which had refused advertisement reconsidered upon reading my article in the *Courier* of June 19 regarding Mr. Van Vechten. Please wire me at my home regarding this.

That evening Vann responded: "Advertisement will be accepted per your statement." A few months later, following Du Bois's critical review of the book in the *Crisis*, White sent him a letter defending the novel. His main argument in support of *Nigger Heaven* was that the book was making many white people who were before completely ignorant of black life aware that there was an educated, refined class of black people living in Harlem. At a dinner party during which White spoke to "about twenty-five people belonging to one of the most socially exclusive and wealthy groups in New York," he was asked:

"Is it really true that there are educated Negroes in Harlem as Mr. Van Vechten shows in his 'Nigger Heaven'? If so, how many are there?" The things that I said are commonplace to those of us who, being Negroes, know about them but to this group it was of amazing newness. Not one of the questions asked intimated any degree of shock or disgust at the characters in "Nigger Heaven" which have given greatest offense to some of the Negro critics of that book. Instead, the amazement was the same as that expressed in many reviews of "Nigger Heaven" in the Southern press—not that there are low Negroes *but that there are so many intelligent and aspiring ones!*

In addition, White noted, many of the people present were anxious to know of works by black artists and what they might do to help "spread this information" to others in the white community who were as ignorant of the subject as they.[114] In closing, White hinted that Du Bois's attack was perhaps intended for Van Vechten's black friends as well as for the book:

I do not agree with you that "Nigger Heaven" is an affront "to the intelligence of white people" for my observations have been precisely to the contrary. And as for its being "an affront to the hospitality of black folk," is such a dictum literary criticism or is it a matter solely for the consideration of those who have shown hospitality to Mr. Van Vechten?

That there was no love lost between White and Du Bois has been a matter of discussion for years; this letter, however, appears to transcend personal animosity in favor of trying to help a friend through some rather brutal critical attacks.[115]

Another prominent figure in American letters with whom White became close in the latter part of the twenties was V. F. Calverton (George Goetz) of the Book League of America and the *Modern Quarterly*. Following their initial meeting in October, 1928, Calverton wrote to remind White about the due date of the latter's review of Stribling's *Bright Medal* and added a note:

May I say what is so uncharacteristic of an American who is always cautious of his sentiments to a point of commercial stinginess, that you are one of the few men whom I have met for the first time and liked immensely and well. I believe, my dear White, that when one feels such sentiments as these, one should be frank in expressing them. I feel them seldom, but when I do I like to express them.

Over the next few months the two men corresponded frequently, mainly concerning the Modern Library's *Anthology of American Negro Literature* (1929), edited by Calverton and dedicated to Walter White: "In admiration of his courage in the cause of his people and in tender appreciation of that fine, inspiring warmth which I have found in his friendship."[116] Calverton included a chapter from *The Fire in the Flint* and White's "I Investigate Lynchings" in his anthology.

The two also corresponded about people Calverton might write "in

onnection with this Modern Library volume," including Claude McKay,
'enton Johnson ("Is he still alive?"), Frank Horne, and Sterling Brown,
hen at Fisk University. Later in the year Calverton wrote White to ask his
dvice about finding a literary patron:

. . you read the first few chapters of my book which I have tentatively en-
itled "This Negro." I sent it to Elmer Carter [at *Opportunity*] and his
:nthusiasm is enormous. He states that he is sure that it will be the most
;weeping presentation of the Negroes that has been made. . . . I can easily
;et a publisher for it but I can scarcely get an advance on it, . . . and I am
wondering if I could not find someone sufficiently interested in the project
:o advance me $500.00 on the book. I mean some individual that is.

White replied: "I hope it doesn't sound selfish but if I knew of some person
who would advance $500 for literary work I am afraid I would have cor-
ralled him long since."[117] After suggesting Calverton try the Guggenheim
Foundation, White noted: "There ought to be patrons for persons doing
reputable work but, alas, those who have the money prefer spending it in
ways less productive!"

In addition to aiding many of the writers of the twenties in their search
for publishers and editors, Walter White also helped the people at the other
end of the publishing exchange, i.e., the publishers and editors. We have
already seen how White coaxed writers to submit their works to the newly
formed Viking Press (e.g., Claude McKay), in response to which George
Oppenheimer wrote: "It is awfully good of you to go to this trouble and we
deeply appreciate not only this but all you are doing and have done for
us." Ruth Raphael and other representatives of Harper and Brothers were
continually writing White for information, lists of people to approach, and
advice, as were representatives at Alfred A. Knopf. When Frederick A.
Stokes published Jessie Fauset's *Plum Bun* in 1929, Mary Mackay of that
firm asked for and received White's assistance. On February 16 she wrote:
"I can't thank you too much for your excellent cooperation on *Plum Bun*.
I have been glad to act on your suggestions and have sent copies to Miss
Jackson and to Mr. Van Vechten. Mr. Thompson of the *Crisis* came in to
see me yesterday and I feel certain that our Advertising Manager will be
interested in considering that publication in her advertising plans for *Plum
Bun*." Finally, on March 4, Ms. Mackay told White: "To say that we are all
most grateful to you and to Mr. Johnson for your marvelous assistance is
phrasing it very mildly. I only hope that I shall be able to reciprocate in
some measure." And when the Literary Guild was formed in 1927, White
sent Samuel Craig the names and addresses of seventy-one people, mainly
"colored people," to whom he might send a copy of the Guild's magazine
Wings. Carl Van Doren, editor-in-chief at the Guild, thanked White for his

help and added: "It is very friendly of you to offer to help the Guild and I am extremely grateful." In a later letter Craig added: "We are indeed grateful to you for the list of names. . . . Enthusiastic support of this kind is bound to make the Guild a success."[118] White's enthusiasm for the Literary Guild reflects his consistent stand that there was a solid reading and book-buying public within the black community; his column for the *Pittsburgh Courier* was used to tap that source and to encourage his black readers to buy books, not only those written by black authors, but any books of merit.

In many ways, then, Walter White functioned as an important catalyst in the Harlem Renaissance. As a writer, as a political figure, as a man interested in helping others, White sought to advance the cause of art from within the black community. In his untiring efforts to help those artists succeed, White added immeasurably to the flowering of the movement. Others may have done as much, perhaps more, to initiate and to perpetuate the New Negro movement, but no one was more committed in his efforts than Walter White. To be sure, Cullen, Hughes, McKay, Van Vechten, and the others would have undoubtedly accomplished their work even if White had not been there to help. But the fact that he was there and that he did help cannot be ignored. He often made the way smoother for a writer or managed to initiate an important contact. Even with a hectic work schedule and an equally demanding speaking schedule, White found the time to offer advice and to give encouragement. Whatever the Harlem Renaissance was, it would have been less without the presence of Walter White.

NOTES

1: THE MAN CALLED WHITE

1.   See, for example, "The Colored Man's White." An interesting study of "the family of George White" was sent to Walter White by Carline [?] Bond Day, another Harvard anthropologist, on April 14, 1930. In that study Day states that "Walter represents the dominant of the group, being most like the mother, with blue eyes, light brown hair, exceedingly thin lips and no trace of prognathism [a projecting of the jaws]." NAACP executive corresondence files, Manuscript Division, Library of Congress, hereafter referred to as the NAACP files.

2.   Walter White, *A Man Called White,* p. 11.

3.   Biographical sketch titled "Walter White / Assistant Executive Secretary / National Association for the / Advancement of Colored People," undated, but probably written in late 1928 or early 1929. Reference is made that *Rope and Faggot* "will be published . . . in February, 1929." NAACP files.

4.   White, *Man,* p. 26.

5.   Ibid., p. 34.

6.   Webster to White, March 22, 1931. NAACP files.

7.   White, *Man,* p. 37.

8.   Ibid., p. 40.

9.   White to Johnson, October 13, 1919. NAACP files.

10.   White, *Man,* pp. 50–51.

11.   Ibid., pp. 74–75.

12.   Ibid., pp. 76–77.

13.   Memorandum on Sweet Case, September 13, 1926. NAACP files.

14.   White, *Man,* pp. 75–76.

15.   Miles Traveled by Walter F. White, During Year 1918; Speeches of Walter F. White – 1919; Speaking Engagements–Assistant Secretary, February 3–14, 1927. NAACP files. These lists are in the publicity (Speaker's Bureau) folders C-185 and C-186.

16.   Lewis to the Guggenheim Foundation, n.d. NAACP files. There is a cover letter from Lewis to White, November 1, 1926.

17.   White to Lewis, November 6, 1926. NAACP files.

18.   Johnson to George E. Haynes, May 22, 1929. Records of the Harmon Foundation, box 53, Manuscript Division, Library of Congress.

19.   Mumford to Haynes, October 28, 1929, records of the Harmon Foundation,

box 30; Spingarn to White, January 9, 1930, NAACP files; Haynes to the judges in literature, December 10, 1929, records of the Harmon Foundation, box 30; Jackson to Haynes, October 28, 1929, records of the Harmon Foundation, box 30.

20. White to Hurst, July 20, 1928. NAACP files.
21. White to Storey, July 22, 1928. NAACP files.
22. White, *Man*, p. 101.
23. Stanley High, "Black Omens," p. 15.
24. White to the Department of Automobile Licenses, New York, April 15, 1924; White to John Drenner, May 1, 1924. NAACP files.
25. Expense Account—Walter White, National Interracial Conference, Dec. 14–21, 1928, December 22, 1924; memorandum from White, September 30, 1929; White to Locke, October 7, 1925; Locke to White, n.d.; White to Locke, October 9, 1925. NAACP files.
26. White to Baer, March 11, 1925. NAACP files.
27. Ransom to White, September 8, 1924; White to Ransom, September 10, 1924; Walker to White, September 25, 1924; Evans to White, October 16, 1924. NAACP files.
28. White to Reipperger, February 14, 1930. NAACP files.
29. White to Bridgman, November 8, 1924. NAACP files.
30. Peterkin to White, n.d. [March 1925]; White to Peterkin, March 27, 1925. NAACP files.
31. *The Souls of Black Folk*, p. 23.
32. White to Trafton, November 25, 1924. NAACP files.
33. Walter White, *How Far the Promised Land?*, p. 28.
34. Sterling A. Brown, interview, July 17, 1974.
35. White to Hamilton, January 16, 1925; Sadie Peterson to White, May 1, 1925; White to the United States Veterans' Bureau, May 5, 1925; Veterans' Bureau to White, May 9, 1925, NAACP files; Edwin Embree, *Thirteen against the Odds*, pp. 94–95. Embree was one of many writers who referred to White as a Little David battling the Goliath of racism.
36. White to Minor, September 23, 1924. NAACP files.
37. Arthur P. Davis, interview, July 29, 1974.
38. White to Hayes, January 5, 1925; White to Hussey, February 5, 1925. NAACP files.
39. Davis, interview, July 29, 1974; Brown, interview, July 17, 1974.
40. See, for example, Nathaniel Patrick Tillman, Jr., "Walter Francis White: A Study in Interest Group Leadership." Many people have noted that *A Man Called White* is, in effect, a biography of the NAACP during White's leadership, rather than a biography of Walter White.
41. Adam Clayton Powell, quoted from the *Congressional Record* (March 30, 1955), in "The Passing of Walter F. White"; Arthur B. Spingarn, quoted in "Walter White"; "Eisenhower Pays Tribute to White."

2: THE HARLEM RENAISSANCE:
A Time of Opportunities

1. Langston Hughes, "Harlem Literati in the Twenties," p. 14.
2. See John Hope Franklin, *From Slavery to Freedom*, pp. 498ff.
3. James Weldon Johnson, "Harlem: The Culture Capital," in Alain Locke, ed., *The New Negro*, p. 311.
4. Carl Van Doren, "The Roving Critic," p. 636.
5. In fact, Van Doren went on to say that "the most striking impression of this book [*The New Negro*] is that the negro is better as analyst than as artist. Perhaps this is because his greatest artistic endowment lies in the direction of dancing and music, which cannot easily be represented in print" (p. 637).

6. Arna Bontemps, "The Awakening: A Memoir," in *The Harlem Renaissance Remembered*, p.1.

7. White, *A Man Called White*, p. 43.

8. Nathan I. Huggins, *Harlem Renaissance*, p. 99. The date of publication of *The Fire in the Flint* was 1924.

9. Langston Hughes, *The Big Sea*, p. 227.

10. Ibid., pp. 227–28.

11. Arthur P. Davis, "Growing Up in the New Negro Renaissance," p. 58.

12. Robert A. Bone, *The Negro Novel in America*, p. 62.

13. Ibid., p. 67.

14. White to McKay (in France), August 15, 1924. NAACP files.

15. White to Mordecai Johnson, March 10, 1925. NAACP files.

16. While Harlem obviously cannot be considered "The Black Community," in the 1920s or in any other era, for purposes of convenience this study will often refer to Harlem as if it were. The reader should mentally note this as the occasion arises.

17. Hughes, *The Big Sea*, p. 228.

18. Arthur P. Davis and Saunders Redding, eds., *Cavalcade*, p. 234.

19. Bone, pp. 88–89.

20. Davis, "Growing Up in the New Negro Renaissance," p. 54. For an excellent study of the evolution of Harlem as a community, see James Weldon Johnson, *Black Manhattan*.

21. George S. Schuyler, "The Negro-Art Hokum," p. 663.

22. Langston Hughes, "The Negro Artist and the Racial Mountain," p. 693.

23. Ibid., 694.

24. S. P. Fullinwider, *The Mind and Mood of Black America*, p. 125.

25. Alain Locke, "Negro Youth Speaks," in *The New Negro*, pp. 50–57.

26. Review of *Home to Harlem*, in the *Crisis* 35 (1928): 202, 211. Quoted in Bone, p. 96.

27. Quoted in Bone, p. 96.

28. "The Negro in Art: How Shall He Be Portrayed?" 31: 219. Since all responses were printed under articles with the same title, subsequent notes will indicate only the specific issue and page numbers when referring to responses to the questionnaire.

29. 31: 219. In a recent article Mark Helbling indicates that it was in fact Van Vechten who drew up the questions used by Du Bois. See "Carl Van Vechten and the Harlem Renaissance," *Negro American Literature Forum* 10 (summer, 1976): 40.

30. 32: 35.

31. 31: 219.

32. Ibid., 220.

33. Ibid.

34. Ibid., 219.

35. Ibid.

36. 32: 36.

37. 32: 193.

38. Ibid.

39. 31: 279.

40. 33: 28.

41. 31: 220.

42. 32: 71.

43. White to Webster, April 14, 1925. NAACP files.

44. 32: 36.

45. 33: 29.

46. 31: 280.

47. Ibid., 278.

48. Alain Locke, "The New Negro," in *The New Negro*, pp. 15–16.

49. Howard W. Odum, "Regional Portraiture," p. 2. A review of *Banjo, Rope and Faggot*, and others.

3: *THE FIRE IN THE FLINT*

1. White, *A Man Called White,* p. 65. For another discussion of the Mencken-White relationship, see Charles F. Cooney, "Mencken's Midwifery," *Menckeniana* no. 42 (fall, 1972): 1–4.
2. Ibid., 66.
3. Ibid.
4. White to Johnson, September 12, 1922. NAACP files.
5. Walter F. White, *The Fire in the Flint,* p. 28.
6. Bone, *The Negro Novel in America,* p. 99.
7. White's concept for his "National Negro Farmers' Cooperative and Protection League" was probably the result of his contact with the Progressive Farmers and Household Union during his lynching investigation in Phillips County, Arkansas, in 1919.
8. See his discussion entitled "The Economic Foundations of Lynch-Law" in *Rope and Faggot: A Biography of Judge Lynch.*
9. White to Wood, October 17, 1922; White to Calvin, December 15, 1922. NAACP files.
10. White, *Man,* pp. 66–67.
11. Saxton to White, June 8, 1923. NAACP files.
12. White to Saxton, July 17, 1923. NAACP files.
13. Saxton to White, July 23, 1923. NAACP files.
14. Saxton to White, August 16, 1923. NAACP files.
15. White to Saxton, August 19, 1923. NAACP files.
16. Saxton to White, August 21, 1923. NAACP files.
17. White to Saxton, August 23, 1923. NAACP files.
18. White to Bishop, May 19, 1925. NAACP files. The conversation referred to in the Saxton letter above occurs on pp. 154–65 in *Fire.* White's widow, Poppy Cannon White, was, before her death in the spring of 1975, at work on a new book about him in which she was to discuss some of the people and events that served as models for his works, information which until now has been unavailable.
19. White to Saxton, August 23, 1923. NAACP files.
20. Saxton to White, August 30, 1923. NAACP files.
21. White to J. E. Spingarn, August 22, 1923. NAACP files.
22. White to Alexander, September 11, 1923. NAACP files.
23. Alexander to White, October 1, 1923; White to Alexander, October 4, 1923. NAACP files.
24. Saxton to White, October 8, 1923. NAACP files.
25. White to J. E. Spingarn, September 12, 1923. Joel E. Spingarn papers, Manuscript Division, Moorland-Spingarn Research Center, Howard University.
26. J. E. Spingarn to White, October 12, 1923. NAACP files.
27. Mencken to White, October 27, 1922. NAACP files.
28. White to Mencken, October 30, 1922. NAACP files.
29. Mencken to White, August 22, 1923. NAACP files.
30. White to Mencken, August 24, 1923. NAACP files.
31. White to Mencken, October 5, 1923. NAACP files.
32. Mencken to White, October 7, 1923. NAACP files.
33. Mencken to White, October 16, 1923. NAACP files.
34. White to Mencken, October 17, 1923. NAACP files.
35. Mencken to White, May 29, no year. NAACP files.
36. Mencken to White, October 18, 1923. NAACP files. In German criticism, a *Tendenzroman* is a novel with a purpose, usually a propaganda piece.
37. Blanche Knopf to White, October 10, 1923; White to Alfred Knopf, October 1 1923. NAACP files.
38. White to Blanche Knopf, October 13, 1923. NAACP files.
39. White to J. E. Spingarn, November 22, 1923. NAACP files.

0.   White to Blanche Knopf, December 27, 1923; Blanche Knopf to White, December 29, 1923. NAACP files.

1.   White to Blanche Knopf, December 18, 1923; Blanche Knopf to White, December 19, 1923. NAACP files.

2.   Blanche Knopf to White, December 29, 1923. NAACP files.

3.   Van Doren to White, January 10, 1924. NAACP files.

4.   White to Blanche Knopf, March 10, 1924. NAACP files.

5.   Robert Vann to White, December 30, 1924; White to Vann, January 3 [1925]; see Charles A. Beard and Mary Beard, *The Rise of American Civilization* 2: 769. By the May, 1927, printing, "Stuart White" had been changed to "Walter F. White."

6.   White to Wells, September 20, 1923. NAACP files.

7.   Wells to White, July 3, 1924. NAACP files.

8.   J. E. Spingarn to White, July 23, 1924. NAACP files.

9.   Lewis to Spingarn, September 6, 1924. NAACP files.

0.   White to Lewis, September 12, 1924. NAACP files.

1.   Included with a letter from White to Van Vechten (through George Oppenheimer), August 7, 1924. NAACP files.

2.   Stribling to White, August 31, 1924. NAACP files.

3.   White to Stribling, September 6, 1924. NAACP files. This second ending, of course, would have made *Fire* even more like *Birthright,* although it does reflect more closely the "true story" on which White based his character Kenneth Harper.

4.   Stribling to White, September 6, 1924. NAACP files.

5.   Stribling to White, January 13, 1925. NAACP files.

6.   From a typescript copy of the *John O'London's Weekly* review, Christmas, 1925. NAACP files.

7.   This part of Stallings's review was included at the top of a list of quotations from various reviews of *Fire* which White compiled and sent to Ira Lewis of the *Pittsburgh Courier* to use in promoting that paper's serialization of the novel. The list is undated, but it was sent to Lewis on January 9, 1926. NAACP files.

8.   White to Stallings, September 2, 1924. NAACP files.

9.   Bercovici to White, February 28, 1924. NAACP files.

50.   Bercovici to White, September 9, 1924. NAACP files.

51.   White to Bercovici (telegram), September 16, 1924. NAACP files.

52.   Konrad Bercovici, "Almost Black and White."

3.   Wood to White, October 7, 1924. NAACP files.

54.   White to Jones, October 7, 1924. NAACP files.

55.   Johnson, *Black Manhattan*, p. 274.

56.   See the list to Ira Lewis mentioned in note 57.

57.   Ibid.

58.   O'Neill to White, October 12, 1924; Peterkin to White, December 9, 1924. NAACP files.

59.   Morris to White, December 8, 1924. NAACP files.

70.   Typescript copy of "Irvin Cobb Talks on 'The Fire in the Flint,' " *Savannah Press,* January 24, 1925. NAACP files. Cobb's charges are an ironic echo of the traditional complaints about the handling of black characters in his own books.

71.   See the list to Ira Lewis mentioned in note 57. Many reviews of *Fire* were mixtures of praise for the novel's theme and the author's boldness and of criticism of what one critic called the novel's "workmanlike" form. See "A Novel by a Negro"; "Justice and the Negro"; and the review of *Fire* in *Independent.*

72.   Mencken to White, December 19, 1923. NAACP files.

73.   White to Mencken, December 22, 1923. NAACP files.

74.   Mencken to White, December 24, 1923. NAACP files.

75.   White to Mencken, August 4, 1924; Mencken to White, September 3, 1924. NAACP files.

76.   White to Irita Van Doren, August 21, 1924; White to Villard, August 22, 1924; White to Smyth, October 14, 1924. NAACP files.

77.   White to Lovett, January 21, 1925. NAACP files.

78.   Lovett to White, January 28, 1925. NAACP files.

79.   White to Blanche Knopf, April 21, 1924. NAACP files.

80.   The letter is undated, but it was written just before publication of the novel. Reference is made to September 5, 1924, as the date the novel was "to be published

81.   White to Merrick, May 8, 1924. NAACP files.

82.   White to Tanter, December 15, 1924. NAACP files.

83.   White, *Man,* p. 68.

84.   White to Johnson, September 5,1924. NAACP files. This letter is in the James Weldon Johnson personal correspondence files.

85.   White to Harry Davis, November 26, 1924; White to Ernest Gruening, December 26, 1924. NAACP files.

86.   White to Hansen, October 7, 1926; Maugham to White, January 1, 1927; Bascom to White, January 21, 1929. NAACP files.

87.   White to Blanche Knopf, October 23, 1925; Pollinger to White, December 10 1925. NAACP files.

88.   White to Harry Bloch, February 18, 1929; White to Mary McDowell, December 5, 1928. NAACP files. In his autobiography White tells of the use of his novel by the Russians and the Japanese for propaganda purposes. See pp. 68–69 in *Man.*

89.   White to Blanche Knopf, March 17, 1925. NAACP files.

90.   White to Blanche Knopf, December 10, 1925. NAACP files.

91.   O'Neill to White, October 24, 1924; White to Blanche Knopf, September 8, 1924; White to George White, September 9, 1924. NAACP files.

92.   Edwin Knopf to White, February 28, 1925; Lemon to White, July 25, 1925. NAACP files.

93.   The correspondence between White and Mason is particularly interesting. For all the rejections, Mason never seemed to lose faith in the possibilities of dramatization in *Fire.* Melvin Tolson did write a successful dramatization of *Fire* a decade later

94.   The correspondence between White and Tully concerning the chances of De Mille's buying *Fire* for a movie began in April, 1926, and extended over several mon White finally heard through Richard Halliday of Putnam that DeMille had bought the rights to *Porgy.* Halliday to White, June 10, 1926. NAACP files.

4: THE SECOND NOVEL: *Flight*

1.   White to Wolfson, September 23, 1924. NAACP files.

2.   White to Johnson, August 29, 1924. NAACP files.

3.   Blanche Knopf to White, October 1, 1924. NAACP files.

4.   White to Blanche Knopf, October 6, 1924; White to J. E. Spingarn, October 2 1924. NAACP files.

5.   White to Blanche Knopf, February 24, 1925; Blanche Knopf to White, May 2: 1925. NAACP files.

6.   White to Locke, August 6, 1925. NAACP files.

7.   "Walter White," n.d., but sent to Butcher March 31, 1925. NAACP files.

8.   Nail to "Madame Francis," August 12, 1925 (attached to a letter to White). NAACP files.

9.   White to Blanche Knopf, September 4, 1925, NAACP files; White to J. E. Spingarn, September 9, 1925, Manuscript Division, Moorhead-Spingarn Research Center, Howard University.

10.   White to Van Vechten, September 9, 1925. NAACP files.

11.   Blanche Knopf to White, September 16, 1925; White to Toms, January 20, 1926. NAACP files.

12.   White to Mordecai Johnson, March 10, 1925. NAACP files.

13.   Walter White, *Flight,* p. 49.

14.   DeFrantz to White, April 1, 1926; White to Holmes, May 6, 1926. NAACP file

5. Review of *Flight, New York Times Book Review.*
6. White to Blanche Knopf, September 26, 1925; Blanche Knopf to White, September 29, 1925. NAACP files.
7. Lewis to Blanche Knopf, October 6, 1925. NAACP files.
8. White to Lewis, October 8, 1925. NAACP files.
9. White to Smertenko, February 19, 1926; Smertenko to Salpeter, February 24, 1926. NAACP files.
10. White to Blanche Knopf, January 12, 1926; A. A. Knopf to various editors, March 16, 1926. NAACP files.
11. Memorandum to the *Crisis,* February 16, 1926. NAACP files.
12. Hughes to White, March 4, 1926; White to Bernd, March 19, 1926; White to Wood, March 20, 1926. NAACP files.
13. White to Wood, July 7, 1926; Stevens to White, July 8, 1926; White to Stevens, July 15, 1926. NAACP files.
14. Lewis to White, August 26, 1925; White to Hussey, September 14, 1925; White to Hussey, September 5, 1925. NAACP files.
15. Hussey to White, September 11, 1925. NAACP files.
16. "Strata."
17. Emma B. Holden, "Notes."
18. J. W. Crawford, review of *Flight.*
19. "Flight," *The Times Literary Supplement.*
20. Lisle Bell, "Easy Going."
21. "Book Chat," April 25, 1926. NAACP files.
22. Bell, p. 89.
23. Review of *Flight, New York Times Book Review.*
24. Review of *Flight, World Tomorrow.*
25. Carl Van Vechten, "Books," *New York Herald Tribune.*
26. Ernest Gruening, "Going White."
27. Frank Horne, "Our Book Shelf," *Opportunity* 4 (July, 1926): 227.
28. White to Charles S. Johnson, July 6, 1926. NAACP files.
29. Charles Johnson to White, July 22, 1926; White to Charles Johnson, July 28, 1926. NAACP files.
30. Charles Johnson to White, August 5, 1926. NAACP files.
31. "Nella" to White, n.d. ("Tuesday, Twelfth"). NAACP files.
32. Nella Imes, Correspondence, *Opportunity* 4 (September, 1926): 295.
33. Frank Horne, Correspondence, *Opportunity* 4 (October, 1926): 326.
34. Charles Johnson to White, October 16, 1926. NAACP files.
35. Walter White, Correspondence, *Opportunity* 4 (December, 1926): 397.
36. DeFrantz to White, April 1, 1926. NAACP files.
37. Smith to White, May 18, 1926; White to Smith, May 29, 1926. NAACP files.
38. Holmes to White, May 5, 1926; White to Holmes, May 6, 1926. NAACP files.
39. Studin to White, April 2, 1926; Brawley to White, September 7, 1926. NAACP files.
40. White to Blanche Knopf, January 5, 1926; White to Haggard, February 19, 1926. NAACP files.
41. Haggard to White, March 2, 1926; White to Haggard, March 3, 1926. NAACP files. The Famous Players–Lasky Corporation later merged with Paramount Pictures.
42. Micheaux to White, April 21, 1926. NAACP files. Micheaux was president of the Micheaux Film Corporation and one of the biggest producers of black films.
43. White to Arthur Spingarn, April 24, 1926. NAACP files.
44. White to Marshall, September 17, 1929. NAACP files.
45. Poppy Cannon White to Edward E. Waldron, August 23, 1974.

5: THE LITERARY COUNSELOR AND FRIEND

1. Hussey to White, September 1, 1925. NAACP files.
2. White to La Violette, February 19, 1931. NAACP files. This letter is in the James Weldon Johnson personal correspondence files.

3. Memorandum from White to Seligmann, February 25, 1931. NAACP files. This memo is in the James Weldon Johnson personal correspondence files.
4. Locke to White, undated, but most probably early 1923. (See letter from James Weldon Johnson cited below.) NAACP files.
5. While there is no date or identification on this memo, it seems safe to assume that it came from Locke. Some handwritten notes added to an attached sheet outlining the Department of Literature and Folklore are in Locke's hand, and Johnson's letter of April 13, 1923 (below), refers to "Locke's Memorandum."
6. Johnson to White, April 13, 1923. NAACP files.
7. Locke to White, April 14, 1924; Locke to White (telegram), April 8, 1924. NAACP files.
8. White to the American Fund for Public Service, Inc., May 20, 1924. NAACP files.
9. Baldwin to White, May 29, 1924. NAACP files.
10. White to Gilbert, March 2, 1927. NAACP files.
11. White to Clark, September 28, 1925. NAACP files.
12. Stewart to White, February 17, 1927; White to Stewart, February 19, 1927. NAACP files.
13. White to Mark Van Doren, January 24, 1929. NAACP files.
14. White to Asher, April 3, 1926. NAACP files.
15. White to Asher, May 11, 1926. NAACP files. Sometimes "Guinsburg" is spelled with a z in White's correspondence.
16. Asher to White, May 18, 1926; Asher to White, May 22, 1926; Asher to White, May 29, 1926; White to Asher, June 2, 1926. NAACP files.
17. Asher to White, September 11, 1926. NAACP files.
18. White to Asher, September 13, 1926. NAACP files.
19. Pitts to White, April 12, 1929. NAACP files.
20. White to Pitts, April 15, 1929. NAACP files.
21. White to Pitts, August 9, 1929; Pitts to White, August 14, 1929; White to Pitts, August 22, 1929. NAACP files. Since White had, years earlier, advised Countee Cullen to delay publishing his poetry in book form until he had enough "first-rate material," we can understand his reluctance to encourage the publication of what must have been much less artistic material.
22. Cora Jordan White to Walter White, February 24, 1927. NAACP files.
23. Walter White to Cora White, February 28, 1927; Cora White to Walter White, March 2, 1927; Walter White to Cora White, March 10, 1927. NAACP files. White frequently referred to Willa Cather as his idea of a good writer or as a model to emulate.
24. Cora White to Walter White, March 21, 1927; Walter White to Cora White, April 29, 1927. NAACP files. White discusses the Lowman case in *Man*, pp. 56–59.
25. Memorandum from White to Mrs. Leland, October 15, 1926. NAACP files.
26. Zackem to White, June 28, 1926; White to Zackem, July 15, 1926. NAACP files.
27. Buster to White, December 28, 1925; White to Buster, January 5, 1926. NAACP files.
28. White to Dameron, February 27, 1926. NAACP files.
29. Shepperson to White, January 27, 1927. NAACP files.
30. Jones to White, September 14, 1923. NAACP files.
31. Richardson to White, June 3, 1926. NAACP files.
32. White to Fisher, February 3, 1925. NAACP files.
33. Fisher to White, February 5, 1925. NAACP files.
34. White to Fisher, February 6, 1925. NAACP files.
35. White to Van Vechten, February 7, 1925. NAACP files.
36. White to Mencken, February 7, 1925; Mencken to White, February 23, 1925. NAACP files.
37. White to Fisher, February 24, 1925; Fisher to White, February 25, 1925; Whit to Fisher, March 12, 1925. NAACP files.

. Fisher to White, February 11, 1925. NAACP files.

. White to Fisher, February 14, 1925. NAACP files.

. Fisher to White, February, 15, 1925; White to Fisher, February 17, 1925. AACP files.

. Fisher to White, March 10, 1925. NAACP files.

. White to Van Doren, March 12, 1925; Van Doren to White, March 13, 1925; hite to Fisher, March 16, 1925. NAACP files.

. White to Fisher, March 12, 1925. NAACP files.

. Ibid. The passage from Ellis is one White quoted frequently during this time in :ters to writer friends, including Claude McKay and Julia Peterkin. The publishers ferred to were undoubtedly Oppenheimer and Guinsburg of the Viking Press.

. White, Confidential Report on Candidate for Fellowship, n.d. [1930]. NAACP es.

. White to Blanche Knopf, January 4, 1925. NAACP files.

. White to Hughes, April 19, 1925; Hughes to White, April 22, 1925. NAACP es.

. White to Hughes, May 27, 1925 (retyped June 2); Hughes to White, June 13, 25; White to Hughes, June 17, 1925. NAACP files.

. Hughes to White, October 29, 1925; White to Hughes, December 15, 1925; ighes to White, December 17, 1925. NAACP files.

. White to Hughes, December 18, 1925. NAACP files.

. Blanche Knopf to White, December 24, 1925; White to Blanche Knopf, Decem- r 28, 1925. NAACP files.

. White to Fay Lewis, January 18, 1926. NAACP files.

. Handy to White, February 3, 1926; White to Handy, February 4, 1926; Hughes White, March 4, 1926; "Harry" to White, June 21, 1926; White to Stephens, July 30, 26. NAACP files.

. White to Haldeman-Julius, January 5, 1927; Haldeman-Julius to White, Janu- y 11, 1927; White to Haldeman-Julius, January 19, 1927; Haldeman-Julius to White, nuary 24, 1927. NAACP files.

. Typescript of White's review of *Fine Clothes to the Jew,* sent to Harry Hansen the *New York World,* February 1, 1927, to be printed on February 6, 1927. NAACP es.

. White to Hughes, February 2, 1927; White to Hughes, February 15, 1927. AACP files.

. Hughes to White, February 5, 1927. NAACP files.

. Ibid.; White to Hughes, February 15, 1927; White to Allen, February 17, 1927; hite to Allen, March 4, 1927; White to Hughes, April 13, 1927; Hughes to White, ay 10, 1927. NAACP files.

. White to Raphael, March 12, 1930; White to Johnson, April 1, 1930; Johnson White, April 2, 1930; White to Johnson, April 4, 1930; White to "B. S.," July 7, 30. NAACP files. White served as secretary to the Harmon Foundation for a num- r of years.

). White to McKay, January 26, 1924. NAACP files.

. McKay to Campbell, January 7, 1924. NAACP files.

. McKay to White, n.d. [1921]; White to Spingarn, December 13, 1921. NAACP es. In his letter to White, McKay used his pseudonym "Eli Edward" for a return ldress name; he was in Berlin at the time.

. McKay to Harrison, January 7, 1922; McKay to White, February 3, 1922; White McKay, February 6, 1922. NAACP files.

. White to McKay, September 12, 1924; McKay to White, December 15, 1924. AACP files.

. White to Lewis (in London), October 15, 1924; White to McKay, November 6,)24. NAACP files.

. Claude McKay, *A Long Way From Home,* p. 259.

. White to McKay, November 6, 1924; McKay to White, December 15, 1924. AACP files.

68. McKay to White, December 4, 1924. NAACP files.

69. McKay to White, June 15, 1925. NAACP files.

70. White to McKay, July 8, 1925; White to Oppenheimer and Guinsburg, May 2? 1925; Oppenheimer to White, May 25, 1925. NAACP files.

71. White to McKay, May 20, 1925; McKay to White, June 15, 1925. NAACP file

72. McKay to White, n.d. [June or July, 1925]; White to Schomberg, July 23, 19 Schomberg to White, July 24, 1925. NAACP files.

73. White to Oppenheimer, August 26, 1925. NAACP files.

74. McKay to White, August 4, 1925. NAACP files. In *A Long Way From Home* McKay insists that *Home to Harlem* was at least partially conceived before the publication of *Nigger Heaven* in 1926: " . . . the pattern tale of the book was written under the title of 'Home to Harlem' in 1925" (p. 283).

75. In this letter, in fact, McKay mentions having another novel "all planned out" this is undoubtedly the germ of the novel referred to in *A Long Way From Home*.

76. White to Schomberg, August 27, 1925; White to McKay, August 28, 1925. NAACP files. "Johnson's Anthology" refers to James Weldon Johnson's *The Book o American Negro Poetry* (1922).

77. McKay to White, September 7, 1925. NAACP files.

78. McKay to White, September 25, 1925; McKay to White, October 15, 1925. NAACP files.

79. Charles Argoff [?] to White, October 27, 1925; Lewis Garnett to White, Octo ber 27, 1925. NAACP files. The note from "JWJ" was attached to the rejection slip from the *American Mercury*.

80. White to Hughes, December 18, 1925. NAACP files.

81. McKay to White, December 4, 1924; McKay to White, November 25, 1925. NAACP files.

82. Claude McKay, "We Who Revolt," typescript dated 1925. NAACP files.

83. White to McKay, July 14, 1925; Johnson to White, February 25, 1928; Johnson to White, March 5, 1928. NAACP files.

84. White to Haynes, September 20, 1928. Records of the Harmon Foundation, box 51, Manuscript Division, Library of Congress.

85. Saxton to White, March 15, 1929. NAACP files. The note White added was dated March 19, 1929.

86. Bradley to White, May 27, 1929; White to Bradley, June 21, 1929. NAACP fil

87. White to Van Doren, April 26 [?], 1924; Van Doren to White, April 22, 1924 NAACP files. The logical sequence of these letters does not correspond with their da

88. White to Cullen, April 14, 1924; White to Liveright, April 25, 1924; White to Cullen, April 25, 1924; Cullen to White, April 28, 1924. NAACP files.

89. Liveright to White, May 2, 1924; White to Liveright, May 3, 1924; Liveright t White, May 5, 1924; White to Cullen, May 3, 1924; Cullen to White, May 6, 1924. NAACP files.

90. White to Trafton, December 23, 1924; White to Thompson, September 28, 1925. NAACP files.

91. White to Saxton, February 13, 1925; White to Allen, February 14, 1925. NAACP files.

92. White to Cullen, March 6, 1925. NAACP files.

93. Cullen to White, June 20, 1925; White to Saxton, July 6, 1925; Saxton to White, June 22, 1925. NAACP files.

94. White to Irita Van Doren, June 19, 1925; Garretta H. Busey to White, July 11 1925; Cullen to White, July 20, 1925. NAACP files.

95. White to Sandburg, October 22, 1925; Raphael to White, December 31, 1925 NAACP files. White had met Sandburg in Chicago in 1919 when they worked togeth investigating housing discrimination in that city. (See *Man*, pp. 44–45.)

96. White to Cullen, January 4, 1926; Cullen to White, January 8, 1926. NAACP files.

97. Cullen to White, January 16, 1926; White to Cullen, January 18, 1926; type-

ript of White's introduction, undated, but sent to Cullen on January 22, 1926; hite to Cullen, January 22, 1926. NAACP files.

)8. White to Cullen, June 14, 1927. NAACP files.

)9. White to *Opportunity,* November 9, 1926. NAACP files.

)0. Typescript copy, n.d., but probably written August 21, 1925 (signed by hite). NAACP files.

)1. Typescript copy, n.d., but probably April, 1927. NAACP files.

)2. White to Raphael, July 11, 1927; White to Ashbrook, July 15, 1927. NAACP les.

)3. Johnson to White, August 1, 1926; White to Johnson, August 3, 1926; John-n to White, August 5, 1926. NAACP files.

)4. White to Johnson, September 24, 1926; Johnson to White, October 18, 1926. AACP files.

)5. White to Imes, October 1, 1926; White to Imes, November 16, 1926. NAACP les.

)6. White to Craig, September 25, 1928; Roderick to White, October 18, 1928; hite to Roderick, October 19, 1928; White to Imes, October 19, 1928. NAACP files.

)7. Typescript of a rough draft, n.d., but requested by Henry Allen Moe of the uggenheim Foundation on November 14, 1929. NAACP files.

)8. White to Farrar, April 3, 1930; Farrar to White, April 14, 1930; White to Bon-mps, April 16, 1930; Bontemps to White, October 17, 1930; Titterton to Bontemps, d.; Alfred Harcourt to Bontemps, n.d.; White to Bontemps, October 21, 1930. AACP files. There was as much confusion over Bontemps's original title for the ovel as there was over White's *The Fire in the Flint.* Farrar referred to it as "The hariot of Wheels," and in his letter of April 16 White called it "The Chariot on heels." *The Chariot in the Cloud,* however, seems to be the most frequent title cited.

)9. Chesnutt to White, December 28, 1926; White to Chesnutt, December 30, 926; Chesnutt to White, January 5, 1927; Chesnutt to White, November 15, 1930; hite to Chesnutt, November 17, 1930. NAACP files.

10. Oppenheimer to White, March 17, 1925; typescript of a letter to the editor, *urvey Graphic,* February 2, 1926; see correspondence between Odum, Guy Johnson, ld White, January, February, and May, 1926. NAACP files.

11. White to Aaron Bernd, May 12, 1927; typescript of a letter to the Pulitzer rize Committee, July 11, 1927; White to Johnson, October 13, 1927; White to litor, *Bookman,* November 15, 1928; White to Johnson, November 3, 1933. AACP files. At one point Johnson was considering using *Along This Way I Came,* hich White preferred to the choice of Carl Van Vechten and Carl Van Doren, *This ay I Came.* George Oppenheimer thought both titles were too long and favored *long This Way.* In this case, the publisher prevailed.

12. White to Cairns, April 17, 1925; White to Robeson, May 12, 1925; Cairns to hite, September 4, 1925. NAACP files.

13. White to Woodruff, July 8, 1927; Woodruff to White, September 1, 1930; hite to Woodruff, September 16, 1930; White to Van Vechten, et al., April 17, 1931. AACP files.

14. See, for example, White to Charlotte Thorne, White to John Work, and White the Hampton Institute Press, all dated May 4, 1925; White to Vann (telegram), ugust 16, 1926; Vann to White (telegram), August 16, 1926; White to Du Bois, ovember 26, 1926. NAACP files.

15. For a recent discussion of the conflict between White and Du Bois, see Eugene evy, *James Weldon Johnson,* pp. 223, 294–95, 339–40. Levy tends to take Du Bois's de of the conflict, perhaps because he is convinced that White was instrumental in moving Johnson from power in the Association before Johnson had planned. The orrespondence between White and Johnson suggests, however, that the two men lt nothing but complete respect and affection for one another.

16. Calverton to White, October 6, 1928. NAACP files.

17. "George" to White, January 27, 1929; White to Calverton, January 29, 1929;

Calverton to White, July 27, 1929; White to Calverton, July 29, 1929. NAACP files.
118.   Oppenheimer to White, May 25, 1925; Mackay to White, February 16, 1929;
Mackay to White, March 4, 1923; White to Craig, January 26, 1927; Van Doren to
White, January 15, 1927; Craig to White, January 29, 1927. NAACP files.

BIBLIOGRAPHY

Most of the information for this study was obtained from the NAACP executive correspondence files, Manuscript Division, Library of Congress. The bibliography is a combination of works cited in the study and a selected bibliography of Walter White. It does not include his newspaper columns or his many book reviews.

Anon. Review of *Flight. New York Times Book Review,* April 11, 1926, p. 9.

Anon. Review of *Flight. World Tomorrow* 9 (April, 1926): 133.

Beard, Charles A. and Mary Beard. *The Rise of American Civilization,* vol. 2. New York: The Macmillan Company, 1927.

Bell, Lisle. "Easy Going." *Nation* 123 (July 28, 1926): 89.

Bercovici, Konrad. "Almost Black and White." *Nation* 119 (October 8, 1924): 386, 388.

Bone, Robert A. *The Negro Novel in America.* Rev. ed. 1958; rpt. New Haven: Yale University Press, 1965.

Bontemps, Arna, ed. *The Harlem Renaissance Remembered.* New York: Dodd, Mead & Company, 1972.

"Book Reviews." *Independent* 113 (September 27, 1924): 202.

Brown, Sterling A. Interview, July 17, 1974.

Calverton, V. F., ed. *Anthology of American Negro Literature.* New York: Modern Library, 1929.

"The Colored Man's White." *Time* 65 (April 4, 1955): 18–19.

Crawford, J. W. Review of *Flight. Literary Digest International Book Review,* July, 1926, p. 519.

Davis, Arthur P. "Growing Up in the New Negro Renaissance." *Negro American Literature Forum* 2 (fall 1968): 53–59.

———. Interview, July 29, 1974.

Davis, Arthur P., and Saunders Redding, eds. *Cavalcade.* Boston: Houghton Mifflin Company, 1971.

Du Bois, W. E. B. *The Souls of Black Folk.* 1903; rpt. New York: Fawcett Publications, Inc., 1961.

"Eisenhower Pays Tribute to White." *New York Times,* March 23, 1955, p. 31, col. 3.

Embree, Edwin. *Thirteen against the Odds.* New York: The Viking Press, 1944.

"Flight." *The Times Literary Supplement,* December 9, 1926, p. 908.

Franklin, John Hope. *From Slavery to Freedom.* 3rd ed. New York: Vintage Books, 1969.

Fullinwider, S. P. *The Mind and Mood of Black America.* Homewood, Illinois: Dorsey Press, 1969.

Gruening, Ernest. "Going White." *Saturday Review of Literature* 2 (July 1 1926): 918.

High, Stanley. "Black Omens." *Saturday Evening Post* 210 (June 4, 1938): 15.

Holden, Emma B. Notes. *New Republic* 48 (September 1, 1926): 53.

Horne, Frank. Our Book Shelf. *Opportunity* 4 (July, 1926): 227.

———. Correspondence. *Opportunity* 4 (October, 1926): 326.

Huggins, Nathan I. *Harlem Renaissance.* New York: Oxford University Press, 1973.

Hughes, Langston. *The Big Sea.* 1940; rpt. New York: Hill & Wang, 1968.

———. "Harlem Literati in the Twenties." *Saturday Review* 22 (June 22, 1940): 13–14.

———. "The Negro Artist and the Racial Mountain." *Nation* 122 (June 23, 1926): 692–94.

Imes, Nella. Correspondence. *Opportunity* 4 (September, 1926): 295.

Johnson, James Weldon. *Along This Way.* 1933; rpt. New York: The Viking Press, 1961.

———. *Black Manhattan.* 1930; rpt. New York: Atheneum Publishers, 1969.

"Justice and the Negro." *New York Times Book Review,* September 14, 1924, p. 9, cols. 3–5.

Levy, Eugene. *James Weldon Johnson: Black Leader, Black Voice.* Chicago: The University of Chicago Press, 1973.

Locke, Alain, ed. *The New Negro.* 1925; rpt. New York: Johnson Reprint Corporation, 1968.

McKay, Claude. *A Long Way from Home.* 1937; rpt. New York: Harcourt, Brace & World, 1970.

"The Negro in Art: How Shall He Be Portrayed? A Symposium." *Crisis* 31 (March, 1926) through 33 (November, 1926).

"A Novel by a Negro." *Survey* 53 (November 1, 1924): 160–62.

Odum, Howard W. "Regional Portraiture." *Saturday Review of Literature* 6 (July 27, 1929): 1–2.

"The Passing of Walter F. White." *Phylon* 16 (1955): 245–46.

Records of the Harmon Foundation, Manuscript Division, Library of Congress

Schuyler, George S. "The Negro-Art Hokum." *Nation* 122 (June 16, 1926): 662–63.

Spingarn, Joel E. Correspondence. Joel E. Spingarn Papers, Manuscript Division, Moorland-Spingarn Research Center, Howard University.

"Strata." *Survey* 56 (September 1, 1926): 595–96.

Tillman, Nathaniel Patrick, Jr. "Walter Francis White: A Study in Interest Group Leadership." Dissertation, University of Wisconsin, 1961.

Turner, Darwin T. *Afro-American Writers.* New York: Appleton-Century-Crofts, 1970.

Van Doren, Carl. "The Roving Critic." *Century Magazine* 111 (March, 1926): 635–37.

Van Vechten, Carl. Books. *New York Herald Tribune,* April 11, 1926, p. 3.

"Walter White." *Crisis* 62 (April, 1955): 227.

White, Walter. *The American Negro and His Problems.* Girard, Kansas: Haldeman-Julius Publications, 1927.

–––. "Chicago and Its Eight Reasons." *Crisis* 18 (October, 1919): 293–97.

–––. *Civil Rights: Fifty Years of Fighting.* Pittsburgh: *Pittsburgh Courier* Publishing Company, 1950.

–––. Correspondence. NAACP executive correspondence files, Manuscript Division, Library of Congress.

–––. Correspondence. *Opportunity* 4 (December, 1926): 397.

–––. "Danger in Haiti." *Crisis* 38 (July, 1931): 231–32.

–––. "The Defeat of Arkansas Mob-Law." *Crisis* 25 (April, 1923): 259–61.

–––. "Election by Terror in Florida." *New Republic* 25 (January 12, 1921): 195–97.

–––. "Election Day in Florida." *Crisis* 21 (January, 1921): 106–9.

–––. *The Fire in the Flint.* New York: Alfred A. Knopf, 1924.

–––. *Flight.* New York: Alfred A. Knopf, 1926.

–––. *How Far the Promised Land?* New York: The Viking Press, 1955.

–––. "I Investigate Lynchings." *American Mercury* 16 (January, 1929): 77–84.

–––. *The Lynchings of May, 1918, in Brooks and Lowndes Counties, Georgia: An Investigation by Walter White.* New York: National Association for the Advancement of Colored People, 1918.

–––. *A Man Called White.* New York: The Viking Press, 1948.

–––. "The Negro and National Defense." *The Role of the Races in Our Future Civilization.* Ed. Harry W. Laidler. New York: League for Industrial Democracy, 1942. Pp. 36–40.

–––. "Negro Literature." *American Writers on American Literature.* Ed. John Macy. New York: Liveright, 1931. Pp. 442–51.

–––. "Negro Segregation Comes North." *Nation* 121 (October 21, 1925): 458–60.

———. "The Paradox of Color." *The New Negro.* Ed. Alain Locke. New York: Albert and Charles Boni, 1925. Pp. 361–68.

———. "Race Relations." *Bookman* 56 (December, 1922): 500–502.

———. "Reviving the Ku Klux Klan." *Forum* 65 (April, 1921): 426–34.

———. *A Rising Wind.* New York: Doubleday, Doran & Company, 1945.

———. *Rope and Faggot: A Biography of Judge Lynch.* New York: Alfred Knopf, 1929.

———. "Solving America's Race Problem." *Nation* 128 (January 9, 1929): 42–43.

———. "The Success of Negro Migration." *Crisis* 19 (January, 1920): 112–1

———. "The Supreme Court and the NAACP." *Crisis* 34 (May, 1927): 82–83 99.

———. "The Sweet Trial." *Crisis* 31 (January, 1926): 125–29.

———. "The Tenth Spingarn Medal." *Crisis* 30 (June, 1925): 68–70.

———. "The Test in Ohio." *Crisis* 37 (November, 1930): 373–74.

———. "U. S. Department of (White) Justice." *Crisis* 42 (October, 1935): 309–10.

——— (with Thurgood Marshall) *What Caused the Detroit Riot?* New York: National Association for the Advancement of Colored People, 1943.

———. "White but Black." *Century Magazine,* 109 (February, 1925): 492–9

———. "The Work of a Mob." *Crisis* 16 (September, 1918): 221–23.

INDEX